Robert Thomas Ketcham
1889—1978

PORTRAIT OF OBEDIENCE

The
Biography
of
Robert T. Ketcham

PORTRAIT OF OBEDIENCE

The
Biography
of
Robert T. Ketcham

J. Murray Murdoch

REGULAR BAPTIST PRESS
1300 North Meacham Road
Post Office Box 95500
Schaumburg, Illinois 60195

Job: Reprint-Info GAL reprint-info
St: b-TR
Operator: csj

PORTRAIT OF OBEDIENCE:
THE BIOGRAPHY OF ROBERT T. KETCHAM
© 1979
2d Printing - 1981
3d Printing - 1986
Regular Baptist Press
Schaumburg, Illinois
Printed in U.S.A.

To
MOTHER
in loving memory of
DAD
They taught me the meaning of service.

Contents

Foreword

This book needed to be written. One could not say the same of many works pouring from evangelical publishers today. Some writers should have spared themselves the effort. But the life of Robert T. Ketcham is a vital message. In fact, several messages.

His platform ministry was unforgettable. Few men have manifested such power and true eloquence in preaching.

His endurance of a severe physical affliction is another message. Mortals of lesser mettle would have given up in discouragement and resigned themselves to a limited, mediocre role in life.

And, of course, his life was woven together with the General Association of Regular Baptist Churches for almost half a century. His biography will provide a better understanding of the background, origin and development of the movement God so evidently honored.

Dr. Murdoch, however, has wisely chosen to center this writing on another word: obedience. This would have been Dr. Ketcham's own choice; he often declared he had nothing to give God but that. And we receive a new insight into the meaning of the word. Obedience, an abstract term, is best understood when personified. That is how we visualize God—as revealed in His Son. So obedience is best understood when demonstrated in a life. May the portrait unveiled in these pages give us all a greater understanding of that blessed quality.

It is an honor for me to write this foreword, and I do so with gratitude to God for Dr. Ketcham's influence in my own life. He performed the marriage ceremony, uniting my wife and me. Later, he was the key factor in our becoming involved with Regular Baptist Press. Before that, my first pastorate was relatively near the city where he was then ministering. The frequent opportunities for observing him and associating with him were immeasurably helpful to a young pastor.

Then it became my rare privilege to be a co-laborer with him for over ten years in the Association's national office. And I came to know Dr. Ketcham in a new way. It is one thing to see a man in a pulpit and hear him preach. It is another to work side by side with him in close, often pressure-filled situations. However, this "knowing by experience" did not extinguish my respect and affection for "Doc." And out of this background I can say with total sincerity that he deserves to be memorialized in biographical form.

I am glad this fine work has been produced. May God use it to deepen discernment, dedication and the spirit of obedience in thousands of hearts.

Merle R. Hull
Regular Baptist Press
Schaumburg, Illinois

Preface

My first contact with Dr. and Mrs. Robert Ketcham occurred approximately thirty years ago in Lock Haven, Pennsylvania. Most of Mrs. Ketcham's family resided in the Lock Haven area, and many attended the First Baptist Church, which my father, Henry Murdoch, pastored at that time. During Dr. Ketcham's visits to Lock Haven, he and my father developed a lasting friendship. This was typical of the relationship Ketcham had with many pastors throughout the country. Thus, my early associations with Dr. Ketcham were of an informal nature. He always had time for a few minutes with the "preacher's kid."

Through the years of my training in both undergraduate and graduate school, Dr. Ketcham manifested a sincere interest in my life. During my graduate school years, we fellowshipped together in the Belden Avenue Baptist Church of Chicago. In this context our friendship grew, and I began discussing with him the possibility of writing his biography.

For many years Dr. Ketcham had been opposed to the idea of anyone writing a book such as this. He was very concerned that the project would appear to be self-vaunting or self-exalting. This was the last thing he wanted. In my contacts with Dr. Ketcham, I found him to be totally committed to the conviction that "in all things" Christ must have "the preeminence." It was only when he became convinced by long-time associates that his experiences might be used of God in the lives of others that he agreed to the project.

Thus, in approaching this volume, I encountered a variety of concerns. How should I write about a man I have known and loved for most of my life? How could I relate his experiences while exalting his Savior? What form should such a volume take?

After much prayerful consideration and reflection, I determined to write a devotional biography. In no sense is this volume a critical analysis of the man's theology or his actions. Instead, it is the account of an Allegheny mountain farm boy with a limited education and a severe physical handicap who promised God the only thing he had to offer—obedience. Each experience in Dr. Ketcham's life reinforced the principle that obedience is all God expects from anyone. The story of Robert Thomas Ketcham is the story of God's sufficient grace in the life of His obedient servant. Thus, the message of this volume is simple: God rewards obedience.

As a historian, I was captivated by the manner in which Dr. Ketcham's life was rooted in the history of fundamentalism. In order to portray him correctly, I felt it important to show some of the conflicts within the Northern Baptist Convention. It also seemed necessary to present briefly the development and decline of the Baptist Bible Union, a movement in which Dr. Ketcham was deeply involved. Finally, since in many respects the story of his life is the story of the General Association of Regular Baptist Churches, some history of the Association has also been included.

Dr. Ketcham was a vital part of the history of the Baptist fundamentalist movement. He was by no means the only figure, but he was an important figure. His life was devoted to the defense of Biblical Christianity. It is my prayer that this volume might help the reader achieve a more complete understanding of fundamentalism in its historic context.

Since no formal bibliography is included, it is important to say a word about the sources used in the preparation of this work. Because the volume revolves around the ministry of one man, I depended heavily on his writing and the material in his personal files (referred to as Ketcham Papers in the footnotes). Ketcham's books and pamphlets, the twelve GARBC literature items and his innumerable articles for The Baptist Bulletin and other Christian publications provided a wealth of information. Many of his sermons have been preserved on tape, and these messages contain significant insights into his personality and life. In addition, between 1968 and 1972, I conducted a series of recorded interviews with Dr. Ketcham. I also conducted recorded interviews with D. A. Waite and Beauchamp Vick, while taped reflections were received from Donn Ketcham and Ruth Ryburn.

Three periodicals were of particular importance. In the early years of the liberal-fundamentalist controversy, the *Watchman-Examiner*, edited by Curtis Lee Laws, was significant. After the formation of the General Association of Regular Baptist Churches, *The Baptist Bulletin* (originally *The Bulletin*) was of utmost importance. The *Fundamentalist*, edited by J. Frank Norris, was of value in researching the contacts between Norris and Ketcham. Other periodicals and monographs of significance are noted with full bibliographic data in the footnotes.

I would also like to say a word about Mrs. Ketcham. She is one of the finest godly women I have had the joy of knowing. As a young adult in her couples Sunday school class at the Belden Avenue Baptist Church, I marveled at her spiritual insights. I am sure that her husband profited frequently throughout the years from those insights. He often publicly expressed his gratitude to God for his beloved wife. I wish more space in this volume could have been devoted to her role in his ministry, but many of those experiences remain hidden in the hearts of Dr. and Mrs. Ketcham.

In conclusion, I would like to thank all those who have contributed in a variety of ways to this project. I will leave most nameless and trust that they understand my gratitude. However, I must publicly thank my former secretary, Miss Mabel Young, who spent countless hours in the preparation of this manuscript. My wife, Ruth, joined Miss Young in typing the final draft. Sons, Jim and Mark, along with their mom, patiently awaited the completion of the project. I am grateful to my family for their encouragement in the past months.

It is my desire that God will use this volume as a testimony to the saving power of Jesus Christ for any who do not know Him as their personal Savior. For those who are born again, may it be a challenge to obedience.

J. Murray Murdoch
Cedarville College
Cedarville, Ohio

1

THE YOUNG MAN'S hand shook slightly as he nervously tore open a letter postmarked Roulette, Pennsylvania. His brow wrinkled in confusion as he quickly scanned the contents of the short note from the church clerk of the First Baptist Church of Roulette. Then, clutching the letter in his hand, he quickly made his way to the Galeton Baptist Church and his friend and pastor, Harry Tillis. Bursting into the church, young Bob Ketcham breathlessly approached his pastor: "Harry, what does this mean? A church at Roulette wants me to candidate! A candidate. Am I running for something?"

Young Bob had absolutely no idea what "candidate" meant. Tillis smiled and replied, "Well, Bob, they want you to come and preach a sermon. If they like you, they'll call you as their pastor."

"SERMON!" roared Bob. It was hard enough to distinguish if the roaring young warrior was asking a question or making a statement, but Tillis recognized the volatile and emotional reaction as being typical of his young parishoner.

"Yes," the pastor chuckled, "a sermon."

This time there was no mistaking the response. It was very clearly a question: "Harry, where do you get 'em?"

"Why, Bob, you make them," Tillis responded. Then recognizing the consternation on the face of the young man, the kindly pastor put his arm around Bob's shoulder and quietly explained to him that sermons had to be developed by carefully studying God's Word.

Young Robert turned and slowly walked away from his pastor to make his way home. He failed to notice the heat of the summer day as his mind was filled with thoughts of "making" and "preaching" a sermon. As he traveled homeward lost in his thoughts, he hardly noticed anything or anyone. He knew that Roulette was a tiny town about thirty miles west of Galeton. He also knew that the Baptist church there was very small. But for someone who had never "made" a sermon, the very thought of "making" one and then "preaching" it—even before a small congregation—was awesome.

As the young candidate sought God's help in preparing that first sermon, he could not help reflecting on his life. In spite of the fact that he had just passed his twenty-third birthday, he felt strangely young, and the memories of his childhood danced vividly across his mind.

Robert Thomas Ketcham was born in Nelson, Pennsylvania, on July 22, 1889, to Charles O. Ketcham and Sarah Bullock Ketcham. His parents were active members of the Methodist church, and his mother was one of the outstanding soprano singers in the area.[1]

Nelson was a small community nestled in the highlands of northern Pennsylvania almost to the New York border. The area was mountainous and rough. Heavy forests surrounded Nelson and the other small towns and draped them marvelously in the beauties of God's creation. Mountains crisscrossed throughout the region, topped by oak, maple, walnut and hickory trees in abundance that stretched lazily upward as if drawn by their Creator. In the autumn months, these stately trees, clothed in the beautiful hues of the rainbow, majestically stood in vivid testimony to the marvels of God's creation.

Bob had little opportunity to know his mother. She died in 1896 before her son was seven years old. This loss was difficult for the youngster to understand. He had not yet learned that his Heavenly

---

1. There were two other children in the Ketcham family. Bob's only brother, Harry, came through this same process, which eventually led him into the Baptist ministry. He was known across the United States as an outstanding preacher of the gospel, ministering for over forty years until his death. When Charles Ketcham married Louise Elliot, Robert and Harry gained a sister, Grace. She is Mrs. Martin Canavan of Elmira, New York.

Father was too wise to make mistakes. In March 1898 God provided a stepmother for the lad when Charles Ketcham married Mrs. Louise Elliot. Widow Elliot was an active member of the Baptist church in her hometown of Wellsboro, Pennsylvania, a community located almost directly south of the Ketcham home in Nelson. Thus Charles Ketcham changed from the Methodist church to the Baptist church.

As he thought back on the years prior to his salvation, Bob marveled at how God had directed his life in such an unmistakable manner. His own mother was a precious and godly woman whom he dearly loved. He often said, "She was a mother beyond description as to her sweet Christian character and godly motherhood." However, had she lived, the Ketcham boys would doubtlessly have been raised in the Methodist church. But the death of his mother eventually led Robert into Baptist circles where he would have opportunity to meet certain people who would shape his life in years to come. Thus, even before he accepted Christ as personal Savior, God was preparing young Robert for the appointed field of service.

When Robert was eleven years old, the Ketcham family left Wellsboro and moved almost due west through the region known as Pennsylvania's Grand Canyon to the little town of Galeton. Pine Creek proved to be a superb fishing place for the Ketcham boys, and the chilling waters of this mountain stream frequently provided a welcome respite from the heat of summer days. The large forests were still another source of recreation.[2] Although he was only eleven, Bob was expected to share in the responsibilities of the farm or on his father's milk route.

As Robert worked side by side with his dad, he closely observed his father's actions. On cold winter mornings, he watched his father breathe heavily on the bit to warm it a little before placing it in the horse's mouth. He was fascinated by the way the steel would become frosted. One day he went out to the woodshed and took down a double-bit ax. He breathed on it and watched it frost. Gradually, the frost dissipated, and the youngster breathed heavily on the ax again

2. The Pennsylvania forests and the resultant paper industry provided the basis for one of Dr. Ketcham's most popular series of messages, "The High Cost of Writing Paper."

and watched it frost. He repeated this process again and again. Unfortunately the lad got his mouth too close, and his tongue froze fast to the freezing ax. Bob ran screaming into the house, holding the ax with both hands while the ax held his tongue.

Charles Ketcham frequently suffered from migraine headaches, and when he had a headache, he did not always think clearly. Instead of pouring lukewarm water over the ax to release the boy's tongue, he ordered his son to put the ax—and his tongue—on the stove. Robert leaned over the wood-burning stove and waited for the ax to thaw. But the combination was too much for his system, and in a matter of moments his nose began to run—as a youngster's nose is prone to do on a cold winter day. This merely added to Robert's horror, as he thought his insides were coming out. He started screaming, "Cut it off! Cut it off!" Eventually the heat loosened the ax's grip on his tongue, and tragedy was averted.

In spite of the testimony of his mother and father, Robert entered his teens without claiming Christ as his personal Savior. He knew the Lord Jesus had died for his sins. He knew salvation came only through Christ. The positive influence of his parents' testimony was such that he knew Christ had performed the miracle of salvation in their lives. But his heart was hardened, and all his head knowledge was to no avail as he steadfastly refused to yield his life to Christ.

One of Bob's favorite pastimes was reading Diamond Dick novels. But these volumes were off limits in Deacon Ketcham's home, and the point was nonnegotiable. The senior Ketcham had a milk route, and his son was expected to help with it. Bob always tried to deliver on the right side of the road. While delivering milk to the drugstore, he would pick up a Diamond Dick novel and smuggle it home. After everyone else was asleep, he would light his lamp and read through the novel. The book was then hidden under his mattress until he could smuggle it out of his bedroom and burn it in the wood-burning stove or dispose of it in some other manner.

While Dad, Bob and Harry did the early morning chores, Mom Ketcham would eat her breakfast and then prepare a large meal of buckwheat pancakes and sausage for her boys. While the fellows ate, she went upstairs to make the beds. One awful morning Bob's mother ordered him up the stairs. By the tone of her voice, Robert knew full well that something was wrong—and he had a pretty good idea what it was. As he started for the stairway, each foot felt as though a cement block covered it instead of a boot. He knew what awaited him. It was more than physical punishment. He knew he would find his godly mother in tears, tears that graphically demonstrated the heartache she felt over his willful disobedience.

As young Bob sat at his desk to prepare his sermon, tears welled in his eyes as he thought of the many times he had broken the hearts of his parents. Though he loved his mom and dad dearly, his personality had borne the unmistakable trait of stubbornness. Stubbornness correctly channeled can be used of God to give a man determination, tenacity and perseverance amid difficult trials. But in Satan's hand, it was a tool used to cultivate rebellion in the heart and life of the young farm boy.

As time passed, the discipline of a Christian home as exercised by godly parents was not acceptable to young Robert. At the age of sixteen he served notice on his father that he was leaving home and would shift for himself in the big, wide world. Charles Ketcham, his heart aching with love, followed his son out of the rugged farmhouse. He tried to embrace the lad, but Bob refused to allow it. As the boy marched stiff-legged out the gate, his father called after him, "Son, if you ever bump up against a row of stumps you can't pull, just call on Dad."

Robert turned, his face reddened by the anger surging within him, and looked back at his father. Glaring directly into those eyes that he knew so well, he assured his dad there would be no such emergencies. Then he turned on his heel and brusquely marched down the road. As he moved away from the family home, he could feel his father's loving eyes burning into his back.

Before he was a hundred yards out of sight, Bob knew exactly where his father was. He had found him there on another occasion when he had broken his father's heart. His dad was in the old hay barn, praying and wetting the hay with his tears. After Bob returned home, he asked his dad if his suspicions were correct. Charles admitted that he had in fact been in the barn at prayer that day. As young Robert walked away from his home, his father poured out his heart to God: "Lord, there goes my youngest son. You follow him and bring him back. I can't."

Thus, off marched the young rebel, sure there was not a stump in all the hills of Pennsylvania he could not pull. Little did he know the emergencies that lurked before him, but he began to learn the truth in a hurry as he encountered stump after stump that he could not budge. Usually these were "stumps" of his own sinful making; and usually he had to have his father come and pull him out of the tangled messes into which he wandered. But still the stubborn lad refused to recognize the God of his earthly father as the answer to the needs of his heart.[3]

Finally the Spirit of God penetrated the hardened heart of young Bob Ketcham. On February 16, 1910, the twenty-year-old Allegheny mountain lad yielded to the Spirit of God and claimed the Lord Jesus Christ as his personal Savior. His conversion took place in the Galeton Baptist Church. Gradually things began to change, but the first year of Ketcham's Christian life was anything but a roaring success. He tried to hang on to all of his old habits, and that simply did not work. He often described those early months of his Christian experience: "I tried the experiment of hanging on to my cigarettes and my pool playing and, my tenor singing and fooling around with the young people in the Galeton Baptist Church on Sundays. I got nothing out of this but a spiritual stomachache, and everybody around me got a spiritual headache."

In 1911 the noted Bible teacher W. W. Rugh went to the Galeton church for a one-week Bible conference. His topic was the Tabernacle. The young convert was not very fond of preachers, regarding them all as "sort of stuffed shirts." The only preacher Bob had any love for or confidence in was Harry Stewart Tillis, the pastor who preached the night he was saved. He liked Harry Tillis, and he liked the two-fisted approach Tillis used in the pulpit. Years later, when thinking about Tillis, Dr. Ketcham would smile and say, "When that man went out of the pulpit, you knew a sermon had been preached!"

But this Rugh fellow was another matter. Bob was not at all anxious for this new preacher to come to town, even for a week, so he did not plan to spend much time in church that week. However, Rugh arrived in Galeton with a huge chart on the Tabernacle that stetched

---

3. This unscheduled trip from home interrupted Bob Ketcham's schooling and was one of the reasons he never got a formal high school education.

across the entire front of the church. This chart attracted Bob. He had never before seen anything even remotely like it.

As Rugh spoke that Lord's Day, he described Jesus Christ through the vivid types of the Old Testament and illustrated his points by frequent references to the mammoth chart. Bob was so fascinated by the messages on Sunday that he decided to go back to church on Monday night instead of going to the pool hall. Again he enjoyed the unique ministry of W. W. Rugh. Consequently, he forsook the pool hall on Tuesday evening and returned to church for an unprecedented third night in a row!

That Tuesday night the preacher made a remark that jarred the young convert as it registered on his mind. Rugh said: "God the Father loves every Christian just as much as He loves His own dear Son." Bob Ketcham sat bolt upright! He looked first at Pastor Tillis, and then at Deacon Playfoot, and finally to his own saintly father. Were these men going to do something to stop this blasphemy? His father was a deacon. He was a man of courage and conviction. Surely he would do something if no one else would! Bob glanced around the sanctuary once more. As it became obvious that the leaders of the church were not going to challenge the remark, he eased back into the pew, but the preacher's statement continued to burn in his mind.

Wednesday night marked Bob's fourth consecutive evening away from the pool hall. As he sat with his eyes fixed on the preacher, Rugh said, "God has given every believer the same standing, favor and acceptance before His holy face that He has given His own dear Son."

Again Bob sat upright. Again he looked to Pastor Tillis, Deacon Playfoot and his deacon father. Again he realized that all these saints were going to allow the preacher's utterance to go unchallenged! Wondering why the "old heads of Israel" were not putting a stop to this kind of "blasphemy," Bob decided it was his responsibility to do something about it. He stood to his feet and shouted: "Mr. Rugh, I don't believe that!"

The sanctuary became silent. Pastor Tillis winced visibly. Deacon Charles Ketcham looked first at his son and then down at his hands as the flush of embarrassment crept quickly up his neck and flooded his cheeks. Meanwhile, Bob stood before Rugh, firm in his conviction that the preacher was doctrinally incorrect. He wondered if the preacher would leave the pulpit and put one hand on his neck and one hand on his head and twist in opposite directions until something cracked! But that was not the way Rugh did business.

Rugh was a warm and compassionate man with a heavenly smile. He unleashed that smile on the tense young man who stood before him and said, "You don't?"

The youth replied, "No, Mr. Rugh, and furthermore, I don't believe what you said last night about God the Father loving every Christian as much as He loves His own Son."

Rugh responded with another question, "You don't believe this is true?"

The quick reply, "No, sir," came back to him.

Rugh continued his interrogation of Bob Ketcham right there in front of the pastor, his family and the whole church: "You don't believe God loves you as much as He loves Jesus Christ, and you don't believe God gave you the same standing before Him that His Son has?"

Again the reply was, "No, sir."

This time Rugh's question was brief but to the point, "Well, Robert, wouldn't it be nice if it were true?"

For the first time in the exchange, the young man's confidence wavered. The preacher had tricked him. The only possible answer to that question was yes, but he still felt the statement was wrong. Instead of answering, Bob's eyes wavered, and he looked to the floor.

When he looked up to Rugh's smiling face, the preacher asked, "Well, Robert, would you believe it if you saw it in the Bible?"

Stunned by the question, Robert realized he was on the ropes. He had stood to question the preacher, but now he was being questioned. He knew there was only one answer to the question he had asked. So he raised himself on his toes and with assurance and finality said, "Yes, I'd believe it if I saw it in the Bible. But it isn't in the Bible, because it isn't true."

Rugh looked at the cigarette-smoking, pool-playing babe in Christ who was telling him what was and what was not in the Bible. With a patience born out of years of experience, Rugh invited Bob to turn in his Bible to John 17:23. This forced Bob Ketcham to admit to the preacher—and to all the congregation—that he did not have a Bible, a fact which Rugh had known all along! Rugh moved from behind the pulpit and made his way to where Robert was standing. He handed

Bob his own Bible and repeated the order to turn to John 17:23. Robert took the Bible and started to search for John. He knew John was in there somewhere, but he had no idea where, so he kept searching. While he searched, Brother Rugh just stood there smiling and let him stew.

Finally Bob found a John way at the back of the Bible near Revelation, but it did not have seventeen chapters. When he informed Rugh of this fact, the congregation snickered in recognition of Bob's mistake. But the preacher took his Bible and explained the difference between the three epistles of John and the Gospel of John. Then Rugh took the Bible, located John 17:23 for the embarrassed lad, and told him to read it. Robert slowly read: "I in them, and thou in me, that they may be made perfect in one; and that the world may know that thou hast sent me, and *hast loved them, as thou hast loved me.*"

As Robert staggered at the impact of those words, Rugh made a few comments that went unheard, and then instructed the youth to turn to Ephesians 1:6. Bob had no idea where, what or who Ephesians was. He decided to start at the beginning in his search. He skimmed past Genesis, Exodus, Leviticus and on through the early books of the Old Testament as Rugh stood watching. Finally, the preacher took the Bible and found the verse for him, and once more Robert read aloud: "To the praise of the glory of his grace, wherein he hath made us accepted in the beloved."

No literal scales dropped from Robert's eyes and rattled onto the seat in front of him, but what transpired could not have been more real. Like the snap of a finger, the scales of confusion fell, and Robert understood the miracle God performed when an individual accepted Christ as personal Savior. He realized that God saved him not only to get him out of Hell and into Heaven, but that He had placed the same arms of love around Robert Thomas Ketcham as had been put around His own dear Son. He understood that God has set him in the heavenlies at His own right hand in the person of Jesus Christ, and that Robert Thomas Ketcham and every other believer was accepted in Christ and reckoned to be as holy and as righteous and as acceptable to God as God's own dear Son!

Robert's knees weakened. He dropped into his seat, laid his head on the pew in front of him and cried like a baby. Finally, with sobs still racking his body, he prayed aloud: "Dear Lord, if this is the way You saved me, then all I ever hope to be or have is Yours forever."

Pastor Tillis, Deacon Playfoot, Charles Ketcham and virtually everyone else in the congregation wept unashamedly as they, too, grasped the beauty and meaning of Rugh's point. That night the whole Galeton church got a new look at what God does when He saves a person. And for the young man who had challenged the old preacher, the new understanding of the miracle of salvation was to be used by the Spirit of God to work a permanent transformation. Old habits began to fall by the wayside, and for the first time since his salvation, Robert realized that normal Christian living involved more than regular visits to the church. It also involved the obedient application of the Word of God to the life of the child of God.

Robert — When Boys wore skirts !!

(caption written by Dr. Ketcham)

BOB KETCHAM thumbed aimlessly through his Bible. His mind was not yet ready to concentrate on the task of sermon preparation. His thoughts continued to drift back to those events that God used to pave the way for his entrance into the ministry.

He recalled how, within a few days of his dramatic challenge of Dr. Rugh, a thing that had been a faint impression since his salvation began to take shape in his mind. He had the vague feeling that God wanted him to preach. Gradually this impression had become an insistent conviction; but in spite of the increased intensity, he said nothing to anyone.

He was certain he was misunderstanding God's signal because he was convinced he could not speak. He never testified in prayer meetings or testimony meetings and could not—or would not—pray in public. Schoolteachers had quickly discovered that to give him a three-stanza poem to recite was a gilt-edged guarantee that he would start in the middle and try to make both ends meet, then go sit down covered with anything but glory! The only thing he felt comfortable doing in public was singing, but God was not calling him to be a gospel singer. God was calling him to be a gospel preacher, and, as far as Bob knew, he had no talent whatsoever for that. But God kept burning the conviction into his heart.

For several nights Bob Ketcham struggled with God. By three o'clock one morning, the burden God had placed on his heart was too great to resist. The young man climbed out of bed, dropped to his knees on the hard wooden floor of the bedroom and prayed: "Dear Lord, I have nothing to give You but obedience. That I do give You. The rest is up to You."

In that moment, Robert Thomas Ketcham gave God the most important thing he had to give, namely, obedience. In the years ahead God would teach him many things. But the lesson that was driven home again and again over the next half century was the same lesson he learned that night—the absolute necessity of obedience. He repeatedly told young preachers: "If God can use this old Allegheny mountain hillbilly, He can use anyone—but you have to give Him obedience."

In 1968 he commented: "My fifty-six years up to this date have proven that all God wants from anybody is obedience. You may have a thousand talents and you may have all the education in the world, and I'm not discounting education. But you can have all of this and if you are not obedient, you are not going to get very much out of life for Christ. But you know something? When you finally yield to the Lord, you discover that He puts talents in you that you knew nothing about. All He was waiting for was possession of the talent box so He could unlock it and let it go. And I found that I had joy in preaching His gospel. I, who couldn't speak. I didn't know that God, when He created me, put that ability in me because He knew He was going to use it some day."

After yielding his life to the Lord, Ketcham said little about his decision to anyone. He was still trying to sort out his confusion. But one day, as he sat on the steps of the church chatting with Harry Tillis, he said to his pastor: "You know, Harry, for two cents, I'd take a church."

At that moment Tillis showed little reaction. Shortly thereafter, however, the Galeton pastor went to Roulette for a Sunday school convention. The First Baptist Church, where the conference was held, was searching for a pastor. When the deacons asked Tillis if he knew of anyone, he immediately thought back to the remark Bob Ketcham had made a few days earlier.

Upon returning home, Tillis saw Bob at a Saturday prayer

meeting. At the conclusion of the service, the pastor approached his young parishioner and placed two shiny new pennies in his hand. The startled Bob began to speak—but the inquiry stuck in his throat as he recognized the implication which Tillis was about to confirm. "You told me for two cents you'd take a church, Bob. The church in Roulette is looking for a pastor, and there's your two cents!" Then Tillis reached his hand into his pocket, drew out two more pennies and said: "And here are two cents more for a postcard to send to the church to tell them you're interested!"

Now Bob Ketcham sat at a table, ready to "make" his first sermon, with two cents in his pocket as a reminder of the manner in which God had worked in his life. For a man who had not even finished the eighth grade, sermon making was a real struggle. Where do you look for a text? And after you find one, where do you go from there?

It seemed logical to preach from the New Testament; and since the New Testament started with Matthew, young Robert turned there. He began reading with verse 1 and stopped with verse 2. There was his text—Matthew 1:2: "Abraham begat Isaac; and Isaac begat Jacob; and Jacob begat Judas and his brethren." The selection of this passage as the text for his initial sermon demonstrates the tremendous impact W. W. Rugh had on him. Rugh, in his messages on the Tabernacle, had dealt in great depth with the types of the Tabernacle; so the would-be preacher was seeing types everywhere he looked.

Therefore, Ketcham thought of the types in Matthew 1:2. As he pondered his text, he started with the fact that Abraham was a man of faith, and he begat Isaac, the son who was faithful and obedient, even unto death. Isaac, in turn, begat Jacob, who later became Israel, representing God's great national servant. The word *Judah* meant praise. So the sermon outline developed: Faith begets sonship; sonship begets service; service begets praise. This was not bad at all for a beginner!

However, that first outline by young Bob Ketcham did contain one serious flaw. In it Ketcham said: "We find that Isaac was an exact type of Jesus, the Son of God. First, in the manner of their birth. Both were conceived by the Holy Spirit." What he meant was that both were miraculous births. Some years later, when he recognized his error, Ketcham added the following note at the bottom of that outline: "Here the young preacher put in one too many virgin births!"[1]

In spite of the extra virgin birth Bob Ketcham placed in his first sermon, the Roulette church extended to him a call to become its pastor. Thus, this young, untrained, twenty-three-year-old lad was to assume the responsibilities of spiritual leadership for an entire congregation. The Roulette church had only thirty-three members, and twenty-eight of them were women. Of the five men, one was eighty-four years old and half dead, and the other four might as well have been! Most of the women were Civil War widows with little to their names but their war pensions. Nonetheless, though the church was small and humble, the task seemed monumental. With neither high school nor seminary training, the responsibility for even this modest flock was awe-inspiring.

As he went over the hill to the Roulette church, Bob Ketcham realized that as a pastor it would be his responsibility to decide issues and answer questions. He had seen and heard enough in his hometown and home church to know he would encounter differences of opinion at virtually every level of his new life. He realized that variant viewpoints were bound to surface among the deacons and in the local congregation. It was not farfetched to imagine that problems could even arise at the upper strata of his denomination.

With this awareness of the potential problems which lay before him, he asked the Lord to give him a verse of Scripture—much as a young person today might search for a life verse. He wanted a passage that would help him out of the tight spots and keep him from getting into the tight spots in the first place; an umpire, a monitor; something he could use as a guideline in all the issues, problems and crises that he would have to face. The desired "yardstick" was not found immediately, but the young man continued to beseech the Lord and to search the Scriptures.

1. The original notes of this first sermon have been preserved and may be seen in the Ketcham Memorial Library at Grand Rapids Baptist College and School of Theology. Dr. Ketcham's first attempt at public speaking was a devotional delivered to the Tioga and Potter County meeting of Baptist young people. He spoke on "Methods of Evangelism by Young People." The notes for this message are also in the Ketcham Memorial Library.

Shortly after arriving in Roulette, the young preacher was reading in the Book of Colossians. As he made his way through the first chapter of the epistle, his eyes stopped at verse 18: "And he is the head of the body, the church: who is the beginning, the firstborn from the dead; that in all things he might have the preeminence." He read the last phrase again: ". . . That in all things he might have the preeminence." Speaking to himself, he said: "There it is; there, right there! So it will be for me. Whenever there is an issue, find out where Jesus Christ stands on that issue and then stand with Him, even if I have to stand alone. If I want to be right, find out where Christ is, and no matter who else passes by, let me stay there."

He pulled his Bible close to him and took his pencil. In the upper corner under his name, he wrote "Colossians 1:18." Then, as he moved the Bible to the side of the desk, a voice seemed to say to him, "Now, son, that isn't going to be as easy as you think it is." As he began to grasp what this verse could mean in his life and where he would sometimes have to stand, panic gripped his heart.

Ketcham honestly did not know whether he wanted to go through with this commitment! Taking his Bible again, he grabbed the pencil eraser and began to remove the reference he had just placed inside the cover. Then he stopped as suddenly as he had begun and forcefully closed the cover. He moved the Bible back and said, "No, sir, it's going to stay." With tears brimming in his eyes and dripping down his cheeks, he asked himself aloud: "What is this going to get me into? What is this going to cost me?"

As the question still echoed in his mind, he once more fingered the eraser. But the passage haunted him. As soon as he started to erase it, he would realize the importance of the message contained in the verse and stop. Over and over he told himself that it had to be that way. For at least an hour he went back and forth, back and forth, again and again and again. One minute he was going to erase the reference; the next minute he was going to leave it there.

As the struggle between the Lord and His servant raged, Bob's mind harkened back to that earlier hour when he had promised the Lord that He would be given the preeminence in his life. Yet ever since that time, he had done nothing but argue with God about his decision. It was time for him to make up his mind; leave it or take it away. Whatever he did was going to be final. If he did not want it, all he had to do was erase the reference. But he knew that if he did so, he could never pretend that he was living as God wanted him. He did not want that for his life.

More than anything else, Bob wanted to be a faithful and obedient servant. He took his Bible once more. This time he took his *pen* from its holder and with a firm hand traced over "Colossians 1:18" with ink. He turned the Bible kitty-corner and stared resolutely at the words he had just traced. Then diagonally, down in the lower right-hand corner of the flyleaf, he wrote these words: "Now, Lord, hold me to it." He then boldly stroked his signature—Robert Thomas Ketcham—beneath it.

This was another crucial hour in Bob Ketcham's life. Had he made the wrong decision that day, it would have formed a vastly different pattern for his life. But he purposed in his heart that from that point on, Jesus Christ—not Bob Ketcham—was to have the preeminence in his ministry. In this context alone was his hope of fulfilling his earlier pledge of obedience. The decision also meant that he would never have to stand alone on an issue. This fact gave him the courage he needed when he encountered crises. As the years passed, Dr. Ketcham signed this verse literally thousands of times. Whenever he autographed a Bible, the verse that always went with his name was Colossians 1:18. The decision he made early in his ministry set the pattern for his life—a pattern that any young preacher would be wise to emulate.

Ketcham's first sermon as pastor in the small, unincorporated village of Roulette was preached September 22, 1912. The ensuing days were busy ones as the Lord began to bless. On the fourth Sunday night of Ketcham's ministry, two important conversions took place. Mrs. Mame Bailey, the daughter of a millionaire oil and lumber man in the town and the belle of the village, trusted Christ as personal Savior. That same evening, her close friend and constant companion, Clella Johnson, also walked the aisle to profess faith in Christ. These two conversions marked the beginning of a dramatic revival in the small community. The next Sunday night others came, and the following Sunday, still others. The only problem was that the young preacher did not know what to do with a revival. He knew that he should have services every night, but the very thought of nightly meetings took on a whole new dimension from the preaching side of the pulpit!

A business meeting of the First Baptist Church of Roulette was scheduled for October 5, 1912. In that session a letter of transfer from the Baptist church in Galeton arrived, and Pastor Ketcham became a member of the Roulette church. Thus, even before the new preacher was officially a member of the church he pastored, the Spirit of God was blessing in a mighty way. Ketcham used this business meeting to recommend that the church begin revival meetings on October 14, a recommendation which the congregation approved.[2]

When Bob Ketcham suggested revival meetings to his church, he knew he could not do the preaching. His heart was burdened for the people, but his experience was too meager. He simply did not have the ability to develop sermons rapidly enough for such meetings. A sermon a day was more than he could handle. He not only lacked experience, he lacked resources. His library consisted of only two volumes: a Scofield Bible and a book of sermons for special occasions.

The book of sermons had been given to him by a superannuated preacher who heard Ketcham was entering the ministry and personally delivered the volume to him. At the time he brought the volume, the old preacher asked young Ketcham if he knew how to preach. Ketcham replied, "No sir."

"Well," the old preacher responded, "this is how you do it. You begin low, and you preach slow. And you rise higher till you strike fire. And then, you burn 'em up!"

Dr. Ketcham told this story to a meeting of the Fundamental Baptist Congress in Grand Rapids in 1963. When the laughter subsided, Ketcham added, "And I never found a better recipe."

Since he could not do the preaching himself, the young pastor sent for an old friend of his family, Fred Slocum. For fourteen days daily meetings were held, with Slocum doing the preaching. At the close of the two weeks, twenty-eight converts were ready for baptism. Ketcham had been told by the denominational leaders that one had to be ordained to baptize. Consequently, Slocum did the baptizing outdoors in an open stream.

This baptismal service took place in late November. The

2. Elwyn C. Cooper, *Memoirs of the Baptist Movement in Roulette, Pennsylvania* (1962), p. 29 (hereafter cited as *Memoirs*).

mountain streams of Pennsylvania, fed by freshwater springs, are always cold; but in late November they are frigid. Nevertheless, one after another the converts marched into the icy waters to be identified with their Savior in His death, burial and resurrection. Ketcham watched from the banks of the stream with a lump in his throat and a song of rejoicing in his heart. His mind went back to his study and the passage in Colossians 1:18: ". . . That in all things he might have the preeminence." It was as though God were saying: "I told you so, Bob Ketcham. All I need is obedience."

Dr. Ketcham at age 23 when he became pastor of First Baptist Church, Roulette, Pennsylvania

ROULETTE WAS only a small town, but in addition to the Baptist and Methodist churches, two Christian Science practitioners were active in the community. The Seventh-day Adventists were so strong in the area that they rented the little village theater every Saturday morning for their weekly service. The tiny theater was then rented every Saturday evening by the Spiritualists for their weekly all-night seance. On top of everything else, Roulette township had 460 registered voters and could count on at least 420 Socialist votes on any issue or for any candidate. Top Socialist leaders frequently came to town for speaking engagements, including Eugene Debbs, the perennial Socialist candidate for president of the United States.

Although Bob Ketcham had no training, he felt that, as a minister of the gospel, it was incumbent upon him to speak to the issues that these viewpoints represented. But every time he spoke in opposition to these various positions and quoted Scripture to support his point, he was told that the Bible was not acceptable evidence.

Because people refused to accept the validity of scriptural teaching on these issues, Ketcham began to read avidly in the writings of the Christian Scientists, the Adventists, the Spiritualists and the Socialists. He was convinced that their teachings were in error, and he reasoned that these errors should surface in their respective writings.

He was so convinced of this concept that he decided if there were not enough errors in the writings of any particular group to condemn them, he would seriously consider joining them! So he subscribed to the *Melting Pot,* the official Socialist paper. He purchased every book and pamphlet that Mary Baker Eddy Glover Patterson Frye had ever written. He bought Conan Doyle's book on his conversation with his deceased son, Raymond. He obtained every piece of Adventist literature he could find. Then he began to read.

For months the young preacher read into the wee hours of the morning, pausing only to prepare sermons for his flock. He read volume after volume as he did everything he could to prepare himself for battle with these enemies of historic, Biblical Christianity.

In this multitude of volumes, Ketcham unearthed some of the weaknesses of Mrs. Eddy's Christian Science teaching. The community in which he lived provided many opportunities to discuss those teachings with some of her followers. He loved to ask Christian Scientists, "Do you know that Mrs. Eddy teaches that heat and cold, rain and sunshine, and climatic conditions in general have no effect on your crops—either in seedtime or in harvest? Do you know she says that?" When they admitted that they did not, he would refer them to the latest edition of *Science and Health with Key to the Scriptures.* He would then remind them that if this was in fact true, they ought to be able to plant potatoes in the hills of Pennsylvania in the middle of winter and have them grow. He used information directly from the source again and again to witness to Christian Scientists. He attacked the Adventists through the use of Ellen G. White's book, *The Desire of Ages,* among others.

Ketcham's in-depth study of the Christian Scientists, Adventists, Spiritualists and Socialists proved to be of tremendous value. In each instance he found weaknesses within the particular position that could be used against it. This confirmed what he already knew on the basis of the Word of God. Further, it provided a context in which he could refute the position from within for those who rejected the validity of the Bible.

Thus, early in Ketcham's career, God armed the young warrior with the weapons to demonstrate the fallacies of the cults. At the same time, God taught His young servant a valuable lesson. The Word of God must be accepted by faith. Those who have placed their faith in

Jesus Christ will readily do this. But unregenerate man, with a variant principle governing his life, may be absolutely unwilling to do so. Consequently, the child of God must be aware of the weaknesses in non-Biblical positions in order to refute them. The Christian is to "be ready always to give an answer to every man that asketh you a reason of the hope that is in you" (1 Pet. 3:15). If a man could show the weaknesses in the cults and defend his own position in the Christian faith, he could be used by the Spirit of God.

His study of the religious cults and Socialism made Bob Ketcham increasingly sensitive to his lack of formal education. He was well aware that the Word of God encouraged the child of God to "study to shew thyself approved unto God, a workman that needeth not to be ashamed, rightly dividing the word of truth" (2 Tim. 2:15). Though he faithfully studied the Word of God in the preparation of his messages, the young preacher was burdened with a desire to further his formal Biblical training. Consequently, while continuing his study of the religious cults and Socialism, he also registered with Crozer Seminary for its correspondence course.

After completing the requirements for the first year of the Crozer program, he received the volumes for the second year. One of the texts was a book by Dr. Stevens on the teachings of Jesus. While reading this volume, Ketcham came across a statement to the effect that since Jesus was human, He was liable to mistakes. Dr. Stevens used as an example the fact that Christ had promised to come back and set up a kingdom. The author indicated that one of two things must have happened: either Jesus made a mistake, or possibly His Jewish nationalist reporters read a Messianic meaning into everything Christ said. Either way, Stevens averred, Jesus could not possibly return to establish a kingdom. The author concluded that traces of Jesus' original meaning were in the Gospels, but that was all.

In spite of his youthfulness and lack of experience with theological issues, warning signals flashed in Ketcham's mind. In future years, looking back on this time, Dr. Ketcham considered the warning signals that he received in those early days to be "an unction of the Holy Spirit." He commented that his ability to remain true to the faith in these formative years and on through his ministry was not because of his sagacity or his astuteness. Instead, it was because God had protected his thinking.

When God revealed the inadequacy and heresy of Stevens' statement to him, Ketcham bundled the whole package of books and shipped them back to the school, addressing them to Milton G. Evans, the president of Crozer Seminary. In an accompanying letter, he indicated to Evans that if there were only "traces" of what Jesus meant in the Gospels, he supposed he could find them as well as anyone else. When reflecting on that event years later, Dr. Ketcham said: "And I think back to that day when, on that little hunch, I bundled the whole business of the bottle of poison they had sent me back and saved myself the danger of following through on that thing. Only God did that. I didn't have sense enough to do it. I didn't know enough, but God . . . but God . . . but God."

Thus in the two years and ten months Bob Ketcham spent in the church in Roulette, God put the young cleric through a seminary course equal to none in this country. To put it in Ketcham's own words: "I got learning back there I never would have gotten in a theological seminary—never."

All these months of intense study hastened the eye trouble with which Dr. Ketcham was to be plagued for the remainder of his life. By late 1913 he had to hold a book within four inches of his face, and by 1914 the volumes were almost rubbing the end of his nose. The first inkling the church had of their pastor's eye problem came on August 30, 1913. Ketcham informed them that he would have to go to Philadelphia to have his eyes treated.[1]

The eye disease that plagued Bob Ketcham was diagnosed as keratoconus, commonly known as "conical cornea."[2] Ketcham's cornea—the transparent structure which formed the front part of the outside layer of his eyeball—increased in convexity and gradually assumed a conical shape instead of the normal rounded configuration. In the early stages, his vision was distorted because his eyes were unable to focus properly due to the cornea's uneven curvature.

1. Cooper, *Memoirs*, p. 29.
2. The cause of keratoconus is unknown, though evidence suggests a significant hereditary component. The above paragraph is based on information taken from these works: Sir Stewart Duke-Elder and Arthur Leigh, *Diseases of the Outer-Eye*, Vol. III: *System of Ophthalmology* (St. Louis: C. V. Mosby Co., 1965) and Merrill Grayson and Richard Keates, *Manual of Diseases of the Cornea* (Boston: Little, Brown and Co., 1969).

Focusing was possible only when the object to be viewed was held extremely close to the eye. As time passed, the progressive thinning of the corneal apex led to the formation of fibrous tissue which caused further deterioration of sight. As a result, Dr. Ketcham was virtually blind for most of his ministry.

Young Ketcham was very sensitive about his eye condition when he was in the pulpit. He felt he was drawing undue attention to himself if he held his Bible up to his nose to read. Consequently, he began to memorize the Scripture from which he was preaching each Lord's Day. He also memorized all the hymns he was planning to use and the announcements he was going to make in each service. Then he would *pretend* to read, because he did not want his people to think that he was memorizing to show off his memory. He did not want them thinking about his memory when they should be thinking about the Word of God.

The practice of memorizing Scripture passages and then holding his Bible at a normal distance while pretending to read it continued throughout Dr. Ketcham's ministry. Much later, when he was pastor in Elyria, Ohio, a deacon in his church, Lou Obitts, met him at the door one morning following the service. He said, "Pastor, I love to hear you read the Word of God."

Dr. Ketcham thought it rather strange that someone would get a blessing out of the way he read the Word of God, but he said, "Thank you, Lou."

Lou replied, "You are a good reader"; then he paused momentarily before adding, "but you're not that good."

Dr. Ketcham looked into the twinkling eyes and smiling face of his deacon and asked, "What do you mean, Lou?"

"You read the whole fifteenth chapter of 1 Corinthians this morning with your Bible upside down!"

Thus in these formative years, young Robert Thomas Ketcham received his "training" at the end of his nose. Book after book after book crossed that nose as the weakened eyes battled their way through a multitude of volumes. Down through the years a series of operations costing in excess of $26,000 attempted to correct the eye difficulty that was first experienced in Roulette. None of these operations was successful, and Dr. Ketcham saw very little for the remainder of his life.

As the months passed, the Roulette church became increasingly aware of the fact that its pastor was not ordained. The church and its pastor continued to believe that ordination was necessary before the preacher could baptize converts. "On December 14, 1912, there was a baptismal service held in Port Allegany [sic] Baptist Church and Pastor Howard Griffith of the Port Allegany [sic] Church baptized twenty-one souls for the Roulette church."[3]

By the next spring the First Baptist Church of Roulette was no longer willing to accept the local Baptist hierarchy's ruling that its pastor could not baptize the converts. At a church business meeting held on May 1, the church "set their pastor apart to administer the ordinance of Christian Baptism."[4] Later the same year the church decided it was time for its pastor to be ordained. "The minutes of the church show that on January 25, 1914, the church voted to call an ordination council for February 9, 1914, to ordain their pastor. The reason the council was not convened is not stated."[5]

Though the reason the council failed to convene was not stated in the official record, it was well known to the people of Roulette. The First Baptist Church was a member of the Allegheny River Association of Baptist Churches which was a subsidiary of the Northern Baptist Convention. Eleven churches comprised the association. When the Roulette church called for Ketcham's ordination and requested a council from the other churches, the pastors of the other churches refused. They indicated that the young pastor was not a graduate of a recognized seminary and was too young and inexperienced; therefore the calling of the council was inappropriate. The Roulette church clerk wrote them a circular letter admitting the validity of the objections but also pointing out that during Ketcham's first year as pastor the church had added more members than the other ten churches in the association put together! Still the pastors of the association churches refused to meet for an ordination council.

Meanwhile the Roulette church was making plans for another evangelistic campaign. Pastor Ketcham contacted John M. Linden, a

3. Cooper, *Memoirs,* p. 30.
4. Ibid.
5. Ibid., pp. 30, 31.

former associate of Billy Sunday, to conduct this series of meetings. Accompanying Linden to Roulette was Harry N. Ross, who had previously worked with J. Wilbur Chapman. The meetings were held in a large tent located next to the C&PA railroad station in Roulette. The meetings opened July 8, 1914, and continued through July 26. "The theme for the meetings was, 'Roulette for Christ,' and by the number of professions it proved to be true."[6] Over 400 people made professions of faith in Christ during the nineteen-day crusade. Some of the converts remained active in the church a half century later!

The village of Roulette had a population of only 400 people. But throughout this two-and-a-half-week campaign, the audiences frequently numbered more than twice that figure as 800 to 900 people a night crowded into the tent. Folks poured out of the Allegheny Mountains from all over Potter County to attend the services. In addition to 443 first-time converts, over 100 backsliders rededicated their lives to the Lord. Every man but one in the local Stave and Heading Mill made a profession of faith, and the superintendent of that plant later became the pastor of the Roulette church. Six of the converts in these meetings later entered full-time Christian service.

Young Bob Ketcham still was not ordained for the ministry, but his congregation was no longer willing to accept the high-handedness of the area pastors. The church members recognized that Baptist churches should be autonomous. They acted accordingly by authorizing Ketcham to conduct the ordinances. This time, Bob Ketcham would do the baptizing.

As Ketcham prepared for his initial baptismal service, he could not help but wonder what it would be like. He would never forget the baptismal service Fred Slocum had conducted for him. The baptism of Mrs. Mame Bailey stood clearly in his mind. It was as though it had happened just hours ago instead of several months earlier.

Because Mrs. Bailey was the leading socialite in the community, her conversion had aroused much attention. Men at the Heading Mill stood by their machines as they talked about Mame Bailey. People gathered in little groups along the streets to speak of her salvation.

6.   Ibid., p. 31.

On the Tuesday before Fred Slocum was to baptize her, she came to Ketcham and said: "Reverend, my husband tells me that if I'm baptized Sunday, he'll leave me."

Ketcham looked at her, grinned and said, "Look, Mame, don't worry about that. When Jim Bailey leaves you, he leaves your father's millions too; you understand?"

This seemed to satisfy the young lady for the moment. But Thursday she returned and said: "Reverend, more trouble. Reverend, more trouble. My father told me last night that if I was baptized Sunday, I could take out all the clothes and everything I had when I went and never come back. Now what do I do?"

The young preacher remembered a verse he had learned long before which said something to the effect that "he that leaveth father and mother and brother and sister and houses and land for my sake, shall receive." He quoted this to her, though if she had asked him the reference, he could never have told her. Mame indicated this was good enough for her; so on Sunday she presented herself for baptism.

As the preliminaries ended and the first candidate was stepping into the water, Mr. Imer, her father, and Mr. Bailey, her husband, rode over the hill and down the dirt road to the site of the baptism. Everyone, including Ketcham and Slocum, was sure there was going to be trouble. As the men rushed up to the people standing there, they inquired as to whether Mame had been baptized yet. When told no, they responded, "Oh, we're so glad. We wanted to see her baptized."

Ketcham chuckled to himself as he recalled that earlier incident. He prepared for the service, his heart pounding with excitement. Seventy-two converts were to be baptized that day, so the preacher had his work cut out for him. As he stepped into the mountain stream, the chill of the water almost took his breath. He smiled to himself as he thought of poor Fred Slocum climbing into the same stream the previous November. But soon his thoughts were riveted to praising God as convert after convert entered the stream and identified with their Savior in His death, burial and resurrection.

Midway through the service, John, a high school senior, left the bank and stepped into the stream. John had been saved and wanted to join the church. He had been examined along with the other candidates who had presented themselves. But a few days before the baptismal service, John came to Pastor Ketcham. "Revener, my dad says that if you baptize me next Sunday, he'll shoot both of us!"

The pastor questioned the boy about his remark. He was convinced his father was not kidding. His dad would do exactly what he had said! So he told the preacher, "I've come to release you. I won't be there."

Pastor Ketcham recalled how he had stopped John and asked him if he still wanted to be baptized. The lad had reassured his preacher that this was his desire, so Ketcham ordered him to be present. As the boy moved through the water toward him, Ketcham could almost hear the excitement in John's voice as he had asked: "You mean you'll baptize me?"

Ketcham remembered replying: "Sure; I'm working for God. I'm not working for your dad. And if you want to mind God, let's both be there and obey Him."

By now John was almost to his pastor. Ketcham looked at the hundreds of people from all over Potter County who lined the banks of the stream. Most of the crowd stood on the opposite bank across from the baptismal class. "Revener" Ketcham had asked two of his deacons to stand close to John's father to watch him. The men had been instructed to do nothing unless the father started trouble.

As John reached Ketcham's side, the deacons moved into position near the youngster's father. The butt of his revolver stuck out the side of his coat pocket. It looked like he had every intention of doing exactly what his son had said he planned to do. As Ketcham spoke to John and moved him into position, the deacons moved closer to the angry man in anticipation. They watched his body stiffen. He was so rigid it was as though he was made of steel. The two men that had been commissioned to watch him got the impression that if they struck him, he would ring like a bell! He stood transfixed, virtually petrified. He was unable to move a muscle! And while he stood stiff as a poker, "Revener" Ketcham baptized his son.

Another incident in the same baptismal service was more humorous than dramatic. Mr. and Mrs. Fred Baker owned the furniture store in Roulette. Fred was a short, thin man with a mop of hair which he wore in a big pompadour. His wife was one of the largest women in the community. Fred wanted to join the Baptist church, but his wife wanted to join the Methodist church. The two simply could not agree, so Fred determined that he was going to go through with the baptism in spite of the fact that his wife refused. The day of the baptismal service, Mrs. Baker requested permission to go to the other side of the creek with the baptismal class so she could stand with Fred. The pastor gladly granted permission for her to do so.

Pastor Ketcham gathered the candidates together to explain to them exactly what they should do when their turn came. He reminded them that it was an open stream with a rocky bottom, and that it was imperative that they follow his orders precisely. The instructions went something like this: "Don't step backwards, because if you do, I must keep up with you, and I may hit a round stone. Just bend at the knees. Don't bend at the knees and hips, because then you sit down and I can't handle you. But if you go back from your knees, back stiff, let me have you. I'll get you out."

Everyone, with the exception of Fred Baker, obeyed the instructions. But as the pastor tipped Fred Baker back, Fred took a step backwards. When Ketcham moved to get into position, he hit an uncertain spot in the streambed. Because he was unsure of his footing, Bob "dunked" Fred very quickly, and in the process missed the big pompadour on the top of Fred's head. The young preacher might have gotten away with this were it not for the fact that Mrs. Baker was standing on the shore. She literally screamed, in a voice that could be heard not only by those gathered on the banks of the stream, but perhaps all over the community of Roulette: "Revener Ketcham, ya didn't put him under! Ya didn't put him under! Ya didn't put him under, Revener! Ya didn't put him under! Put him under again!!" So Ketcham put him under again!

As the preacher turned Fred to start him back to the shore, Mrs. Baker splashed into the water in her street clothes. She moved toward the pastor with tears streaming down her face and indicated that she, too, wanted to be baptized. Though she had not been before the deacons for approval, the "Revener" baptized her anyhow, telling her he would take her to the deacons subsequently.

As Ketcham finally emerged from the stream after the lengthy service, his back and limbs were already stiffening. But he felt like he was floating on the crest of the stream. It was easily one of the most thrilling days of his young life. The value of giving Christ the preeminence was already evident as he thanked God for the blessings of obedience.

4

SUBSEQUENT TO the successful revival campaign with Evangelist John Linden, the First Baptist Church of Roulette again sought the ordination of its pastor. On December 23, 1914, the church voted to call a council for January 12, 1915. "The council convened on this date with the following churches represented: Smethport, Eldred, Port Allegany [sic], Shinglehouse, Ulysses, Annin Creek, Brookville and there is no mention in the minutes but there is some evidence that Coudersport was also present."[1] The pastors had little enthusiasm for ordaining Robert Ketcham, but the obvious blessing of God on the Roulette church left them no alternative.

When the council met, it was obvious that the pastors who served were divided in their theology. The inroads of modernism were already visible in the tiny hill churches of Pennsylvania, and the modernist-fundamentalist clash was apparent as the council discussed the Virgin Birth and the inspiration of the Scriptures. The controversy raged as both sides asked questions of the candidate. Most of the questions related to the issue of verbal inspiration. Ketcham made his fundamentalist position clear at the outset. He then defended that

---

1. Cooper, *Memoirs*, p. 32.

position by re-preaching a series of messages he had been presenting to his church from the Book of Ruth. For three and one-half hours the council fired questions, and for three and one-half hours Ketcham preached Ruth. Finally, the council decided to pursue the matter no further. In frustration, they voted to go into executive session.[2]

The liberal faction of the council opposed Ketcham's ordination because of his "narrow" fundamentalist position, his lack of education, his unwillingness to attend a denominational seminary (which he declined doing because of the modernism in the seminary), and the fact that he built his theology on the Book of Ruth! The fundamentalists admitted that many of these objections had merit, but they pointed to the blessing of God on his ministry. Finally, the pastor from the Port Allegheny church, after lengthy discussion, stood to his feet. He told the council that while Ketcham would obviously never be able to carry the responsibilities of a large church, and while he would never be able to preach to lawyers or doctors and other educated men, somebody had to preach to the little country churches. In spite of Ketcham's obvious shortcomings, the pastor opined, he could probably serve in some of the small country churches with reasonable effectiveness. Therefore, the Port Allegheny pastor moved that Bob Ketcham be recommended to the First Baptist Church of Roulette for ordination.[3] With the fundamentalists in the majority, the vote went in favor of the candidate.

Bob Ketcham's ordination council, with its conflict between the liberal and conservative factions, was a microcosm of a much broader conflict that was rapidly developing throughout the Northern Baptist Convention. Indeed, the entire religious community in America was being shaken to its foundations by Darwinism, German rationalism, naturalism and pragmatism. These movements undermined the traditional foundation of the Word of God and replaced it with a man-centered, relativistic world and life view.

The dramatic shift in American spiritual values became clear in the

---

2. Ibid.
3. Ketcham's father was invited to sit in on the council's deliberations, and he provided the above information concerning the discussion and the comments of the Port Allegheny pastor.

years after 1865. Prior to the Civil War, most Americans lived on the farm, and each farm was, for the most part, a self-contained unit. A father and his sons were responsible for building and maintaining the house, clearing the fields, planting and harvesting the crops, and keeping the livestock—if the family was fortunate enough to have livestock. The mother and her older daughters cared for the younger children, prepared the meals, and made the butter, soap and family clothing. The life of this typical rural family was one of never-ending toil. Yet, after years of labor, their homes and furnishings were still crude and their clothing still coarse.

Following the Civil War, all this began to change. The nation experienced an industrial revolution that was unparalleled in human history. As agricultural technology developed, many men were freed from working the soil for food and were available to move into the strange, man-made world of the city. Here they provided the needed manpower to staff the growing industrial structure. Meanwhile, economic catastrophe in Europe uprooted many peasants, who viewed the United States as the great land of freedom and opportunity. Consequently, hundreds of thousands of immigrants left their native lands and flocked to America. In spite of this influx of foreign laborers, the appetite of American industry could not be satisfied. The need for manpower persisted as factories and plants continued to emerge, particularly in the northeast.

The development of city life brought a growing rebellion against traditional values. Biblical concepts of right and wrong were increasingly rejected. Man preferred, as did Israel of old, to do "that which was right in his own eyes" (Judg. 21:25).

Soon the academic community was seeking to provide new philosophies to help men justify their actions. Some turned to Darwin's idea that man evolved from lower life forms through the process of natural selection. They argued that man was a slave to his environment and therefore not responsible for his actions.

Others, such as William James, claimed that man had the right to do anything he wanted. In fact, according to James, man had the ability both to learn truth and to create truth by his actions. He believed that "the truth of a proposition is determined by its practical consequences."[4] In short, truth was whatever worked! This relativistic approach elevated man to the status of a god.

Thus men had a choice. If they wanted to deny responsibility for their actions, they could blame their environment. If they chose to elevate themselves, they could deny the validity of scriptural absolutes. Right and wrong were relative, and only man himself had the right to determine which was which. At the same time, the development of liberal theology provided a convenient framework for the individual who wanted to embrace the changing value structure of the world while maintaining the name Christian.

Secular movements in the United States were unleashing rapid changes in American life, and the impact of these changes upon the Christian community was tremendous. Many members of the clergy felt it was necessary to incorporate the new ideas of science, literature and philosophy in their theological systems.

> During the same period German methods of Bible investigation claimed eager disciples among American students. Men went abroad to pursue graduate work and returned to occupy theological chairs in seminaries and to command pulpits of influence. They used the Scriptures historically and advocated inductive theological thinking.[5]

As the new theologians returned from the schools of higher criticism in Germany and began to preach and teach in America, it was evident that their modern theology was incompatible with the conservative view of the Word of God. Nothing made this fact clearer than Bob Ketcham's ordination council. Higher criticism had stripped orthodoxy of its meaning. Indeed, higher criticism struck to the very core of orthodox Christianity by challenging the inspiration of the Scriptures. Rather than the Holy Spirit inspiring the authors, it was argued that real men had written the words of Scripture and thus the

---

4. Dagobert D. Runes (ed.), *Dictionary of Philosophy: Ancient-Medieval-Modern* (Ames, IA: Littlefield, Adams and Co., 1955), p. 245.

5. Stewart G. Cole, *The History of Fundamentalism* (Hamden, CT: Archon Books, 1963), p. 48.

Bible was much like any other book. "Whether the Bible 'was' or 'contained' the Word of God became an open question for the clergy."[6]

Another area that surfaced in Ketcham's ordination related to the person of Jesus Christ.

> Liberals began to preach about the human side of Jesus' life, and the national development of Hebrew ideals was indicated. The ethical values of the Cross took precedence over the substitutionary theory of the atonement in evangelistic appeal. Toward the end of the century certain ministers began to cast discredit upon the dogma of the Virgin birth. They appealed to the "experience" of Christ as their basis of religious authority. The theory of evolution gained in recognition, so that a reasonable gospel was displacing a miraculous one.[7]

The disagreement between the modernists and fundamentalists was argued loud and long in this regard at Roulette.

In light of the fact that the modernist theologian challenged the validity of Scripture and the Biblical doctrine of the deity of Christ, he naturally recognized little value in Christ's substitutionary death for the sin of man. The gospel of Jesus Christ was no longer necessary. In its place the liberal theologian fashioned a new social gospel in which individual salvation of the soul by Jesus Christ was eliminated. In place of individual salvation he inserted the collective salvation of society through social action.

> There were grievous wrongs incident to congested urban quarters that required correction. Spokesmen felt burdened for the salvaging of victims of the liquor traffic. They knew from sad experience that simply waiting upon God would not relieve the national menace, but that public opinion inducing legislative action was necessary. These reformers preached temperance and organized anti-saloon leagues to demand constitutional reparation.[8]

The liberal pastors at Ketcham's ordination viewed with contempt his

6. Ibid., p. 50.
7. Ibid.
8. Ibid., p. 48.

emphasis on evangelism and personal salvation. They argued that it was not in keeping with the realities of the new age.

Many of the causes espoused by the social gospelers were worthwhile. Clearly, human needs should be met. The problem with the social gospel was that it assumed that by meeting those needs men were fulfilling their responsibility to God. Having rejected the Biblical account of the nature of man and the purpose of Jesus Christ in coming to redeem man, they substituted a message which enabled man to save himself by helping others. Having rejected the Biblical premise that all man's "righteousnesses are as filthy rags" before God (Isa. 64:6), they sought to clothe themselves in good works. In this context, they felt salvation was achieved through patterning the life after the example set by the Lord Jesus Christ. Though they rejected the deity of the man Jesus, they recognized Him as their pattern and sought to walk "in His steps."[9]

Thus, Bob Ketcham's ordination council provided the young preacher with graphic proof that new ideas were penetrating the religious community. The controversy that raged among that group of preachers which examined him was but a shadow of things to come. But Ketcham knew full well where he would stand in that controversy. He would stand firmly on the position that the Scriptures were the verbally inspired Word of God and that the Bible was written by "holy men of God" who "spake as they were moved [that is, borne along] by the Holy Ghost" (2 Pet. 1:21).

His ordination council was not the only brush Ketcham had with modernism during the Roulette years. He also encountered a problem with the Northern Baptist Convention's Sunday school literature. A denominational Sunday school quarterly was sent to him. This literature asserted that the story of the translation of Elijah was the most picturesque "description of death" found anywhere in the Scriptures. This concept did not impress the young preacher. Indeed, it contradicted what his Bible said.

The young, upstart preacher took his pen in hand and wrote a letter to the convention editors. He instructed them to stop sending

---

9. This concept is clearly seen in the volume *In His Steps*, written by Charles M. Sheldon (Chicago: Advance, 1898).

literature to him and to his church. In the letter he told them: "You are several thousand years too late. The Jericho seminary sent out their group to hunt for the dead body of Elijah. After thirty days of searching, they had to come back and admit that maybe it had happened the way Elisha said."

Even during his first pastorate, Bob Ketcham was moving into the pattern that was to characterize his ministry. Though he had little education, he utilized as his guiding principle a desire to be faithful to the Word of God and obedient to the God of the Word. No matter how much education others might have, if they were not faithful to the Scriptures, Ketcham was ready to challenge them, even as he had challenged Rugh a few years before.

In these formative years, God was molding the stubbornness that had caused the youngster to march away from home at the age of sixteen into a usable strength of conviction that was to keep him true to the Word of God. The battle lines were being drawn for the titanic struggle between the forces of orthodoxy and liberalism in the United States, and God was preparing men to defend the faith. One of the warriors being thus set apart by God was a young, uneducated farm boy named Robert Thomas Ketcham.

First Baptist Church, Roulette, Pennsylvania

Evangelistic meeting with Linden and Ross, Roulette,
Pennsylvania, 1915

5

AS MODERNISM (or liberalism) continued its rapid growth during the early years of the twentieth century, those committed to the principles of the Word of God became increasingly alarmed. In denomination after denomination conservative Christian scholars realized that their number was diminishing. The principles which they held dear were being forced into a secondary position by liberal clerics. The initial response of conservative pastors was very disorganized. Individuals would defend the faith in their pulpits and before their congregations, but no organized resistance could be found. However, by 1910 conservative theologians became aware of the need for some form of structured resistance to the insidious development of modernistic theology.

One of the first to act was A. C. Dixon, pastor of the Moody Church in Chicago, who organized a small firm called the Testimony Publishing Company. With the financial assistance of two Los Angeles oil men, Milton and Lyman Stewart, Dixon began the ambitious project of issuing ten volumes called *The Fundamentals: A Testimony to the Truth.* This series of lengthy pamphlets took as its motto Isaiah 8:20: "To the law and to the testimony." *The Fundamentals* were replete with doctrinal studies. The orthodox Biblical scholars who wrote articles for this publication stood firmly for the traditional principles of Biblical Christianity. The infallibility of the scriptural account and the verbal inspiration of the Scripture were clearly set forth. Jesus Christ was recognized as the virgin-born Son of God, conceived by the Holy Spirit.

On the basis of the scriptural account, man was regarded as a lost sinner, hopelessly condemned apart from God. Jesus Christ, however, died a substitutionary death in order that man might avoid condemnation and become the recipient of everlasting life. This everlasting life was guaranteed to those who placed their faith in the Person of Jesus Christ on the basis of the bodily resurrection of Jesus from the dead. Every believer was assured that Jesus, Who had ascended into Heaven to sit at the right hand of the Father, would return again for those who had believed in order that they might spend eternity with Him.

In addition to explicating the basic principles of orthodox Christianity, *The Fundamentals* devoted a number of articles to the liberal challenge. Essays designed to refute modernist views of higher criticism and evolution, in particular, were to be found. By the time the last volume of *The Fundamentals* appeared, the battle lines between orthodoxy and liberalism were clearly drawn. As a result of this significant editorial project, "the conservatives' creed was now reduced to clear essentials."[1] R. A. Torrey subsequently continued the process in a work entitled *The King's Business.*[2]

Historians generally credit the publication of *The Fundamentals* with launching the fundamentalist movement. Stewart Cole, while describing *The Fundamentals* as a "reactionary protest," found in the project "the clear emergence of Fundamentalism." Then Cole went on to give his definition of the fundamentalist movement:

> Fundamentalism was the organized determination of conservative churchmen to continue the imperialistic culture of historic Protestantism within an inhospitable civilization dominated by secular interests and a progressive Christian idealism. The fundamentalist was opposed to social change, particularly such

1. Norman F. Furniss, *The Fundamentalist Controversy, 1918-1931* (New Haven, CT: Yale University Press, 1954), p. 13 (hereafter cited as *Controversy*).

2. *The Fundamentals: A Testimony to the Truth* (Chicago: Testimony Publishing Co., n.d.), vol. XII, pp. 4, 5.

change as threatened the standards of his faith and his status in ecclesiastical circles. As a Christian, he insisted upon the preservation of such evangelical values as at one time had been accepted universally, but in recent years were widely abandoned for more meaningful ideals. Those churchmen who attempted the task of re-defining Christianity to meet the conditions of shifting culture became known as modernists.[3]

Cole's sympathies are obvious in his definition. It is somewhat difficult to understand how one with so little doctrinal sympathy with orthodox Christianity could adequately write a history of fundamentalism. To describe orthodox Christianity as perpetuating "the imperialistic culture of historic Protestantism" and opposing "social change" reflects a total misunderstanding of the principles of the movement.

Norman Furniss reflected much the same weakness in his work. In discussing the causes of the fundamentalist controversy, Furniss stated: "The principal cause for the rise of the fundamentalist controversy was the incompatibility of the nineteenth-century orthodoxy cherished by many humble Americans with the progress made in science and theology since the Civil War."[4] This statement obviously reflects the opinion that evolution and higher criticism demonstrate religious progress. The clear implication is that anyone who would attempt to defend the validity of traditional Christianity is in some curious way out of step with the modern world. A more sympathetic general history of fundamentalism has yet to be written, though several defenses are to be found in the recent histories of various fundamentalist groups.[5]

Bob Ketcham's early awareness of the conflict between liberalism and conservatism—gained from his dissatisfaction with the

3. Cole, *The History of Fundamentalism,* p. 53.
4. Furniss, *Controversy,* p. 14.
5. An example of this kind of writing is Joseph M. Stowell's brief volume, *Background and History of the General Association of Regular Baptist Churches* (Hayward, CA: J. F. May Press, 1949) hereafter cited as *Background and History,* and Bruce L. Shelley, *A History of Conservative Baptists* (Wheaton, IL: Conservative Baptist Press, 1971) hereafter cited as *Conservative Baptists.* The excesses of George W. Dollar limit the usefulness of his volume, *A History of Fundamentalism in America* (Greenville, SC: Bob Jones University Press, 1973).

Convention's Sunday school material and the conflict on his ordination council—served to confirm his commitment to orthodox Biblical Christianity. He concluded his ministry in Roulette at approximately the same time the last volume of *The Fundamentals* was being published. After the thirty-four-month tenure of his first pastorate, the Roulette church had multiplied six hundred percent, growing from 33 members to nearly 200. A firm and thriving testimony for the Word of God had been established, and a young preacher had learned by experience that God would bless obedience.

In 1915 Ketcham answered the call of God to the pastorate of the First Baptist Church of Brookville, Pennsylvania. Interestingly, he followed his friend and former pastor, Harry Tillis, to the Brookville church. The Brookville years may be viewed as a continuation of the educational process in the life of the young preacher. The church was a member of the Northern Baptist Convention, though Harry Tillis had expressed his displeasure with some aspects of Convention life. When Ketcham arrived on the scene, he, too, expressed displeasure with certain characteristics of the Convention on the basis of his experiences in Roulette.

But Ketcham was still learning the issues, and he also was still learning the Word of God. Though he had been pastoring approximately three years, he had not yet mastered the homespun eloquence for which he was to be known in later years. Many hours were spent in the preparation of sermons. Outlines were worked and reworked, illustrations were sought, and examples from Scripture were researched as the young minister sought to clearly portray the message of the Word of God. But, in spite of the careful preparation, sometimes he would enter the pulpit and struggle for words.

Recognizing His servant's need for encouragement, God provided a man to aid the young cleric over some of the rough spots in those years. Many a preacher of today can look back on the early years of his ministry and point to a godly lay person whom the Holy Spirit used to provide prayer support, mature wisdom or spiritual encouragement. The man for that hour in Dr. Ketcham's ministry was George Stahlman. Stahlman was a man who had become dissatisfied in the Brookville church because of its relationship with the Northern Baptist Convention. He eventually left the church, but he returned when Ketcham came as pastor. He approved of the way in which the young preacher fearlessly pointed out some of the problems of Convention life. When he rejoined the church, one of the deacons said to him, "Well, Brother George, it's good to see you change your mind and come back in with us." Stahlman replied, "Well brother, it isn't me that's changed my mind; it's you fellows!"

Stahlman became one of Ketcham's most ardent supporters. He would watch his pastor closely as he preached, and when the words flowed freely, George would sit in silence. But, if he saw his pastor struggling, he would begin offering verbal encouragement, most frequently saying, "That's so!" As the verbal encouragement continued, the young preacher would regain his momentum, and the old layman would lapse into silence. This verbal reinforcement from the pew helped Ketcham through many a message in those early days of his ministry.

The Brookville church experienced both numerical and financial growth during Ketcham's pastorate. The missionary giving of the church doubled in the three-year period, and a parsonage was purchased and almost paid for in the space of two years. A newspaper report following Ketcham's farewell message indicated that the church had advanced in virtually every area.

That same newspaper account told the story of Ketcham's last service in Brookville. Prior to preaching, Bob reviewed the years of his ministry and thanked the deacons for "their always unanimous support of every suggestion which he had presented to them concerning the spiritual matters of the church." He also conveyed similar gratitude to the trustees for their support in material matters.

His message that evening was entitled, "The Power of a Clean Testimony." It was based on the testimony of the apostle John concerning the Lord Jesus Christ, when John said, "Behold the Lamb of God" (John 1:36). In this message, Ketcham said:

> The message of John is the message of 1918. Times have changed 'tis true, but men's hearts have not and neither has the Lamb of God. The membership of this church is ready to acknowledge the fact that the thing which, in the last three years and more, has put this church on its feet and made it one of the strongest Baptist churches in this section of this state, both in ability to finance its obligations and in things spiritual, has been the

constant exaltation and honoring of Jesus Christ, the Lamb of God, as the only hope for the world.[6]

Once more the meaning of obedience became obvious. In reflecting on his three years in the Brookville pulpit, Ketcham was acknowledging that any success, financial or otherwise, experienced in that church was the result of giving God the preeminence. Ketcham's closing prayer in that last service provided a beautiful picture of a young preacher's responsibility to be faithful and to leave the harvest to God. The prayer demonstrated the degree to which Ketcham had learned his dependence upon God and therefore the degree to which he was prepared for the struggle against liberalism which rested on the immediate horizon:

> Father, my work here is done. I come to Thee with weary body and on bended knee. I bring an offering of my work and way, and for a blessing on the efforts, I pray. Thou knowest all. 'Tis sweet to think that Thou canst read the heart, and that Thou knowest how I strove to win to Thee lost souls, who strayed afar from Thee and from the narrow way. I have gazed on faces that were strangers to me, but all, O Lord, are known and loved by Thee. Their lives to me are as a sealed book, but Thou dost know their nature's inmost nook. But some there are whose natures I know well. I know and love them and would feign compel them to come in unto the marriage feast, but these they are who seem to heed me least. I gave the message and the arrow sped just where Thy hand—divine-directing—led. I cannot tell, but Thou dost know, Dear Lord, if hearts have found comfort from Thy preached Word. I leave it all with Thee. I did my best. Dear Father, it is Thine to do the rest. Drive home conviction to the stubborn heart and to the one in doubt sweet peace impart. I ask thy blessing on the Scriptures read, on hymns of praise, on words of warning said. Let not my prayer to Thee unheeded fall. My work is done; with Thee I leave it all.[7]

Ketcham's farewell message to the Brookville church was literally one of the most painful of his life. Not so much because of his departure from the church, for he knew full well that God was leading

---

6. This statement was taken from a typed copy of an article that appeared in the Brookville newspaper following Ketcham's resignation. *Ketcham Papers.*
    7. Ibid.

him to new responsibilities in Butler, Pennsylvania. Instead, the pain was literal and physical. Ketcham's resignation came in November, and November 1918 is known as the key month in the dreadful flu epidemic that engulfed the entire world. At times "epidemics become world-wide or pandemic, and during these periods, as in 1918, the severity of the disease and the frequency of complications may attain terrifying proportions."[8]

Many outbreaks of influenza had been recorded by medical science, dating back into the early seventeenth century. A generation earlier (1889-1890) an outbreak had occurred. But at no time in human history has there been a pandemic to compare with the one that occurred in the second decade of the twentieth century.

> The 1918 epidemic was the most destructive in history; in fact it ranks with the plague of Justinian and the Black Death as one of the severest holocausts of disease ever encountered. It was estimated by E. O. Jordan that more than 20,000,000 persons perished of influenza in a few months and more than 50 times as many were sick. In India, 12,500,000 persons, or 4% of the total population, are said to have been killed by influenza in the autumn of 1918. In the United States 548,000 died.[9]

A curious feature of this outbreak of influenza was the impact it had on young adults. Usually this age group offers the greatest resistance to disease. However, in this instance, "young, vigorous adults, those between the ages of twenty and forty, were most susceptible to the ravages of the disease and suffered approximately half the deaths."[10]

Bob Ketcham fit right into the middle of the twenty-to-forty age group. The night of his farewell message, when in his prayer he referred to his "weary body," he was truly weary. His sermon was completed only with great effort. Following the service that evening he returned to the Brookville parsonage and went to bed. It was over two

---

8. "Influenza," *Encyclopedia Brittanica,* XII (1971), 242.

9. Ibid.

10. Robert S. Katz, "Influenza 1918-1919: A Study in Mortality," *Bulletin History of Medicine,* XLVIII (February 1974), 416. Katz attributes this to the failure of this age group to build immunity to influenza. He also points to immigration and the unhealthy nature of urban life at this time.

months before he was well enough to leave that parsonage! While Ketcham struggled to recover from his illness, influenza raged through Brookville. This Pennsylvania community of 5,000 buried over 300 of her citizens during the epidemic.

The physical pandemic that was sweeping the world in 1918 represented an overt physical dilemma which men encountered. However, beneath the surface the insidious pandemic of modernism was creeping into the warp and woof of American life. Liberal theologians achieved professorial chairs in the colleges and seminaries that were training young pastors. They brought with them a bushel of contemporary solutions to old spiritual problems. But the new solutions were rooted in humanistic principles that were contrary to the Word of God. The plague of liberalism that was soon to sweep the nation was a far greater spiritual dilemma than anything prior to its time. This "spiritual epidemic" swept through the Northern Baptist Convention and soon Bob Ketcham would stand at the turning point of his career. Before the next year was completed, he would face a spiritual crossroad of far greater significance than his physical crossroad of 1918.

WHEN BOB KETCHAM became pastor of the First Baptist Church of Butler, Pennsylvania, in early 1919, the United States was rejoicing over the end of World War I. The armistice concluding the war was signed in the early morning hours of November 11, 1918. In January 1919, President Woodrow Wilson led the American contingent to Paris for peace negotiations. Wilson met with Georges Clemenceau, "the tiger" of France; David Lloyd George, the clever but shallow premier of Great Britain; and Vittorio Orlando of Italy. The clash between Wilson's idealism and the desire of the representatives of the other countries to see Germany pay for the severe losses they had incurred during the war led to sharp conflict.

Clemenceau, Lloyd George and Orlando viewed peace in terms of the destruction and dismemberment of Germany by territorial concessions and huge war reparations. Wilson had a much more benevolent spirit. The ensuing compromise in reality pleased no one. In practical terms, the Treaty of Versailles was too severe to conciliate the German people, but not severe enough to destroy Germany's potential for war. Adolph Hitler later rode to power on the crest of German dissatisfaction with the treaty.

International unrest relating to the Treaty of Versailles was matched in America by domestic unrest. Wilson had gone to France with a desire for a League of Nations. The League was organized, but it was doomed from the beginning because the treaty carved in Paris was unacceptable to the United States Senate. As a result, the Senate refused to ratify the treaty, and the United States never joined Wilson's beloved League. Meanwhile, the unrest created by war and postwar international tensions caused many in America to retreat to an isolationist philosophy. Americans could not understand why the allies were not more grateful for America's belated but pivotal involvement in the war. Dissatisfaction swept the nation as Americans failed to experience the gratification they felt should accompany victory in a world war.

Some historians have viewed the war as a primary cause in the emergence of fundamentalism. Stewart G. Cole proposed that "much of the intolerance absorbed in Protestantism . . . was due directly to the technique and spirit of wartime carried over into the days of social reconstruction."[1] Cole unhesitatingly placed Bible-believing Christians in rather contemptible company: "The Ku Klux Klan, the anti-World Court crusade, 'one hundred per cent Americanism,' tirades against labor and bolshevism, sabbatarianism, *fundamentalism* [italics mine], suggest the new cults."[2]

Norman Furniss makes the same connection between World War I, the Klan and fundamentalism:

> . . . Vaguely defined fear was one of the most obvious traits of the Fundamentalists. Just as the Kleagles and Kluggs of the Ku Klux Klan worked upon the unrest of millions throughout the United States after 1918, so the fundamentalist leaders, experiencing obscure apprehensions as a residue of wartime fever, satisfied themselves and their followers that two sinister forces, evolution and modernism, were the evil agents producing their uneasiness.[3]

Furniss then goes on to describe "violence in thought and language" and "abusive personal attack upon Modernists or evolutionists" as two basic characteristics of fundamentalism.[4]

Ketcham's position in the Klan controversy was made very clear in the mid 1920s. The Klan reached its apex in the United States in this

1. Cole, *The History of Fundamentalism,* p. 26.
2. Ibid., p. 25.
3. Furniss, *Controversy,* p. 35.
4. Ibid., p. 36.

time period. It was so powerful that in 1924 the Democratic National Convention rejected a resolution that would have denounced Klan activities. At that time Ketcham was pastor in Niles, Ohio. In response to the Democratic Party's decision, he preached a series of messages in opposition to the Klan. Indeed, if Bob Ketcham is typical, the attempt of historians to link fundamentalism and the Ku Klux Klan is an unwarranted generalization and a manifestation of a deeply rooted misunderstanding of the purposes of orthodox Biblical Christianity.

In the midst of the domestic and international unrest that came in the backwash of World War I and the Paris Peace Conference, American religious leaders proposed a new movement which was designed to affect not only America but the world. The program was known as the New World Movement and, in Ketcham's opinion, was liberal from the outset.

> It was a 5-year program launched simultaneously by all the great denominations through which and by which they were going to bring in the Kingdom. Their own word for it was "creating a civilization Christian in spirit and in passion." Each of the co-operating denominations was to make a contribution to the big Central Committee which would in turn do most of the propaganda work for all of the co-operating bodies.[5]

The Northern Baptist Convention's share of this total program was a stunning one hundred million dollars, which was to be raised over the five-year period. But in the minds of many, the problem was not the number of dollars demanded. The real concern was that everyone had to participate. Bob Ketcham was but one of many who became concerned about the development of a denominational hierarchy which sought to control the local churches.

> This New World Movement was the first organized attempt to compel everybody to support the modernistic program. It was the inauguration in 1919 of the famous "Unified Budget" system where, instead of supporting individual agencies and missionaries, a church was compelled to support the "Budget." It was this new twist which aroused pastors and churches and caused us to begin

---

5. R. T. Ketcham, "Lest We Forget," *The Baptist Bulletin*, XXI (September 1955), 6.

examining our beloved Convention and denomination—and
what we discovered there gave many of us some bad hours.[6]

The New World Movement was launched by the Northern Baptist
Convention when it met in Denver in 1919. By this time Ketcham was
thirty years old and had been in the ministry for seven years. He had
just started his third pastorate when the document that launched the
New World Movement reached his desk. Along with it came a request
for $17,000 to be paid over the next five years by the First Baptist
Church of Butler.

Bob's initial reaction centered on the document's purported
desire to create a "civilization Christian in spirit and in passion." He
came erect in his chair and said to himself (talking to himself was a
characteristic of Ketcham), "Whoa! Wait a minute. That is
postmillennialism—pure unadulterated postmillennialism—and I'm a
pre! I don't know any place that I'm ordered to create a world
Christian in spirit and in passion, but I am ordered to get people out of
this one that's going to the dogs and over the abyss into the pit. So,
there's something wrong with this program."

With that warning signal erected in his mind, Ketcham thoroughly
read and digested the Convention's document. Uneasiness continued
to engulf him as he recognized the implications of the program his
church was being urged to support. He was convinced that the
autonomy of the local congregation was being threatened by a
procedure that was not even Baptistic. The more he read, the more
uneasy he became over the implications and complications of the
commitment that was being asked of his church.

He realized that he could not in good conscience support the
program. The Convention had taken the records of the missionary
giving for each of their member churches over the previous three
years, and on that basis had made an assessment upon each church.
The $17,000 assessment for the Butler church was to be over and
above their regular missionary giving. What could a pastor do in the
face of this denominational dictum?

In light of all these facts, and because he had to make a proposal
to his congregation concerning the assessed $17,000, Robert Ketcham

6. Ibid.

felt compelled to do further research. He expanded his study of the problem beyond the Convention pamphlet by reading several books and documents—particularly those written by professors of the suspect Crozer Seminary. Volumes by men such as Shirley Jackson Case, George Berman Foster and James Franklin were studied in great detail, after which Ketcham concluded that "the whole administrative structure of the Northern Baptist Convention was honeycombed with modernism."

Ketcham sat down at his desk and began to write a document to his church in longhand. In an introductory paragraph he expressed his concern for the growth of liberalism in the Northern Baptist Convention, while admitting that "the great majority of Baptist laymen and laywomen are today true to the 'faith once delivered.' "[7] But Ketcham noted the apparent discrepancy between what was believed by the people in the pew and what was taught by many who were now preaching in the churches of the Convention. He pinpointed the problem as denominational education and isolated four areas within the denomination that were of utmost concern to him: the colleges and universities, the seminaries, the publication society and the General Board of Promotion.[8] In its final form, Ketcham's research became known as *A Statement of the First Baptist Church Butler, Pennsylvania, with reference to The New World Movement and the $100,000,000 Drive.*

In the first section of the pamphlet, Ketcham dealt with the situation in denominational colleges and universities. He wrote: "We deplore and protest the presence of Unitarian professors in our colleges and universities endowed with Baptist money."[9] Ketcham went on to quote several denominational faculty members who denied the Virgin Birth, the deity of Christ, redemption through the blood of Christ, and other basic tenets of orthodox Christianity. He concluded that if a school was willing to allow men who espoused such positions

7. R. T. Ketcham, *A Statement of the First Baptist Church Butler, Pennsylvania, with reference to The New World Movement and the $100,000,000 Drive* (Butler, PA: Citizen Printing Co., 1919), p. 2. A copy of the original pamphlet is in the *Ketcham Papers.*
   8. Ibid., p. 3.
   9. Ibid.

to remain on the faculty, "then we believe that such institutions should turn over their endowment and property to the Baptist denomination and seek their future support from the Unitarians, to whom they truly belong."[10]

In the second section of this pamphlet, Ketcham turned his attention to the denominational seminaries. He quoted a letter from a seminary student who was about to graduate. The youth indicated that his seminary career had caused him to doubt everything. For a preacher whose theory of knowledge was rooted in the principle of faith in the Word of God, this letter was a serious indictment. Ketcham also protested the use of G. B. Stevens's volume, *The Teachings of Jesus,* as a seminary textbook because it taught that Christ was "limited in knowledge" and "liable to mistakes." Finally, he pointed out that at least two seminary professors were serving as pulpit supplies in Unitarian churches.

The third section of Ketcham's pamphlet dealt with the denominational publication society. In this segment he began by protesting the nature of some of the materials being sold in denominational bookrooms, referring in particular to Sir Oliver Lodge's volume, *Raymond, or Life and Death,* which was accepted as an "authoritative text" of the Spiritualists. Ketcham identified specific problems and doctrinal disagreements he had with the denominational Sunday school literature.

The fourth section of the pamphlet dealt with the General Board of Promotion and comprised almost two-thirds of the total pamphlet. Ketcham began this section with the following statement: "We deplore the fact that the General Board of Promotion has set before the Baptist masses a program which that Board calls 'The Program of Jesus Christ,' whereas that program is in large measure foreign to the Revealed Program of Jesus Christ as outlined in the New Testament."[11] Ketcham listed two basic objections in this category.

First, he averred the Board's program was "foreign in its objective." This objection dealt with the aforementioned phrase taken from the first article adopted by the Northern Baptist Convention in

10. Ibid., p. 4.
11. Ibid., p. 6.

Denver in May 1919 where it proposed to establish a civilization Christian in spirit and in passion throughout the world. Ketcham began his argument with a question and a statement. "Is there any hint in Scripture of such a civilization brought about by the activities of the church in this age? If there is, the Bible record of the entire cycle of time does not declare and reveal it."[12] Ketcham then reviewed and quoted several Scriptures, beginning in Genesis 6 and moving on to Psalm 14, the Book of Isaiah, and, in the New Testament, Mark 7, Romans 3 and Paul's description of the last days in 2 Timothy.

Ketcham concluded this review of Scripture by saying, ". . . Nowhere is there an intimation that that circle is to be broken into by 'a civilization Christian in spirit and in passion.' "[13]

Ketcham continued his defense of the premillenarian position by reviewing several parables of the Lord Jesus Christ. Then, looking at the program of God outlined in Acts 15, he concluded that "the immediate program of God is not to present and establish a kingdom on earth now, but to take out His bride to become associated with Him in the rule of that kingdom when it is established."[14] Ketcham closed this section by quoting Dr. S. E. Taylor and Mrs. Cronk, leaders of the New World Movement, to the effect that evil was continuing to grow in the world.

Ketcham's second objection to the program of the General Board of Promotion was that it was foreign in its method: "Were it possible to endorse the program itself, it would still be utterly impossible to endorse the method by which it is to be put across."[15] Here Ketcham particularly objected to the proposal that the church should solicit funds from the unregenerate in the community on behalf of their program:

> It is an admitted fact that the cause of Christ would be over-financed if the Christian people would practice the principles of New Testament stewardship, but, since they have not done so, and the cause is suffering for funds, shall we seek, therefore, to

12. Ibid.
13. Ibid., p. 9.
14. Ibid., p. 12.
15. Ibid., pp. 12, 13.

force enough money from the world to make up for the failure of the saints?[16]

In consequence of his findings, Ketcham concluded his pamphlet by suggesting a course of action for his church. This proposal formed the concluding paragraph of the pamphlet and is here repeated in its entirety:

> AND NOW, WHEREAS: We feel that we cannot enter into the New World Movement, even exercising our right of designation, without becoming a part of it and thereby endorsing it;
>
> AND WHEREAS: In view of facts cited above, we cannot conscientiously endorse the Movement as at present outlined:
>
> THEREFORE BE IT RESOLVED, That we, the First Baptist Church of Butler, Pennsylvania, withhold our financial support from the movement entirely.
>
> AND WHEREAS: This action is not meant as a withdrawal from the Baptist denomination, but simply from a denominational program which we believe to be unscriptural in purpose and method:
>
> THEREFORE BE IT FURTHER RESOLVED: That we shall make just as earnest and honest an effort to raise $17,000.00 for benevolent purposes during the next five years as we should have made had we entered the Movement, and that we shall administer our own funds so raised, forfeiting denominational credit, and that worthy objects, institutions and individuals within the scope of our denomination and elsewhere that to our mind are worthy of Baptist support shall be the recipients of our gifts.[17]

This document was signed by Rev. R. T. Ketcham, Pastor, and Mrs. Rella F. Ellenburger, Clerk.

When Ketcham completed the handwritten version of his paper, he reworked it and typed it in a manuscript of some fifteen to twenty pages. After making sure that the manuscript read exactly as he felt it should, he took the document into the pulpit with him one Sunday morning and read the prepared statement in its entirety.

For the next five weeks, the church reviewed the document

16. Ibid., p. 14.
17. Ibid., pp. 15, 16.

section by section. On a Sunday morning following this detailed review, Ketcham again read it in its entirety and said he would entertain a motion to either accept or reject the proposal. He made no coercive threats, but simply said, "What is your pleasure?" Someone made the motion that the First Baptist Church of Butler refuse the $17,000 assessment of the Convention and decline to cooperate in the New World Movement. The motion was seconded and a standing vote was taken: 131 in favor, 5 opposed. "Some of the five opposed voted thus because the Resolutions were not drastic enough."[18] Two of the five were convinced that the church should have voted to withdraw from the Convention immediately.

As he put it at a later date: "We were going to clean the mess up, you know. We were going in like the Gold Dust twins, and clean the place up, brother. We were going to get rid of this bunch of Matthew 13 birds in the mustard tree." The dream of "cleaning up" the Convention was destined to turn into a nightmare in the years ahead. For the moment, however, it was the challenge of obedience.

Sometime after the vote had been taken by the First Baptist Church of Butler, Bob Ketcham's people began to ask if they could have a copy of the document he had prepared. Ketcham visited the small Citizen Printing Company in Butler and had 500 copies of his manuscript prepared in pamphlet form for distribution to his church. Little did he realize the chain of events that would be set in motion by the printing of this pamphlet.

18. Ibid., p. 1.

An original copy of this pamphlet is in the *Ketcham Papers.*

Dr. Ketcham at age 27 when he became pastor of his second church, Brookville, Pennsylvania

7

THROUGHOUT THE country other fundamentalist
ministers were developing some of the same concerns over the New
World Movement that Ketcham had expressed to his church. Like
Ketcham, most of these people had no intention of leaving the
Northern Baptist Convention. Curtis Lee Laws, editor of the
conservative *Watchman-Examiner,* was also concerned about this
movement. Before the Denver convention ever met, Laws pleaded
with the Convention to spend time examining the new program before
launching it.

His concerns revolved around three basic problems. First, he felt it
would be necessary to teach people the value of a unified budget
before asking them to accept this new approach. Second, he was
convinced that the Northern Baptist Convention would not support
the New World Movement because $30,000,000 of the $100,000,000
was to be distributed to colleges and seminaries, many of which were
suspected of liberalism by the rank and file of the denomination. Third,
Laws was convinced that the prohibition against designated giving was
"un-Baptistic" and that the Convention had no right to force
congregations to give to projects that violated their conscience.[1]

1. *Watchman-Examiner,* XI (1923), 165.

In spite of his serious reservations, however, Laws urged support of the program once it was adopted. He pled with his readers to fulfill their pledges to the New World Movement, though he remained vitally concerned about the growth of liberalism in his beloved denomination. Thus, while his approach was somewhat different, his desire was the same as Ketcham's:

> Meanwhile, our Baptist people everywhere should use their influence to see to it that the leaders in our Baptist organizations of every kind, and in our institutions of every grade, shall be men who cling tenaciously to the evangelical doctrines of God's Word and to the time-honored principles of our beloved denomination. Everywhere it is being said that nine-tenths of our people hold to the faith of our fathers. If unity and aggressiveness are desired in our denomination, the time has come for the evangelical nine-tenths of our denomination to assert itself and take the reins of our government in its hands. Thus, and only thus, can confidence be restored and can the denomination go forth like a conquering army.[2]

Another clergyman to be concerned over the New World Movement was the dynamic William Bell Riley, pastor of the First Baptist Church of Minneapolis. Riley was one of the leading spokesmen for fundamentalism in the 1920s. As early as 1909, he had attacked modernism in his volume, *The Finality of Higher Criticism.*

> His First Baptist Church of Minneapolis, which by 1925 reported annual receipts of over $200,000, and his ever expanding Northwestern Bible and Missionary Training School were known throughout the upper Middle West. His opinions influenced not only the people who heard his many speeches and sermons but also those who read his periodicals—*Baptist Beacon, Christian Fundamentalist, Christian Fundamentals in School and Church*—and his books and articles.[3]

Somehow, Riley, who assumed a major role in the leadership of the fundamentalist forces during the 1920s, received a copy of Ketcham's pamphlet. The old gentleman liked what he saw in the pamphlet and penned a letter to Ketcham, requesting 20,000 copies.

2. Ibid., p. 167.
3. Furniss, *Controversy,* p. 110.

When Ketcham prepared the pamphlet, he had no realization that anything like this would occur. He had not designed his work for anyone but his local congregation. He could not believe that a man of such distinction as Riley would want a single copy of the pamphlet, let alone 20,000 copies!

But it turned out that this little pamphlet, designed to express the young pastor's convictions to his church, was destined to be "the first of its kind published and distributed in what later proved to be the long, bitter struggle in the Northern Baptist Convention to cleanse it from its modernism. Dr. R. E. Neighbour, then pastor in Elyria, Ohio, came out with another exposé some time later, but so far as is known this little 16-page pamphlet was the first to be released."[4] Requests poured in for the pamphlet, and Ketcham had more and more copies printed. Before the end of 1920, over 200,000 copies of the pamphlet had been distributed throughout the country.[5]

The ability of the fundamentalists to carry on such a mass distribution of literature was the result of their forces becoming more organized in response to the threat of modernism. As early as 1916, a group of preachers meeting at Montrose, Pennsylvania, had laid the groundwork for an organization known as the World's Christian Fundamentals Association. In the ensuing years many fundamentalists were attracted to this organization. In May 1918 they held a prophetic conference in Philadelphia which drew over five thousand people.

In light of the success of the Philadelphia conference, the fundamentalists decided to reconvene at Moody Bible Institute in 1919. The Moody conference proved to be of great significance. "Whereas prior to this convention spokesmen for orthodoxy had been content to affirm their faith and deplore unbelief, the men assembled at the Moody Bible Institute in 1919 showed a determination to take the offensive."[6] Men such as James Gray, dean of Moody Bible Institute, and the aforementioned W. B. Riley, along with Amzi Clarence Dixon, became prime movers in the new association.

4. Ketcham, "Lest We Forget," p. 6.
5. Ibid.
6. Furniss, Controversy, p. 50.

At the same time key fundamentalists within the Northern Baptist Convention were also organizing their forces. The fundamentalists became concerned over a Convention vote establishing a new weekly periodical called *The Baptist.* Curtis Lee Laws, editor of the *Watchman-Examiner,* led the opposition. He "was not afraid of a new competitor: his own periodical was a popular one; rather he was convinced that Modernists in the church would use this official organ to disseminate their ideas."[7] With Laws joining Riley and Jasper C. Massee of Brooklyn as the guiding forces, a committee of fundamentalists was established. The group called for a preconvention conference prior to the convening of the Northern Baptist Convention's 1920 meeting. This body provided the appropriate vehicle for the distribution of literature to the fundamentalists in the Northern Baptist Convention, and Riley, Ketcham and Neighbour saw to it that the vehicle was adequately employed!

The preconvention meeting of 1920 marked the initial organization of the fundamentalists inside the Northern Baptist Convention. "When the first assembly appointed a commission to investigate conditions within Northern Baptist educational circles and to report its findings to another preconvention conference in 1921, it in effect made itself a permanent body, soon to carry the impressive title National Federation of Fundamentalists of the Northern Baptists."[8] This group was to lead the battle against liberalism in the Convention for several years to come.

The unexpected demand for his pamphlet marked an important transition in the life of Robert T. Ketcham. The first seven years of his ministry had been conducted almost exclusively at the local level. The young preacher was learning to preach and to care for the many administrative details in the local church. To the best of his knowledge, this was his life calling: to faithfully proclaim the Word of God and care for the needs of the local congregation. But unbeknown to him, God had been preparing him for a broader ministry. While continuing his responsibilities as the pastor of a local church, beginning in 1920 he would assume an increasing influence in his denomination.

7. Ibid., p. 103.
8. Ibid., p. 104.

Ketcham's trip to the 1920 Northern Baptist Convention and the preconvention meeting of the fundamentalists was both encouraging and discouraging. He was greatly encouraged by the enthusiasm and the organization of the fundamentalists, and he was convinced that victory was assured. However, W. B. Riley declined taking the active leadership of the fundamentalist cause, preferring J. C. Massee as the leader. Riley expressed the desire to be free to work from the floor of the Convention.

Massee was a mild man who was reticent to force issues. In Ketcham's mind, his appointment as leader turned out to be a critical mistake. "J. C. Massee proved to be a pussyfooter. There were two or three times in that Buffalo meeting when we had the victory right in our hands and J. C. Massee took it out." Ketcham's response to Massee was the result of the latter's willingness to allow key issues to be delayed until the next year's Convention, thus giving the liberal faction time to regroup their forces.

The 1920 Northern Baptist Convention meetings in Buffalo proved to be very dramatic. Courtland Myers, who had been decrying modernism in the colleges and seminaries, made a firm denunciation of modernists from the floor of the Convention. J. C. Massee introduced the World's Christian Fundamentals Association's proposal for examining conditions in the colleges and seminaries. W. B. Riley immediately followed him in support of the motion and indicated the men he felt should serve on the committee. Naturally, all of the men named were solid, Bible-believing fundamentalists, and the liberal response was immediate and loud. The fundamentalists were accused of railroading and cheap politics, and the liberals asserted that the committee members would naturally hang everybody they found.

Bob Ketcham once admitted: "I'm a little ashamed of some of the things that happened there. But I want to tell you, emotion was at a high pitch, and there was one time when we were standing up on our chairs."

Ketcham attended the conference with his friend and confidant, Harry Tillis. At one point, Tillis and Ketcham were separated from the group of fundamentalists with whom they had been seated. They found themselves right in the middle of a rather large coterie of modernists. As the debate raged, Tillis and Ketcham were applauding and shouting, "Amen! Amen!" to the remarks of W. B. Riley. As they finally were seated, one of the liberal clerics turned to Tillis and shouted, "Steam rollers! Steam rollers! Steam rollers!" Tillis looked at him and responded, "Yes sir, yes sir, we've been rolled under the thing so long that it seems good to get on it and ride it for once."

In reflecting on that event and the ensuing years, Bob Ketcham said: "Nobody will ever know what we went through in those days. But we lost the battle there, and the next year they were ready. And the next year we got whipped and whipped and whipped. For twelve long years, from 1920 to 1932, there was an effort made to clean up the camp, and it got worse. And we went home more defeated than ever."

Bob Ketcham returned to Butler following the convention weary in body and in soul. He was deeply distressed that the fundamentalists in his denomination had not been able to effectuate a swift and sure victory over the liberal forces.

His mind was troubled by his personal life also. A cousin, who had been like a brother, and a grandmother, who was like a mother to him, had died. In addition, his father-in-law had died. At the same time, his wife, Clara, was in Crest Sanitorium near Altoona, Pennsylvania. Clara had come through the flu epidemic of 1918 with much greater ease than Bob. But in 1919 she had contracted tuberculosis, and the doctors offered little hope of her survival. Because the physicians were unable to help her, they granted permission for her to return home. Ketcham's father journeyed down from Elmira to meet Bob after he returned from the convention. Bob and his father made the trip to Crest Sanitorium and back to Butler together. Ketcham's father provided much needed comfort as Bob brought his wife home to die.

After returning from Altoona, the weary preacher placed his dying wife in bed and went into his study to visit with his father. The senior Ketcham was returning home the next morning. As they visited, a rap came at the door. The preacher called "Come in," fully expecting to see one of the members of his congregation. But when the door opened, seven men and one woman paraded into the parsonage. Ketcham was startled. He immediately recognized all the men as pastors in the Pittsburgh Baptist Association. The woman was the wife of one of the pastors.

The visitors waited silently as Bob and his father got out chairs and arranged them in the living room so the guests could be seated.

When everyone was in place, the younger Ketcham asked what he could do for his guests. It quickly became apparent that his pamphlet had had a marked effect on the Northern Baptist Convention.   Mr. J. A. T. Marstellar, serving as the group's spokesman, announced that the seven preachers had come to request the withdrawal of the Butler church's pamphlet and the retraction of its contents. Further, they wanted to urge the Butler pastor to put his church into the denominational program and assume responsibility for the $17,000.

Ketcham sat silently, peering into the eyes of one after another of his guests. Finally, fixing his gaze on the spokesman, he said, "Mr. Marstellar, what's the matter with it? Isn't it true?" Marstellar's reply was that the pamphlet was harmful to the denominational program. To this Ketcham responded, "Is that the issue? Well, to me the issue is, is it true? Is what I said in that pamphlet true?" At this point Marstellar pleaded ignorance, admitting that he had not even read the pamphlet.

Without a word, Ketcham arose from his chair and went to his study. He returned, carrying a copy of the much-circulated pamphlet, and suggested that in the light of the fact that the chairman of the committee had not read it, perhaps others on the committee were also ignorant of its contents. He handed the pamphlet to Marstellar and asked him to read it aloud, so that "we will all know what we are talking about." In a few moments, Marstellar was reading the Butler church's pamphlet aloud to his committee! Meanwhile, Ketcham's father sat in a corner with a sizable grin splitting his face. He was later to commend his son for his cleverness in getting the information disseminated in this manner!

When the pamphlet had been read in its entirety, Ketcham again asked if it was true, and his guests again repeated the charge that it was harmful to the denomination. For three and one-half hours the debate raged, with the committee demanding retraction and Ketcham refusing to back away from the pamphlet he had prepared. At one point one of the men became so incensed at Ketcham's intransigence that he jumped from his chair, dashed across the room and grabbed Bob by the coat collar. In describing this portion of the incident, Ketcham stated: "He shook me so hard that if I had had the kind of teeth in my head then that I have now, they would have been all over the place."

The committee member's face was livid. He drew the young preacher by the collar until they stood nose to nose, and he shook him again and said, "You get down on your knees and ask God to forgive you. You get down right here and tell God to forgive you and tell your church to forgive you and get back on this thing." It seemed incredible to the fundamentalist preacher that this liberal was telling him to ask for forgiveness for being faithful to the principles of Scripture!

In spite of the tenseness of the situation, Ketcham was struck by the irony of such a demand. As a smile crept across his face, his protagonist became further enraged. Everyone in the room stiffened as the liberal preacher prepared to strike his opponent. As Ketcham subsequently described it: "I thought he was going to strike me, but this one dear woman proved to be his wife. The only time she made any movement the whole day was now. She came over and took him by the arm and said, 'Now come on, Papa, now come; come on, sit down, Papa.' And 'Papa' went and sat down; otherwise, I might have gotten smacked."

It became obvious that things were at a stalemate. Tempers were frayed, and everyone was on the edge of exhaustion. Finally, Ketcham stood and said: "There's no use talking about it anymore; I'm not going to do it." Silence fell over the entire room. It finally was broken by the scraping of Marstellar's chair, as the spokesman for the delegation stood to his feet and approached the young Ketcham. In staccato-like tones, he said: "I'm here to tell you, then, that you either put your church into this movement and pay this assessment and withdraw that pamphlet, or I will personally see to it that you never get another Baptist church as long as you live."

Again silence engulfed the room, broken for several moments only by the sound of Bob Ketcham's labored breathing. The gauntlet had been thrown. The challenge was there, and the young preacher's career appeared to be on the line. He did not have time to say, "I'll pray about it, think it over, and get back to you in a few days." So far as he knew, he stood at that moment in danger of losing all he had prepared to do in the previous years.

As he stood there, Ketcham's mind flashed back to that hour in 1911 when at three o'clock in the morning he had promised God obedience. He recalled how he had entered the ministry with that promise of obedience as his only qualification for the job. Then his mind raced back to that day in his little study in Roulette when the battle had raged in his heart and soul over Colossians 1:18. He vividly recalled how he had affirmed his commitment to give Christ the preeminence in all things by inking the penciled inscription in the flyleaf of his Bible.

As he thought back to those earlier moments, tears brimmed in his eyes. But they were not tears of defeat, for behind the tears shone the fire of resolution. The silence was broken as Ketcham hoarsely whispered, "Well, Mr. Marstellar, if you are asking me to buy a church for $17,000 through the nose of my local church, your price is too high. I can get a soapbox for a dime."

Marstellar turned without speaking and stalked to the door, and the committee of liberal clergymen slowly filed out of the house. Ketcham and his father sat engulfed in silence for several minutes.

Without question, this was one of the great crises in the life of Robert Thomas Ketcham. At the tender age of thirty, with most of his ministry still ahead of him, he had faced the pressure of a coercive attempt on the part of the liberals to gain his cooperation. The challenge came at a time when his eyes were growing dimmer by the month. It came at a time when he knew his wife was dying and he would be left with two motherless daughters. Now he was faced with the realization that he might have to care for Lois and Peg in some different vocation than the ministry. But he also realized that his commitment was to obedience and that God could overrule the political machinations of man.

This event in Bob Ketcham's life would not be complete without reference to a sequel that occurred some seventeen years later. At that time Ketcham was pastor of the Central Baptist Church of Gary, Indiana, a church with one thousand members. One day a man approached Pastor Ketcham with a letter that had been written by Marstellar to one of his friends in New York State. One paragraph of that letter read as follows: "Dear Bill: For God's sake try and get me a church somewhere. I must have something within six months or I will have to crawl out of Pittsburgh on my hands and knees after dark." In reacting to this letter, Dr. Ketcham said, "Here was the tragic story of a man who had sold his ministerial soul to the Convention, and this was the payoff!"[9]

9. Ketcham, "Lest We Forget," p. 6.

Conversely, Ketcham's pastorate of the vigorous Central Baptist Church in Gary provided the blessed story of a man who had sold his ministerial soul to the Lord Jesus Christ. Indeed, the years of Bob Ketcham's ministry graphically demonstrate that you never lose when you obey the Lord Jesus. It is when you fail to obey, or when you fail to stand for the Word of God, or when you only halfway follow through, that you get into trouble. But if you find out where Jesus Christ stands and stand with Him, you do not lose. Every would-be preacher must learn there is no substitute for obedience to the Lord Jesus Christ and for faithfulness to His Word. For "in all things," *He* must "have the preeminence."

8

THE DAYS FOLLOWING his confrontation with

the area ministerial representatives were filled with sorrow and
heartache for Robert Thomas Ketcham. Clara's physical condition
deteriorated rapidly. While he watched and prayed, his wife grew
weaker daily. Meanwhile, in the midst of these family trials, the pastor
and his church were buffeted by criticism for their stand against the
denominational program. Further, Ketcham was becoming
increasingly aware of the severity of his eye disease and the
implications of this ailment for his future ministry.

Less than two months after his dramatic meeting with the
convention clerics, Bob's Clara went to be with the Lord. The full
burden of raising his daughters, Lois and Peg, fell squarely on his
shoulders. Shortly thereafter, the brokenhearted Ketcham lost his
godly father to whom he had turned many a time in periods of trial.

During these months of testing, Ketcham learned anew his
absolute dependence upon God. He came to know more about the
sufficiency of God's grace than he had ever known. In the stillness of
the night he would water his pillow with his tears and plead for divine
strength for his broken heart. In much smaller crises many a man has
reverted to blaming God for his problems. Yet it was in this context
that God began to impress upon Ketcham's mind the very precious
truth that years later was to become his familiar motto: "Your heavenly

Father is too good to be unkind and too wise to make mistakes."

In the perspective of time it can be seen that those days of heartache and heartbreak were important in the life of Bob Ketcham. God was molding His servant for future ministry. Devoid of formal college or seminary training, Ketcham was learning through the experience of personal heartbreak that a vital aspect of obedience was a complete submission to whatever God chose to bring into the life of His servant. In the midst of deep trial, Ketcham spent his days in his study pouring over the Word of God and his nights praying for the strength of God. Thus he learned the importance of total dependence upon Christ and total submission to God's will. He began to understand as never before Paul's response to God's sufficient grace when the apostle said: "Most gladly therefore will I rather glory in my infirmities, that the power of Christ may rest upon me" (2 Cor. 12:9).

The manner in which God used these days of personal trial to train his servant can be seen in a visible and tangible illustration. For several years, Ketcham had been puzzled by Psalm 147:3 and 4: "He healeth the broken in heart, and bindeth up their wounds. He telleth the number of the stars; he calleth them all by their names."

These verses had been a conundrum to Ketcham ever since he read them. He found it difficult to understand why two apparently disparate thoughts were placed back to back by the psalmist. What did they have to do with each other? Why were they linked? Why would God in one breath of inspiration bring together such diametrically opposite concepts?

It was simple for Ketcham to picture the austere, mighty, magnificent, sovereign God of Heaven and earth standing in His spaceless eternity. It was easy to picture God perfectly at home in the midst of the stars and planets that were His creation. It was no problem to picture God in all of His majesty directing the stars by name as to which way they should go. But it was difficult to understand how suddenly this great and mighty God would drop here to earth, right into the basement of human suffering and human living, to bind up the wounds of mankind.

In the days of his own heartache and suffering, suddenly the meaning of Psalm 147:3 and 4 came thundering to him like a solid piece of heavenly steel. The meaning was simple yet beautiful: the God of the stars is the God of broken hearts. God is not so busy in

Heaven numbering the stars that He cannot hear the faintest whisper that comes from the distraught and bothered soul. This precious thought subsequently became a portion of a beautiful volume that God has used to challenge the hearts of many. Notice the full value of the educational process through which Bob Ketcham was passing as he expressed it in his own words:

> This intimate association of Himself with us in our sorrow is beautifully set before us in Psalm 147:3-4, "He healeth the broken in heart and bindeth up their wounds. He telleth the number of the stars; he calleth them all by their names." Two more widely separated spheres could hardly be imagined—*shining heavenly stars and broken human hearts!* In the one, we are taken on an excursion through the starry heavens. We are called upon to take note of the uncountable millions of celestial bodies reaching out into uncountable billions of miles in space, and there we are introduced to a Being who knows their exact number and the name of every one of them. We quail before such a Being. We fall upon our faces in fear and terror as we glimpse the majestic presence of the *God of Stars.*
>
> The contrasting sphere is that of broken human hearts. It is as though the floor of heaven had suddenly opened and dropped us down to earth, but not into the homes and halls of earth where mirth and happiness reign. We crash on down through all of that into the very depths of human experience where broken hearts and blasted lives lie all around us. And here in this realm, too, strangely enough, we find God at work. Not now making and naming a few new stars, the greatness of which *drives us from Him* in *awful fear,* but healing and comforting broken hearts and binding up their wounds with a tenderness that *draws us to Him* and causes us to pillow our head upon His breast while with His own nail-pierced hand of love, He wipes every tear from our eyes.
>
> For years I struggled with these two verses trying to understand why two realms so vastly different and so infinitely far apart were crowded into one breath in the inspired Scriptures. Then one day I learned the truth. It was back in 1920 when, in eleven short months, four of my most precious ones on earth were, one after the other, suddenly snatched from me in death. It was in those hours of darkness that could be felt, shut away alone in my study by day and my room by night, that I learned what God the Lord was trying to say to me by putting these two verses so close together and yet dealing with realms so far apart. I learned in that black night that God was trying to teach me that the *God of stars IS the God of broken hearts.*

In our experiences of sorrow we are apt to feel that God is so far away, that He is so busy numbering and naming stars and manipulating His vast universe that He has no time to hear our feeble gasp, as with uncontrollable sorrow we turn our tear-stained faces to the sky, begging for some relief for our aching hearts. What God would have us to know from these verses is that He is never so busy manipulating the universe, as vast and intricate as it is, that He does not have time to come into our little home and stand with us at the bedside of a loved one fast slipping away, and to travel with us to sustain us at the open gravesides; then He returns with us to our homes and walks with us in all our ways, drying our tears, healing our hurts, and sanctifying to us our sorrows.

It was such a God who left His stars to come to the side of a brokenhearted Hagar when she cried over the imminent death of her only son. It was such a God who came to the desolate little home in Moab where sat a brokenhearted Naomi, thinking of the three graves which contained the bodies of husband and two sons, and whispered in her ear words of hope and blessing and restoration back in the homeland of Bethlehem-Judah. It was such a God who could leave His complex universe and stand at the sealed tomb of Lazarus and weep, and in the next moment open the tomb and bring forth Lazarus. It is this God in the person of Christ who is waiting today to walk straight into the very heart of your sorrow and heal it by the touch of His nail-pierced hand. The Lord is my Shepherd, therefore I shall not want for *comfort*.[1]

While God in His sovereign wisdom continued to educate Bob Ketcham for future battles, other fundamentalist preachers prepared to carry on the struggle implemented in 1920. A second preconvention meeting of fundamentalists was called in Des Moines in June 1921. It was in this meeting that the concept of urging the Northern Baptists to formulate a doctrinal statement for fellowship was born. J. C. Massee, in his role as chairman of the fundamentalists' preconvention session, pointed out that a basic doctrinal homogeneity was a prerequisite for the Convention. The orthodox delegates voiced hearty approval.

However, the fundamentalist action of the preconvention period did not carry over into the 1921 Northern Baptist Convention sessions.

1. R. T. Ketcham, *I Shall Not Want* (Chicago: Moody Press, 1953, 1972), pp. 79-82.

The committee that had been assigned to examine the schools expressed dissatisfaction with some faculty members but did little more. The idea of adopting a creed such as the New Hampshire Confession of Faith was presented to the preconvention fundamentalists but was not pushed in front of the convention as a whole.

At the same time liberal opposition began to emerge in an organized fashion, led by such individuals as Cornelius Woelfkin. At this point in the developing conflict neither side was characterized by good organization. But the liberals had the distinct advantage because they were seeking to maintain the status quo. Gradually the fundamentalists came to recognize that basic changes would be necessary in the Northern Baptist Convention itself if the rapidly rising tide of modernism was to be stemmed.

Even as the realization of this need gripped the hearts of key fundamentalists, liberal theologians were beginning to recognize the "threat" of fundamentalism. In response to the two-year-old movement among preconvention fundamentalists, in February 1922, Cornelius Woelfkin of New York City announced a new organization designed to defend the Northern Baptist Convention against "factious" elements. The new group was to be called the "Evangelical Movement."[2]

While Woelfkin was expressing his dismay over fundamentalism in terms of an organizational structure, Harry Emerson Fosdick was becoming the emotional spokesman for the liberal position. He equated fundamentalism with hypocrisy and narrow-mindedness. Fosdick called forth the "glories" of open-minded liberalism and attacked the fundamentalists. In a sermon entitled "Shall the Fundamentalists Win?" he made a convenient differentiation between fundamentalists and conservatives:

> We should not identify the fundamentalists with the conservatives. All fundamentalists are conservatives, but not all conservatives are fundamentalists. The best conservatives can often give lessons to

2. *Watchman-Examiner,* X (1922), 198.

the liberals in true liberality of spirit, but the fundamentalists'
program is essentially illiberal and intolerant.[3]

Clearly Fosdick had no quarrel with anyone who would leave him
completely alone. He demanded the freedom to do what he wanted
and to believe what he wished. A man could be a conservative
theologically as long as he allowed Fosdick to deny the essentials of the
faith and still bear the name Christian.

The real problem, Fosdick complained, rested in the fact that the
fundamentalists insisted upon absolute doctrinal principles. He listed
five: the virgin birth of Jesus Christ; the inspiration of Scripture; the
inerrancy of Scripture; the substitutionary death of Jesus Christ; and
the second coming of Christ. Having pointed to these, Fosdick
averred:

> If a man is a genuine liberal, his primary protest is not against
> holding these opinions, although he may well protest against their
> being considered the fundamentals of Christianity. This is a free
> country and anybody has a right to hold these opinions or any
> others, if he is sincerely convinced of them. The question is: Has
> anybody a right to deny the Christian name to those who differ
> with him on such points and shut against them the doors of the
> Christian fellowship?[4]

Fosdick went on to plead "the cause of magnanimity and liberality and
tolerance of spirit."

He then began a treatment of each of the aforementioned
principles. In the process he applied what he called "modern
knowledge" to the traditional teachings of Scripture. "The church,"
Fosdick said, "needed to recognize that there were only two solutions
to its problems—and fundamentalism recognized neither of them."
The first solution was a "spirit of tolerance and Christian liberty." The
second was "a clear insight into the main issues of modern
Christianity." In Fosdick's opinion the main issues were social. He
talked of the international problems of his day, and indicated that the

---

3. Harry Emerson Fosdick, "Shall the Fundamentalists Win?" (a
sermon preached at the First Presbyterian Church, New York, May 21,
1922), p. 4.
4. Ibid., p. 6.

church should concern itself with these problems rather than fuss over doctrine. After describing what he felt were prime international needs, he concluded:

> And now, in the presence of colossal problems, which must be solved in Christ's name and for Christ's sake, the fundamentalists propose to drive out from the Christian churches all the consecrated souls who do not agree with their theory of inspiration. What immeasurable folly![5]

Though Harry Emerson Fosdick had been ordained a Baptist, at the time he preached this sermon he was pastoring a Presbyterian church. As time passed, he became more and more a focal point in the argument between the conservatives and liberals in the Presbyterian Church. Fosdick ultimately resigned and shifted back to Baptist circles, but always he remained a spokesman for liberal theology.

Fosdick and Woelfkin represented the solidification of liberal thinkers. Their movement to the front helped crystallize the controversy that was developing. The main issue became painfully clear: Were there any absolutes in Christianity? The fundamentalist said yes while the liberal said no. In response to fundamentalism, the modernists were recognizing the desirability of organization. Thus the battle lines were being more tightly drawn in the great struggle for the faith.

5. Ibid., p. 14.

Dr. Ketcham with his daughters Peg (left) and Lois (right).
The picture was taken just after the death of their mother.
Dr. Ketcham noted:

*I washed them
Combed their hair
and dressed them*

IN THE MONTHS following his wife's death, Bob Ketcham was called upon to serve as both father and mother to his daughters. The people in his congregation were responsive to the young widower's needs, and they sought to aid in every way possible. But Ketcham was lonely and fully aware that his home lacked the woman's touch. In June 1922 Bob married Mary Smart of Lock Haven, Pennsylvania.

The town of Lock Haven was nestled among the Pennsylvania mountains along the Susquehanna River. It was a center of the paper industry. The trees were harvested from the mountains and floated down the streams to the Susquehanna River. The logs were then moved into the waiting paper mills in Lock Haven. This milling community provided the backdrop for one of Dr. Ketcham's most popular series of messages, "The High Cost of Writing Paper."

Little did Ketcham realize that he and Mary would spend more than half a century together serving the God they so dearly loved.[1] But Mary Smart Ketcham was destined to learn quickly what marriage to Bob would mean in her life. Their "honeymoon" was spent at the Northern Baptist Convention meeting in Indianapolis!

1. Bob and Mary Ketcham had one son, Donn, who is a physician, serving God in Bangladesh.

As the bride and groom traveled through western Pennsylvania, across Ohio and into Indiana, Bob's mind already was preoccupied with the struggle to come. Liberal literature had served to sharpen his mind to the impending crisis. He constantly thought of what course of action would be best. He prayed for wisdom and direction from God.

As the Ketchams approached Indianapolis, their excitement greatly increased. Earlier publicity had promised that one of the nation's best-known fundamentalists would be their preconvention speaker. Soon they would be listening to William Jennings Bryan! The 62-year-old statesman had left government service by this time and was conducting an ardent campaign against evolution in public education. Bob Ketcham had been but a young school lad when Bryan narrowly lost to McKinley in the presidential election of 1896. As Ketcham grew to manhood, Bryan continued to be a dynamic force on the national political scene, while losing the presidential elections of 1900 and 1908. He was a prime mover in the selection of Woodrow Wilson as the Democratic standard-bearer in 1912. As a result, Wilson had named him Secretary of State. Bryan held that lofty position from 1913 to 1915 when differences with Wilson led to his resignation.

Brilliant oratory had always been a trademark of Bryan. In spite of the fact that by 1922 he was showing his age, he did not disappoint his Indianapolis audience. He spoke sternly on the theme, "Tampering with the Mainspring." In this address he lashed out at liberal theologians for their denial of the inspiration of Scripture. The Word of God was the mainspring with which they tampered.

The preconvention session of the Federation of Fundamentalists was held in the magnificent Claypool Hotel ballroom. Following the stirring presentation by William Jennings Bryan, the fundamentalists got down to the problem of how to deal with those who were "tampering with the mainspring" of Christianity. It was in this session that the Bible-believing pastors determined their course of action. The plan was simple yet direct. They would propose that the New Hampshire Confession of Faith become the creed of Northern Baptists.

The Northern Baptist Convention had never had a confession of faith. Indeed, many Convention members were proud of the fact that they were a creedless body and preferred to remain that way. The orthodox clerics, however, felt that it was this fact that had created the doctrinal breakdown within the structure of their denomination.

Between 300 and 400 Bible-believing preachers were gathered in the Claypool Hotel when W. B. Riley stood to his feet. He began to read the New Hampshire Confession to the men seated before him. As Dr. Riley slowly read the beautiful doctrinal creed, a hush fell over his audience. Men who had come to the meeting, agitated by the theological struggle they were encountering, sat quietly in reverence for the truths being intoned.

Bob Ketcham sat in choked silence and looked about him as he listened: "I saw great men, like Curtis Lee Laws and others, sit with their shoulders shaking with sobs of downright sensitivity and sensibility to the glory and wonder of this marvelous statement about God and His truths. Oh, the Spirit of God was in that room that night as we saw the beauty and the grandeur of what Baptists had loved, believed, lived for and died for through the centuries."[2]

The fundamentalists were so moved by the New Hampshire Confession that Riley was appointed to read it on the floor of the convention the next day. The men left that room convinced that they would be able to close ranks around this marvelous creed and bring the Northern Baptist Convention to the point of accepting it.

The next day W. B. Riley stood to his feet to address the Convention. He was a striking figure, dressed in a white suit, accented by his great mop of snowy white hair. As this prestigious and dignified gentleman stood to his feet, he made the motion that the New Hampshire Confession of Faith be adopted as the doctrinal statement and creed of the Northern Baptist Convention. As he had done the night before in the hotel, Riley read in stirring tones the precious truths of that document. Having read the entire document and moved that it be accepted as the confession of faith of Northern Baptists, he sat down.

Riley was no sooner in his seat than Mr. Colgate (of Colgate toothpaste fame) stood to his feet. This was the same man after whom the Colgate Seminary in Rochester was named. Colgate, the treasurer of the Northern Baptist Convention, moved quickly from his chair to the podium, leaned over and said, "Hmm, so that's the New

2. R. T. Ketcham, *taped interview,* 1969.

Hampshire Confession of Faith, huh? I thought Mr. Riley was reading from the back of a Western Union telegraph blank."[3]

While the fundamentalists sat in stunned silence, Cornelius Woelfkin, the organizer and spokesman of the liberal faction, jumped to his feet, calling for recognition from the moderator. When the chairman recognized him, Woelfkin proposed his famous motion: "That the New Testament is all-sufficient ground of our faith and practice, and we need no other statement."[4]

Woelfkin's substitute motion was a brilliant piece of political strategy for the liberal faction. It proposed to maintain the Northern Baptist Convention as a creedless body, but at the same time did so within a context which was difficult for the fundamentalists to fight. A rumble stirred throughout the Convention. The fundamentalists wanted to vote for the New Hampshire Confession of Faith as their creed, but what of the Woelfkin resolution? Could they vote against it? If they voted against the liberal theologian's motion, were they in effect voting against the New Testament?

W. B. Riley later estimated that from 200 to 300 men had written or spoken to him to the effect that while they had wanted to vote for his motion, they could not bring themselves to vote against Woelfkin's resolution. Robert Ketcham had many tell him the same thing. "See the strategy of it? They said they could not bring themselves to vote against the Woelfkin resolution because it made them vote against the New Testament. That's the strategy of this crowd of apostates that we fought for years and years and years."[5]

When the moderator called for the vote on Woelfkin's substitute proposal, it was approved by a lopsided margin of 1,260 for to 637 against.[6] The liberals had won an important victory, and the fundamentalists sat in stunned silence and confusion. Bob Ketcham recognized in his heart more than ever before the battle that was raging. He sat with head bowed, clutching the hand of his new bride, and purposed in his heart to be faithful to the Word of God. He

---

3. R. T. Ketcham quoting Colgate, Ibid.
4. *Annual of the Northern Baptist Convention*, 1922, p. 133.
5. R. T. Ketcham, *taped interview*, 1969.
6. *Annual of the Northern Baptist Convention*, 1922, p. 133.

continued to recognize the absolute necessity of obedience, and he knew that obedience would place upon him new demands in the great struggle for the defense of Scripture against the forces of heresy in his denomination.

In the months following their defeat in Indianapolis, the fundamentalists continued to search for a strategy which could be effectively used against liberalism. Already, however, it was becoming apparent that not all orthodox believers agreed as to the procedures that should be used. Some seemed to favor appeasement, while others favored greater militancy. At this time few were considering the option of leaving the Convention.

The decision to form some kind of formal permanent structure among fundamentalists dates back to the Indianapolis convention. Though the exact roots are difficult to trace, gradually the idea for a new organization took shape in the minds of key men who were to form an executive committee.[7] This organization was to be designed to effectuate the cooperation of Bible-believing Baptists throughout the entire nation (not just the north) against the forces of liberalism. Finally, the call was issued for "the First Annual Conference of the Baptist Bible Union of America" to be held in Kansas City, Missouri, May 10-15, 1923.[8]

The executive committee of the new organization indicated they would not publish their objectives prior to the initial meeting, though these objectives had been clearly demarcated. Instead, they would wait until these principles had been "submitted to and passed upon by the assembly itself."[9] After making it clear that the Baptist Bible Union

7. The executive committee was composed of R. E. Neighbour, First Baptist Church, Elyria, Ohio; J. Frank Norris, First Baptist Church, Fort Worth; O. W. Van Osdel, Wealthy Street Baptist Church, Grand Rapids, Michigan; William Pettingill, North Baptist Church, Wilmington, Delaware; and W. B. Riley, First Baptist Church, Minneapolis. At the same time, a confession of faith was being prepared by the aforementioned Riley along with T. T. Shields, Jarvis Street Baptist Church, Toronto, and A. C. Dixon, University Baptist Church, Baltimore.

8. The call appeared in the *Watchman-Examiner*, XI (April 12, 1923), 470.

9. Ibid.

recognized "no Mason-Dixon or national lines so far as the North American continent was concerned," the executive committee went on to make its purposes and objectives clear. It pointed out that the "Baptist Council" had existed for years "solely for the purpose of propagating Liberalism." This fact, they admitted, "had something to do" with the calling of the first conference sessions of the Baptist Bible Union.

> The tares of rationalism have been sown in both our schools and churches, and they have not only taken root but are now developing to such proportions as to demand attention. It should be remembered that in the parable, the field is the world, and at the present time the worldly schools are broadcasting these seeds increasingly, and many of them fall on church soil and spring up. There is nothing in the parable to indicate that such tares are to be left to grow in the church until the harvest, or that such sowers are to be encouraged in evangelical bodies. Conservatives are increasingly alive both to the menace of this matter and to the necessity of meeting this menace with more and better Bible teaching.[10]

By March 1923 a doctrinal statement based on the New Hampshire Confession of Faith had been prepared for distribution.

Bob Ketcham was sympathetic to the call for the Baptist Bible Union. He had been wounded deeply by the failure of the Northern Baptist Convention to adopt the New Hampshire Confession. He was horrified by the attitudes displayed by men like Colgate and Woelfkin. He was appalled by the growth of liberalism, not only among Northern Baptists, but in all denominations. In the months following the Indianapolis convention, Bob Ketcham pondered the problems that plagued his denomination. He avidly consumed the early information concerning the Baptist Bible Union as he sought the path of obedience in the impending crisis.

10. Ibid.

10

EVEN BEFORE THE first sessions of the Baptist Bible Union of America were held, the new group was embroiled in controversy. Many felt its existence was totally unnecessary and would serve only to divide the ranks of Bible-believing clergy. Others contended that any organization which would stress the fundamentals of the faith would serve a useful purpose. But there were many questions. Would the new group work with the older organization of Convention fundamentalists? Would the two bodies duplicate efforts? Were the groups different enough to justify the existence of both? And if differences existed, should they be resolved for the unity of the cause?

The week after he published the call for the Baptist Bible Union in his paper, Curtis Lee Laws addressed himself to this controversy. By this time Laws was the possessor of a brief paper which stated the aims of the Baptist Bible Union. These aims were to be presented in the Kansas City meeting. He also had a copy of a confession of faith that had been prepared for consideration. Laws pointed out that many denominational papers in both the North and the South were discussing the question as to whether ''the Baptist Bible Union and the Fundamentals Movement of the Northern Baptist Convention'' were the same. In responding to this question, Laws listed six basic differences that he saw between the two groups.

Bob Ketcham studiously observed the two groups of fundamentalists. He was interested in both, having deep roots in one and seeing dynamic possibilities in the other. Ketcham carefully analyzed the six differences.

First, Laws pointed out that "the Baptist Bible Union includes in its membership Baptists from all over America; whereas the Fundamentals Movement of Northern Baptists has been composed of Northern Baptists only, and has done its work wholly within the Northern Baptist Convention."[1] Indeed, locating the first meeting in Kansas City was in a large measure the result of trying to attract representatives from the South. Earlier plans had called for the conference to be held in Evansville, Indiana, but that plan was scrapped in order to facilitate travel arrangements for southern representatives.[2] The active involvement of T. T. Shields and the statement that the Baptist Bible Union recognized "no Mason-Dixon or national lines so far as the North American continent is concerned" further indicated the national intentions of the new organization. Certainly the selection of T. T. Shields as the first president may be viewed as an important step in fulfilling the objective of a broad base. The original executive committee had representatives from Canada as well as northern and southern United States, and "a Council was also selected composed of representatives from every State in the United States and from every Province in Canada."[3]

The second difference observed by Laws was that the Baptist Bible Union was "an organization definitely inviting churches and individuals to membership on the condition of subscription to its confession of faith; whereas the Northern Baptists Fundamentals Movement, has never had or desired a membership roll, but has invited all Baptists of the North who accept the Faith of our Fathers to unite in holy warfare against rationalism in our pulpits and in our schools."[4] The confession of faith was published over the names of T. T. Shields, A. C. Dixon and W. B. Riley.

1. *Watchman-Examiner*, XI (1923), 487.
2. Ibid., p. 470.
3. Stowell, *Background and History*, p. 24.
4. *Watchman-Examiner*, XI (1923), 487.

In reality the confession was not totally new. The Baptist Bible Union organizers continued to reflect the strong impression the New Hampshire Confession had made on them. A comparison revealed "that of the eighteen points of the Baptist Bible Union confession, thirteen were taken directly from the older [New Hampshire Confession]. Only the statement on civil government was taken intact, the other twelve all involving the change of at least a few words, and some of the changes were major revisions."[5] This adoption of a creed by the Baptist Bible Union was indeed an important point of differentiation between the two fundamentalist groups. The more militant fundamentalists were determined to structure a basis for association in which they would be able to exercise doctrinal control. This characteristic continued through subsequent decades as a mark of fundamentalist, separatist groups. It was a position which Bob Ketcham found very appealing.

A third distinction between the two fundamentalist bodies was the fact that "the Baptist Bible Union frankly declares that it will not lend its support to missionary organizations and schools whose officers and teachers do not accept its confession of faith; whereas the Northern Baptist Fundamentals Movement is determined to use to its utmost every atom of its power in saving its missionary organization and schools to our denomination by freeing them as rapidly as possible from the pernicious influence of rationalism."[6] In this statement, perhaps more than any other, Curtis Lee Laws showed his preference for the Fundamentalist Movement. He continued to believe that the fundamentalists within the structure of the Northern Baptist Convention could save the mainline denominational mission agencies and schools.

Yet, throughout the early years of the Fundamentalist Movement, the leadership had been totally unsuccessful in driving the rationalists and modernists out of the church-related schools. By 1923 that failure was making itself manifest in the kinds of people who were being

---

5. Robert George Delnay, *A History of the Baptist Bible Union* (Winston-Salem, NC: Piedmont Bible College Press, 1974), p. 40 (hereafter cited as *Union*).

6. *Watchman-Examiner,* XI (1923), 487.

enlisted to serve under the missionary agencies. It seemed to many fundamentalists in the Baptist Bible Union absolutely incongruous that mission agencies would send out missionaries who denied the inspiration of Scripture and the deity of Christ. The leadership of both fundamentalist groups recognized the same problem, but the Bible Unionists wanted to drop totally all support of suspect institutions, while the Northern Baptist Fundamentalist Movement determined to continue supporting these agencies while attempting to purge them.

The missions question was vital to Bob Ketcham. It was the unified missions program, the New World Movement, that he had so violently opposed in his early days at Butler. His categorical refusal to permit his church to be dragged into that program meant that he would naturally be enthused over the Baptist Bible Union position on this strategic question.

The fourth difference perceived by Curtis Lee Laws was: "The Baptist Bible Union seems to insist that the premillennial interpretation of the doctrine of our Lord's Second Coming shall be considered essential to membership in the organization; whereas the Northern Baptists Fundamentals Movement has always invited the cooperation of all who believe in the actual and visual coming of our Lord, and among its proponents both pre-millennialists and post-millennialists have been prominent from the very start."[7] Laws saw this point as being so clear-cut that he said, "It would seem that all members of the Union must be acknowledged pre-millennialists."

But the premillennial position of the initial confession of faith provoked considerable controversy in the Baptist Bible Union, particularly from the southerners. In response, W. B. Riley argued that the term had not been used in the first statement. "Actually Riley's argument looks thin; the confession in its original form is simply premillennial, word or no. Nevertheless a change was voted at Kansas City to soften the language, and a new edition appeared in the summer of 1923."[8] But the language of the original statement did not

7. Ibid.
8. Delnay, *Union*, p. 40. Laws, writing before the Kansas City meeting, had no way of realizing that the Kansas City meeting would reduce the original emphasis on premillennialism.

have to be watered down for Bob Ketcham. He was thoroughly committed to a premillennial position.

The fifth difference perceived by Laws was:

> The Baptist Bible Union believes the time has come for those who accept the faith set forth in its confession to unite in a fellowship which excludes all who are not of like mind; whereas, the Northern Baptists Fundamentals Movement, while recognizing the incongruity of attempting to walk with those with whom we have little agreement, has sought in season and out of season to preserve our denominational unity by making war on rationalism and by pleading with our denominational societies and schools to shake off this demon from the pit which is seeking to destroy them.[9]

In this case, Laws seems to feel the Unionists had a viable position.

It is important to note, however, that while the Baptist Bible Union sought to unite those of like precious faith, at this point they were not planning separation. In this regard, the Union underwent a significant transition in the early formative days. Robert G. Delnay in his *History of the Baptist Bible Union* contended that the Union was "originally a separatist movement." He argued that men such as Neighbour, Van Osdel and Norris were clearly separatists, although in the case of Norris, it was "not so much by conviction as by nature." His argument was based on an early pamphlet which treated the Convention as beyond saving and clearly moved toward separation.

Apparently W. B. Riley blocked the separation movement by refusing to endorse it. Delnay indicated that Riley "caused the destruction" of the pamphlet and thus "turned the direction" of the movement.

> The pamphlet makes no mention of the confession, but the confession's introduction disavows separatism, hence the conclusion that Riley had turned the Baptist Bible Union from separatism well in advance of the Kansas City meeting of May, 1923. If this conclusion is correct, ... it leads to a second probability, that Riley brought Shields into the movement to

9. *Watchman-Examiner,* XI (1923), 487.

counteract the separatist tendency. Riley was no separatist, as he repeatedly demonstrated.[10]

Thus, while many in the Baptist Bible Union in the early days favored a separatist position, the Union itself maintained a framework in which members could remain in the structure of the Northern Baptist Convention. However, because of their doctrinal statement, they were in a position to guard against the inroads of modernism within the new body. This would have been inadequate for today's separatists, but the decision to break away from the traditional Convention was a difficult one for all concerned.

The sixth difference observed by Laws related to the development of agencies:

> As we understand it, the Baptist Bible Union reserves to itself the right, if it becomes necessary, to establish schools and to organize missionary societies to promote the faith of our fathers; whereas the Northern Baptist Fundamentals Movement, having from the beginning emphasized the fact that our societies and schools were established and endowed by thorough-going evangelicals, and unwilling to concede that rationalism has any rights whatever in these societies and schools, is seeking from within to so influence these societies and schools as to make unnecessary and undesirable new societies and new schools for the promotion of the faith of our fathers.[11]

At this point in time the Union had no plans for establishing societies or schools, but it recognized that the necessity to do so might be imminent.

It would appear that Laws and the others within the Fundamentalist Movement were guilty of looking through rose-colored glasses. Though they were unwilling to make concessions to the legitimacy of rationalism within their schools and missionary agencies, they had been totally unsuccessful in their quest to purge liberalism from either area. But the difference mentioned by Laws is certainly a significant one. Though the Union had not positionalized itself on separatism, the basis for such a stand was visible within the concept of establishing independent agencies if necessary. In this framework,

10. Delnay, *Union,* pp. 41, 42.
11. *Watchman-Examiner,* XI (1923), 487.

subsequent movements would be able to develop independent agencies exclusively for fundamentalist spokesmen.

Norman Furniss contended that "the difference between the two groups [of fundamentalists] lay not in doctrine, for both were amply endowed with fundamentalist conviction, but rather in the intensity of their agitation. The Federation, pursuing a more gentle line of attack, never permitted its activities to reach the point where they became a disruptive force within the church, as did the Baptist Bible Union." He goes on to contend that this "conflict in policy between the two groups, one desirous of maintaining some peace within the church, the other eager to stamp out heresy cost what it might, kept them at odds during most of the 1920's."[12]

Yet Curtis Lee Laws was very careful to point out that he had no argument with the Baptist Bible Union and urged his readers not to consider his analysis of the differences between the two groups as an "attack" on the Union. He reminded his readers that all those involved in the Union were "thorough-going fundamentalists." He concluded:

> They have been in line in all the battles which have been fought during the past three years in the Northern Baptist Convention, and we have no doubt that they will stand up to be counted with the fundamentalists in all future Northern Baptist meetings. The conservative forces in the North are apparently divided by the organization of the Baptist Bible Union, but as a matter of fact, the fundamentalists and the Bible Union are one in the battle which will continue to be waged against rationalism.[13]

Laws continued to provide information concerning the Baptist Bible Union in subsequent issues of his Watchman-Examiner.

Bob Ketcham found much in the early plans of the Baptist Bible Union that appealed to him. He was frustrated by the inability of the Federation to stem the tide of rationalism and liberalism. Because his stand against apostasy had already won the approval of some members of the executive committee, Ketcham was invited to speak at one of the sessions of that first Baptist Bible Union conference. He readily accepted. On May 14, 1923, Robert Thomas Ketcham

12. Furniss, Controversy, p. 106.
13. Watchman-Examiner, XI (1923), 488.

delivered the first of what was to be many messages to national audiences. For the next half century he was destined to defend the truth of the Word of God from pulpits throughout the world.

Dr. Ketcham preaching in chapel, Baptist Bible College of Pennsylvania, October 1968

11

1923 MARKED THE beginning of the Ohio years in the ministry of R. T. Ketcham. For the first time he moved out of his home state of Pennsylvania, going west in response to the call of the First Baptist Church of Niles, Ohio. Ketcham pastored in Niles until 1926 when he moved to Elyria and assumed the pastorate of the First Baptist Church of Elyria. Ketcham gradually moved to the foreground in the great battle for the faith.

The Ohio years were of vital importance in the development of Ketcham's long-range ministry. He became increasingly aware of the inroads of liberalism. He observed firsthand the growth of apostasy in institutions and agencies in Ohio, and he saw church after church depart from the faith. He was still idealistic enough to assume that the "mess could be cleaned up." In describing his attitude at that time, Ketcham remarked, "Nobody had launched any idea of separation. This was something we had run onto under the covers, and we were going to change the linen on the bed and get it straightened out. So when I went to the Niles church, I was not at all exercised about withdrawal, but I was exercised about letting people know what the situation was that we had discovered."[1]

1. R. T. Ketcham, *taped interview,* 1969. It is important to remember

Ketcham was not the only man in Ohio concerned about stemming the tide of liberalism. Dr. Earle G. Griffith, pastor of the Emmanuel Baptist Church of Toledo, and Dr. H. O. Van Gilder, Sr., pastor of the Central Baptist Church of Columbus, were also deeply involved in the defense of the faith. Many others across the state helped, but Griffith, Van Gilder and Ketcham kept the ball rolling. Joined by area pastors, they held rallies throughout the state, attacking the presence of modernism in the colleges and mission agencies.

One of the primary fundamentalist concerns was the fact that modernism was permitted on the foreign mission field. It seemed absolutely incongruous to them that men who denied the foundational doctrinal principles of the Word of God should be supported and sustained by the Northern Baptist Convention mission agencies. How could a man who denied the validity of the Word of God be sent to a foreign field? Ketcham identified one such missionary and made him a focal point of attack. Cecil G. Fielder, missionary to Assam, India, wrote a lengthy confession of faith while in Assam. His statement was mailed to the mission board in New York. Ketcham received a copy of the Fielder confession and immediately isolated a host of basic errors. Ketcham used Fielder's statements repeatedly in rallies throughout Ohio.

Another area of grave concern to Ketcham was the fact that two denominational schools, Rio Grande College and Denison University, also showed the marked impress of modernism. Again Ketcham documented his case carefully and presented it throughout the state. He called for the purging of textbooks and faculty in these denominational institutions.

This research was crystallizing in Ketcham's mind, as never before, the issues of the age. With each passing day his frustration with the denominational machinery grew increasingly intense. Ketcham was an emotional and dynamic man. In his presentations in defense of the faith he was alternately moved to tears of sorrow and shouts of righteous indignation. Those who had contact with him recognized him as a man who would express his convictions with candor.

that men like Ketcham turned to separation only after being frustrated in their attempts to purge the Northern Baptist Convention of liberalism.

This quickly became a trademark of Robert Thomas Ketcham. He was a man who would address issues in a direct and forthright manner, whether those issues were local, state or national. More and more people recognized him as a spokesman for fundamentalism. His local congregation flourished, and his statewide ministry became increasingly effective. The Spirit of God made him a blessing for Bible-believing Christians and a blight for those of the liberal persuasion.

While gaining a statewide reputation for being a defender of the faith, Ketcham continued to minister to the spiritual needs of his local congregation. He developed a flare for rather dramatic sermon titles. His congregation enjoyed them, and Ketcham believed that the titles often helped his people to remember important spiritual principles contained in the message. One week Ketcham advertised his message for the following Sunday on small cards. On the card he challenged the people of Niles to come to the Baptist church to hear the message "Three Persons Out of Place, or What's the Matter With Niles?" The three persons involved in Ketcham's sermon were Christ, the Jews and the Devil. "The Lord Jesus Christ is out of place. He's not on His Father's throne. He's not even on His own throne. The Jews are out of place. They are everywhere, and they ought to be in Palestine. And the Devil is running around loose, and he ought to be in Hell." Ketcham then planned to describe the implications of these three persons being out of place for the city of Niles.

Obviously Ketcham's message was not the least bit controversial. On the day of the service, the preacher went through his usual preparations for his activities of the day. The parsonage was located next door to the church. After breakfast Ketcham gathered his Bible and notes and went to the parsonage door. As he opened the door and started across the lawn to the church, he encountered a throng of people. The crowd was so tightly packed around the church that Ketcham could not get through. The building itself was already filled to capacity.

Finally a young man approached Ketcham. He pulled on his lapel until Ketcham looked down at his badge. The sheriff said to Ketcham, "You follow me, Reverend. I'll get you in." So the law officer led Ketcham into the church building. As they shouldered their way through the crowd, several comments were made to both the preacher and the sheriff. Ketcham tried to learn why the sheriff was there but could not do so until they were safely within the confines of the church.

In answer to Ketcham's inquiry, the sheriff indicated that the people of Niles thought that the Baptist preacher was going to expose three members of the community in his message that day. One of the three was the leader of the town gang, Jim Jennings. The sheriff warned Ketcham: "Jim Jennings thinks that he's going to be one of the three men that you expose today, and he said that if you mention the name of Jim Jennings, he's going to blow up the church with the congregation in it!" The sheriff went on to warn Ketcham that no one in town doubted for a moment that Jennings would take such action. When the sheriffs' department became aware of his threat, they assigned virtually their entire force to be at the First Baptist Church of Niles. Twenty-seven deputies were scattered throughout the crowd.

The service began, and Ketcham described the three people who were out of place. He wove into his message the plan of salvation. He preached to people he had never before seen and described for them why Jesus had left His throne, why the Jews were out of place, and why Satan was loose for a season. He also indicated what would happen when all these were in their proper place and pointed to eternity, explaining how men could enjoy eternal life with Jesus Christ. Those who had come to the meeting expecting an exposé may have been disappointed. But many of them left having heard for the first time the message of salvation through the blood of Jesus Christ.

Incidents such as this provided comic relief for Bob Ketcham, but that did little to alleviate his growing concern about the trends in his denomination. On both the state and national levels, the fundamentalists were being frustrated at every turn. The power of liberalism seemed to grow stronger with each passing day.

Efforts toward achieving doctrinal purity in the Northern Baptist Convention in the 1923 Atlantic City conference proved fruitless. The liberals became more aggressive, passing an amendment to the constitution which would deprive churches of the right to vote in the Northern Baptist Convention if they failed to support the Convention financially.[2] It was in the 1923 Atlantic City meetings that J. C. Massee

2. Stowell, *Background and History,* p. 22.

began to move back toward the Convention and away from the fundamentalist group. Massee, who had assumed a leadership role in the early organization of fundamentalists within the Convention, was a man who could not bring himself to separate from his denomination or to live in a state of conflict within it. Consequently, after 1923, he sought to ease the differences between the liberals and the conservatives.

In the Milwaukee conference of 1924, the fundamentalists tried a new approach. "Abandoning their attempts to purge the church's schools, a line which they had followed without results since 1918, they made another effort to secure a doctrinal declaration, a drive started in 1922, and brought forward a new issue, modernism in the missions." Again Massee neutralized the more rigid fundamentalists, this time on the question of the foreign missionary society.[3]

By the Seattle convention in 1925, fundamentalist attitudes were inflamed. In addition to the inroads of modernism in the mission agencies and the continuing unwillingness of the Convention to accept a confession of faith, they were confronted now by yet another crisis. Harry Emerson Fosdick announced that in his Baptist church he would not only baptize by immersion but would also baptize by sprinkling. When the Northern Baptist liberals merely expressed "mild concern" at this unprecedented action, the fundamentalists were outraged. In the same convention, "the Hinson motion, that the Convention instruct the Mission Societies to recall at once all missionaries who were not orthodox, was voted down."[4]

The Seattle convention marked the final great effort of fundamentalism in the minds of many. "If there were ever a time when the fundamentalists could have won a battle on the floor of the convention, it would have been at Seattle."[5] From this point on the fundamentalists in the Convention grew weaker with each passing year. Within a year the Baptist Bible Union had formed its own missionary agency. The concept of separation became a focal point of conversation on the part of some. But separation was still not the objective of most fundamentalists. Most continued to cling to the idea

3. Furniss, *Controversy*, p. 114.
4. Stowell, *Background and History*, p. 23.
5. Delnay, *Union*, p. 81.

of purging the Convention. Men began speaking of separation as a last resort, but the establishment of the Baptist Bible Union's missionary agency, and the existence of the threat of separation, provided a hint of what was to come.

By the time of the Northern Baptist Convention meeting in Washington in 1926, the fundamentalist forces were beginning to divide on the question of reconciliation. Men such as Massee and J. Whitcomb Brougher were in favor of trying to restore some semblance of unity in the Convention. Massee suggested a six-month truce on theological argumentation and proposed an evangelistic campaign. The Convention approved his suggestion. Meanwhile the more militant fundamentalists attempted to replace modernists on the missionary board with fundamentalists. This attempt was overwhelmingly defeated.

By this time Bob Ketcham was a man whose heart was torn. He continued to attend Northern Baptist Convention meetings whenever possible. He was also actively involved in the programs of the Baptist Bible Union. His concern for missions and educational institutions in Ohio occupied much of his attention. But more and more frequently he found his mind turning to the thought of separation from the Convention, though he knew his friend W. B. Riley did not agree. "We had no idea of separation at first, but the longer the controversy raged and the more hopeless it became to correct it, gradually we got the idea that if we can't clean the leaven out of our house, then we must leave the house."[6]

As that idea laid hold of Ketcham and others, it started to creep into their public addresses. Ketcham, Griffith and Van Gilder began to discuss with each other the possibilities of a break with the Convention. Their early public references to separation continued to recognize it as a last resort. They had not yet locked into it as the only course of action. They continued to cling to the ever thinning thread of hope that their denomination could be purged.

From a historical perspective it is evident that "Fundamentalism had run its course [in the Convention] when the Northern Baptist Convention met in Chicago in 1927."[7] But Bob Ketcham did not

6. R. T. Ketcham, *taped interview,* 1969.
7. Cole, *The History of Fundamentalism,* p. 95.

realize this. He still had hopes of a fundamentalist victory, though victory had thus far proved elusive. What plan of action could be taken? Was there really hope? If there was no hope, how long should the struggle be continued? How long could a man dedicated to obedience continue to function in a denominational structure with men who disavowed everything to which he was obedient? With these many questions burning in his mind, a deeply troubled Robert Ketcham left for Chicago to attend the convention sessions.

Dr. and Mrs. Ketcham are on the right of this picture, taken in 1935. Their son, Donn, is standing in front.

Belden Avenue Baptist Church, Chicago

12

DURING HIS TRIP to the Windy City, Bob Ketcham was lost in thought. He remembered his ordination council and the conflicts which he had experienced with the liberal clerics. He remembered the excitement of his first pastorate and the thrill of seeing God's blessing. He recalled his promise to be obedient to God, that "in all things he might have the preeminence." A smile crept across his face as he realized he had already been in the ministry fifteen years. The years had been good to him in many ways. Treasured friendships had been developed among the people in his churches and among other Bible-believing pastors. He had been thrilled to see souls saved and lives transformed. Again and again he rejoiced over God's blessing on his life.

It was good to remember the blessings, for the storm clouds of liberalism threatened to distort a man's perspective if he was not careful. Ketcham thought of the battle against modernism. He remembered standing with men such as W. B. Riley, John Straton, Courtland Myers and many others in the great battles on the floor of the Northern Baptist Convention. But even as Ketcham treasured the recollection of these men with whom he stood for the faith, tears welled within his eyes, and his determined jaw clenched as he remembered that their efforts had accomplished nothing. Would 1927 be any different? Ketcham had every hope that it would be.

The fundamentalists at the Chicago convention decided that they would meet together in the hotel each night after the sessions. They would review the activities of the day and determine a course of action for the following day. They were seeking an opportunity to attack liberalism on the floor of the Convention.

The evening before the election of officers for the Foreign Missions Board, approximately 300 fundamentalist preachers gathered. Someone on the floor rose and suggested that the Bible-believing segment of the Convention should submit an opposition slate of officers for the following day's election. This was not a new idea. It had been tried the previous year, and the liberals had won a resounding victory. Nevertheless, the fundamentalists spent almost two hours preparing a substitute ballot. They carefully reviewed each nomination for the mission board. For every modernist nominated by the Convention committee, the name of a known fundamentalist was substituted. When the process was finished, every name on the ballot was a solid Bible-believer.

Once the ballot was completed, Bob Ketcham stood to his feet and stunned his colleagues by saying, "Now look, brethren, we're not going to get to first base with that." Ketcham waited for the rumble in the room to die down and then continued: "Dr. James Whitcomb Brougher will rule us out of order." (Brougher was the Convention president.) "When we make these nominations from the floor, he will say that no group can remember all these names; and he'll rule the whole thing out of order."[1] A murmur of agreement moved quickly through the room. Most of the men assembled had witnessed Convention parliamentary procedures long enough to recognize that Ketcham was undoubtedly right. W. B. Riley was moderating the session, and when he was able to restore order, he offered Ketcham the floor once more. Ketcham then suggested that rather than go to the Convention floor with all of these nominations, which could be ruled out of order, they should prepare a printed ballot. This fundamentalist ballot with its substitute nominations could be placed in the hands of every delegate. Thus, each voter would have the opportunity to vote a fundamentalist, a modernist or a mixed ballot.

1. R. T. Ketcham, *taped interview,* 1969.

Nods of approval spread through the room, and chairman Riley said, "That's a good idea; that's a good idea, Bob." As often happens in such situations, Riley then appointed Ketcham to see to it that printed ballots were available the next morning. He further assigned to Ketcham the responsibility of presenting them on the floor of the Northern Baptist Convention.

Ketcham looked at his watch and discovered it was two o'clock in the morning. He solicited the help of a young pastor, and the two men set out in search of a print shop that was open. After walking a few blocks and discovering nothing, they realized that treading the streets of Chicago could be a long and fruitless process. Ketcham reasoned that a telephone would be easier to find than a print shop!

In a matter of moments he was on the telephone, calling the Chicago police. He explained to the officer that he was in desperate need of a print shop. He stressed the importance of the job he had to have done and explained that it was imperative the task be completed before ten in the morning. The desk sergeant, contrary to the picture many have of people in a large city, was very helpful. While he did not know of a print shop himself, he indicated he would light up all his patrol boxes. When the patrolmen called him in response to the lights, he would inquire of them concerning a print shop that might be open. The officer instructed Ketcham to stay put and await a return call.

Within five minutes the sergeant called back with a list of approximately a dozen print shops. After discovering Ketcham's location, the policeman indicated that some of those shops were within easy walking distance of the phone booth. Following the sergeant's directions, Ketcham quickly found a print shop. He showed the manager a copy of the substitute ballot and explained that he needed at least 4,000 copies of it at the auditorium no later than nine-thirty in the morning. The printer promised that the job would be completed and the ballots delivered in plenty of time.

The next morning when Ketcham entered the auditorium, he found 4,000 ballots printed on green paper. He entrusted the ballots to some of his colleagues while he sought Convention president Brougher. When he found him, Ketcham said: "Dr. Brougher, I have some names to nominate from the floor this morning. When election time comes, I'd like to be recognized."

Brougher responded by saying, "OK, Bob, sit here on the

platform so you won't have to take time getting up here. Just stay right here on the platform." Ketcham concurred and sat down.

When election time came, the regular ballots were distributed, and President Brougher instructed the delegates to mark their ballots. Ketcham jumped to his feet and said, "Mr. President, Mr. President," but he got no reply. Finally Bob walked over to the podium and said, "Mr. President, I told you I had some names to present from. . . ."

Broughter turned, saw Ketcham and interrupted him in mid-sentence: "Oh, yes; just a minute folks. Bob Ketcham has some names to present from the floor."

Ketcham took the podium and said, "We have forty-two substitutions to make this morning."

Immediately the president rapped the gavel and said, "I rule you out of order. Nobody can remember forty-two substitutions."

Ketcham again took the podium and said: "Dr. Brougher, we're ready for that. A new ballot with forty-two substitutions put in for the ones we took out is right outside in the hall. We have 4,000 copies of it. If you'll just have your ushers pass them out, all these voters will have to do if they want to vote the fundamentalist ballot is vote the green one. If they want to vote a mixed multitude, they can vote the white one. There will be no confusion whatsoever."

Brougher was taken by surprise. He had no alternative but to have the fundamentalist ballot distributed. Ketcham watched with a tremendous sense of anticipation and excitement as the ushers distributed the green ballot containing the names of the fundamentalists. Eager orthodox Christians excitedly seized this opportunity to vote for men who stood for the Word of God. Ketcham and Riley anxiously awaited the results of the Convention vote. But their anticipation quickly turned to agony. They lost! The vote was not even close. Modernism was once more victorious in the Northern Baptist Convention.

When the vote was announced and the cheers and jeers of the modernists stopped echoing in his ears, Ketcham turned to W. B. Riley and said, "I'm through. I'm never coming back. There's no use."

Riley tried to console his friend: "Bob, look; if we can get a resolution and motion through to disenfranchise every salaried servant, we can win this battle."

Ketcham understood immediately what Riley was saying. For

years the fundamentalists had realized that in all close elections and close votes they lost because of the votes of the paid staff members of the Convention. Many fundamentalists were convinced that the majority vote, even in 1927's lopsided decision, was a result of the fact that all of the paid employees of the Northern Baptist Convention had the right to vote. There were secretaries of the various state conventions; officers of the city mission societies and the mission fields, home and abroad; and stenographers in the offices of the denomination throughout this country and the foreign fields. All these people who were salaried by the Convention, and who usually had their way paid to the convention by the denomination, were given the right to vote. For years the fundamentalists felt that if they could disenfranchise all these paid staff members and allow the average man and woman who belonged to the local church to vote, they would be able to win.

Ketcham looked straight into the eyes of this man he loved so dearly. His admiration for Riley knew no limits. He grasped the older man by the shoulders and gently said, "Yes, that's right, Dr. Riley. But do you really have any notion that you're going to get this crowd to disenfranchise themselves?"

Suddenly Riley looked very old. He seemed to wilt before Bob's gaze. He finally responded, "Oh, I guess not, Bob; I guess not."

Bob's eyes softened as he saw the dreadful realization of the totality of their defeat creep across the countenance of his stately friend. In a voice choked with emotion, Bob softly said, "No, I guess not. I'm through, Dr. Riley; I am going home and I will never be back!"

Following the Chicago convention, Curtis Lee Laws evaluated the fundamentalist movement in an article entitled "Has Fundamentalism Accomplished Anything?" His greatest disappointment with fundamentalism was the failure of the movement to bring together "the conservative forces of our denomination." He continued to hope that "out of this Fundamentals Movement will come some kind of a union of conservative forces that will stand like a wall in the path of liberalism."[2]

2. Curtis Lee Laws, "Has Fundamentalism Accomplished Anything?" *Watchman-Examiner*, XV (1927), 1639.

Laws was of the conviction that in spite of their failures the fundamentalists had accomplished much. He argued that they had the entire denomination "thinking about doctrinal questions." As a result of the revival of doctrinal preaching by the fundamentalists over the previous half dozen years, "liberal preachers are no longer able to deny the great doctrines of our faith without having their position questioned."[3] Laws also argued that, because of fundamentalism, "our seminaries, our colleges and our academies have been forced to a higher regard for Scriptural teaching. In other words, they have been placed on their guard."[4]

In this regard, Laws seemed to feel that the educational institutions were, for the most part, still conservative. This was a posture with which men like Bob Ketcham disagreed. In the closing paragraph of his article, Laws voiced the plaintive tone of those conservative, Bible-believing Baptists who chose to remain within the structure of the Northern Baptist Convention:

> The WATCHMAN-EXAMINER is convinced that fundamentalism, under some name, will exist until Christ comes again. As long as it exists this paper will continue its advocacy, "re-stating and re-emphasizing" the great fundamentals of our faith. At the present time it feels that it is by this method that it can best advance the cause that is so dear to our hearts. We are in no sense discouraged, although, as we have said in a foregoing paragraph, we long for the union of all of the conservative people of our denomination in some movement to stem the tide of liberalism.[5]

Though Ketcham had vowed never to attend another meeting of the Northern Baptist Convention, he still had not crystallized the concept of separation in his mind. By this time, he was pastoring the First Baptist Church of Elyria. His predecessor in that ministry was Ralph E. Neighbour. Neighbour and Ketcham were cut out of the same cloth. Shortly after Ketcham had published his pamphlet in Butler, Neighbour had published a pamphlet along the same lines. Neighbour had consistently battled the modernists. He had instructed

3. Ibid., pp. 1639, 1640.
4. Ibid., p. 1640.
5. Ibid.

and educated the people of his local congregation on the issues of liberalism to the point that they wanted nothing more to do with the Convention. Thus, under Dr. Neighbour's ministry, the First Baptist Church of Elyria had withdrawn from the Northern Baptist Convention. So Ketcham's new church was already out of the Convention, and this set the stage for his subsequent activities.

Ketcham, Van Gilder and Griffith were joined at this time by Chester Tulga who had recently accepted a pastorate in Columbus. These four men conducted an intensive statewide barrage against modernism. Their efforts culminated on February 21, 1928, when a group of Ohio pastors met with state officials of the Northern Baptist Convention. "We laid before the convention group the difficulties in the way of our co-operation with the present denominational program, and asked them to state what they would do to assist in the removal of these difficulties."[6]

For almost six hours the fundamentalists presented evidence of modernism to a convention group that included the state secretaries and the presidents of the two Ohio colleges, Rio Grande and Denison. At the end of the protracted session, Ketcham and his friends were requested to submit their complaints in writing. In response to this, Ketcham compiled a lengthy document. He divided his charges against the state convention into four categories: foreign missions, home missions, education and leadership. In each of the four categories he first listed the charges that the fundamentalists had been leveling against the modernists in the preceding months. Then he marshaled evidence in support of each charge.

Four charges were leveled against the Convention-supported foreign missions program. First, modernism was permitted on the foreign field. Second, educational missions were pursued "out of all proportion to Evangelistic Missions." Third, the board had not been honest in its dealings with the constituency. Fourth, large sums of money were wasted.[7]

6. R. T. Ketcham, *Charges and Proofs of Doctrinal and Ecclesiastical Deflections from the Baptist Faith on the Part of our Denominational Leaders and Programs* (printed for R. T. Ketcham, n. d.)(hereafter cited as *Charges and Proofs*).
7. Ibid., p. 3.

In support of his first charge, Ketcham pointed to the case of Cecil Fielder. He listed several quotations from Fielder's doctrinal statement which indicated that the missionary to Assam denied the deity of Christ, the Genesis account of creation, and atonement through the blood of Christ. At the same time he demonstrated that Fielder accepted the theories of evolution and a concept of salvation based on man's efforts. Ketcham then referred to his recently published volume, *Facts to be Faced*, in which he dealt with the Fielder case in great detail.

Ketcham continued in a similar vein to prove each of the other charges he had made. In the second section of his pamphlet he asserted that the home mission board permitted "Modernism to be taught by their missionaries."[8]

His argument against the educational system was twofold. First, he charged the denominational schools with teaching evolution as the most logical explanation of the universe. Second, he stated that the fundamental doctrines of the Word of God were denied. He went into great detail on the problems at Rio Grande College and Denison University and included a number of letters he had written and received. Most of this discussion centered around textbooks that denied the principles of Christianity. Complaints were also registered against other institutions.

When Ketcham discussed the problem of leadership, he recognized that the officials of the Northern Baptist Convention in the state of Ohio included both modernists and fundamentalists. But he complained that the leaders who were "fundamental in their own theology" were "at the same time silent about, or sympathetic with, the modernistic leaders and their policies."[9] As far as the more militant fundamentalists were concerned, Ketcham charged, it was the failure of orthodox leaders within the Convention structure that led to repeated fundamentalist defeats. "We are convinced that the war against Modernism in our denomination would have been won in two-years' time had state convention groups like yourselves stood

8. Ibid., p. 7.
9. Ibid., p. 14.

openly against all approaches of it no matter what personal friendships may have been affected by such a stand."[10] Ketcham went on to name individuals who had been guilty of such compromise.

In their original meeting with the board, the fundamentalists had warned state officials that unless the un-Baptistic doctrines and procedures of the Northern Baptist Convention were abandoned, serious consequences would ensue. "We told them that we would go back to where Baptists belonged scripturally and denominationally, and that we would have to pull our churches out of the convention."[11] It was in this context that state convention president Lloyd urged the fundamentalists to put their charges in writing. After submitting all of his evidence, Ketcham concluded with these words:

> At our Columbus conference you committed yourselves to a promise to go over these charges and proofs, and state in writing either your affirmation or denial of their truth. If convinced of their truth, you were to state in writing what, if anything, you would do to correct the same.[12]

The answer of the state convention group to the charges summarized by Ketcham was a masterpiece of subterfuge. The state board denied any responsibility to correct anything. They apparently felt to do so would be an admission of guilt. After accusing the fundamentalists of misunderstanding, they devoted most of their statement to the charge of wasting money. Very little was said about the doctrinal deviations seen in the mission agencies and schools. "We feel that the way to secure redress for these or any other grievances lies in the proper presentation of the same to the various Boards concerned."[13]

The folly of this suggestion was evident to all. For years fundamentalists had been vigorously corresponding directly with the schools and agencies. In short, the conservatives were being given the runaround. Leadership in the various institutions and agencies would

10. Ibid.
11. R. T. Ketcham, *taped interview,* 1969.
12. Ketcham, *Charges and Proofs,* p. 18.
13. Ibid., p. 19. In the pamphlet in which Ketcham published the charges he submitted to the convention, he included its reply.

refer the fundamentalists to the state board. Now the state board was referring them back to the institutions.

Ketcham responded to the convention answer in a letter addressed to state president J. H. Lloyd. This letter began:

> We have received your reply to our document in which we submitted charges and proofs of departure from Baptist faith and practice on the part of our conventions. While your reply is a distinct disappointment to us, it is by no means a surprise. It is, for the most part, a repetition of the same old method of meeting an issue, namely, by refusing to meet it at all.[14]

Throughout the letter, Ketcham accused Lloyd of evading the issue. Near the end of his epistle, he complained: "The policy of evasion and cover-up is so thoroughly rooted in the attitude of our denominational leaders, and it has become such a persistent practice, that we are not at all surprised to find it revealed in every page of your reply."[15]

Lloyd never replied to Ketcham's letter. As the days passed, it became evident that no course of appeal to the convention authorities in Ohio was going to bear fruit. The face-to-face confrontation in Columbus had failed. The preparation of formal charges had failed. By this time the fundamentalists had come to expect failure. Following the fruitless Columbus meeting, they spoke more and more of withdrawal. Dr. H. O. Van Gilder was strong and eloquent in his messages on withdrawal, as was Dr. Earle Griffith. Bob Ketcham joined his friends in the conclusion that there was no longer any hope of saving the Convention at either the state or national levels. The situation had gotten beyond control. It was time to separate.

Late in 1928, Van Gilder, Griffith and Tulga converged on the Ketcham home in Elyria. The purpose of their meeting was to discuss the concept of separating from the Northern Baptist Convention. They began their conference shortly after noon with a lengthy season of prayer. Then they shared together what the Word of God had to say about doctrinal purity. They reflected upon the circumstances and situations of the previous years. A variety of alternatives were

14. R. T. Ketcham to J. H. Lloyd, September 18, 1928.
15. Ibid.

suggested, but gradually, with heavy hearts, they moved closer and closer to seeing separation as their only option. It took them until three o'clock in the morning to conclude that the only thing left to do was withdraw.

Even then only three of the four men were convinced. Chester Tulga, the most recent addition to the group, was not excited about the idea. He said: "I don't like to walk out. I'd rather stay in until we're thrown out." Every man in the room was exhausted. It was H. O. Van Gilder who responded: "Brother Tulga, when I leave, I'm going to walk out with my phylacteries intact and my garments carefully drawn about me."

Years later Ketcham reflected: "I'll never forget Van Gilder's reply. We were all so tired and groggy, but you know how dignified Dr. Van Gilder usually is. Though he was sleepy, he still had his dignity. Nobody was going to mess him up by throwing him out!"[16]

Thus the die was cast. The battles within the Convention were finished. Months earlier Ketcham had vowed never to return to a meeting of the Northern Baptist Convention. Now he also was finished with the state Baptist convention. From this point on, any criticisms Bob Ketcham made of the Northern Baptist Convention would be as an outsider.

The next move was the organization of the Ohio Association of Independent Baptist Churches. This association was formed in the Central Baptist Church of Columbus where H. O. Van Gilder was pastor. In the Elyria area, Ketcham founded a small fellowship composed of churches that had withdrawn from the Convention. This group came to be called the Hebron Association. The name Hebron was taken because of a message delivered by Ketcham at the time the group was organized. It reflected both the heartaches and the hopes of a separatist.

HEBRON

I. Place of Separation—Genesis 13:18; Abraham from Lot.

II. Place of Worship—Genesis 13:18; built an altar.

16. R. T. Ketcham, *taped interview*, 1969.

III. Starting Point for Victory—Genesis 14:13; Abraham went out and whipped four kings.

IV. Place of Communion—Genesis 18; Abraham and three heavenly visitors.

V. Place of Promise—Genesis 18:10-14; Sarah *shall* have a son.

VI. Place of Intercession—Genesis 18:23-32; save Sodom for 50? 10?

VII. Place of Conquest—Joshua 10:36-37; Joshua took Hebron. There is more ahead!! The grapes are better farther in!!

VIII. Place of Refuge—Joshua 21:11-13; what a refuge!

IX. Place of Weeping over Betrayed Friends—2 Samuel 3:32; David, Abner, Joab. Here let us weep over the knife thrusts of "modern" Joabs which take the lives of our own fellow Baptists.

X. Place of Union—2 Samuel 5:1: "Then came all the tribes of Israel to David unto Hebron, and spake, saying, Behold, we are thy bone and thy flesh." Here we recognize the headship of Christ.

XI. Place of Anointing—2 Samuel 5:3; anointed David king at Hebron. Oh, for His anointing these two days!!

XII. Place of Fellowship—meaning of the word.

XIII. Place of Sovereignty—2 Samuel 5:5: "In Hebron he reigned." Grant a duplicate.[17]

Thus independent Baptists began to organize at both the local and state levels in Ohio. For Robert Thomas Ketcham, this path of obedience was new and uncharted. He did not know what the future held, but he knew Who held the future. He faced that future with a keen sense of anticipation. He was convinced that his course of action was scripturally defensible as seen in his Hebron outline. He knew that God was faithful, and he was determined that in all things He would have the preeminence.

17. Typed outline; *Ketcham Papers.*

THE DECISION TO break away from the Northern Baptist Convention marked the dawn of a new era for Ohio fundamental Baptists and necessitated answers to several dynamic questions: To what extent do you separate? How do you form a new organization? What criteria do you use for defining the nature of that organization? Earlier separatist movements in Michigan and Ontario, Canada, provided some experience for the Ohio churches. Though neither of these organizations was initially designed to be separatist, both had moved in that direction by the time the Ohio organization was forming.

Consequently, Ketcham sent a telegram to T. T. Shields seeking his advice on how to formulate the new group in Ohio.

> Shields' answer began: "Your telegram received today. From my own experience in Jarvis Street Church the last seven years, I conclude that you need to cut entirely clear of the old Convention. If we had had in this church one member remaining who had any kind of association with the outside, it would have been possible for outside influences to register their will." There follows a detailed explanation how to proceed: begin with a doctrinal statement and make it the basis of union.[1]

1. Delnay, *Union*, p. 131.

The organization of the Ohio Association of Independent Baptist Churches, with Ketcham as its president, apparently sounded the death knell for the Baptist Bible Union in Ohio. The Baptist Bible Union movement was in serious trouble. Bob Ketcham was on the executive committee of the Union in 1927, but by this time his confidence in the organization had started to waver. He was deeply troubled by the failure of some leaders in the Union to disassociate themselves from J. Frank Norris, the volatile southern preacher who had become involved in a dramatic shooting incident.

Norris was an extremely intense individual who seemed to thrive on controversy. Throughout his ministry he was on the offensive. In the summer of 1926, he preached a series of messages attacking Fort Worth business and political leaders.

> Late Saturday afternoon, July 17, it appears that Norris received a threatening telephone call from one D. E. Chipps, a wealthy lumber dealer and a friend of Meacham. H. C. Meacham was at that time the mayor of Fort Worth and an enemy of Norris. At the time a friend of Norris was present in the church office, L. H. Nutt, auditor of the Farmers and Mechanics National Bank. Some time after the telephone call, Chipps appeared at the office, and according to Nutt's account, there followed a long argument coupled with threats; Chipps insisted that Norris stop attacking Mayor Meacham. In the course of the heated conversation Chipps apparently threatened Norris' life. Presently Chipps turned to go. At the door he apparently stopped as if with an afterthought, and reached behind him. In Texas such a gesture could have only one meaning, and it would be readily understood. Norris, sitting at the desk facing the door, may already have had his hand on the watchman's revolver. He lifted it from the drawer and fired four times. Chipps was dead before the ambulance arrived at the hospital.[2]

Though Norris withdrew from the Baptist Bible Union following this dramatic affair which received nationwide publicity, the damage was done. His previous associations with the movement were destructive. Many members of the Union were deeply troubled that T. T. Shields did not publicly disassociate himself from Norris. Bob Ketcham was but one of many who publicly expressed concern over

2. Ibid., p. 100.

the actions of Norris in spite of the fact that the southern preacher was ultimately acquitted.

Shortly after the Norris incident, the Baptist Bible Union took a step toward developing an educational program. Des Moines University, under the control of the Iowa Baptist Convention, was in serious trouble. In spite of the fact that the Northern Baptist Convention poured hundreds of thousands of dollars into that institution, it was on the verge of bankruptcy. The existence of several modernists on the faculty of the institution caused the fundamentalist preachers to organize an attack against it. In addition to verbal assaults against the school for its liberalism, several conservatives withheld support from it. Following the decision to close Des Moines University, the Baptist Bible Union, under the driving influence of T. T. Shields, purchased the institution and reopened it. Bob Ketcham was among the new trustees. The faculty was restructured to include only fundamentalists.

Des Moines University was a troubled institution from the outset. The fundamentalists, much like their predecessors, struggled with financial problems. Many Union men were not sympathetic to the involvement of the Union in an educational venture, particularly a financially implausible one. In addition, many of the same students who had attended under the old regime remained in the student body. This harbored the seeds of disaster. The student body was divided on the new leadership from the beginning. Many had strong loyalties for the old administration. Though all the faculty was conservative in its personal theology, some were not at all sympathetic to the separatist tendencies of the new administration. A trustee decision to eliminate fraternities and sororities further added to the tension.

As feelings heightened, a variety of indiscriminate charges were hurled at faculty members and trustees. Tensions continued to mount throughout the 1929 school year until things were completely out of hand. The administration had lost control of the institution, and community leaders were appalled, not only with Shields, but with the entire situation. The chaotic dilemma reached the point of no return in May when the trustees' meeting was interrupted by a student riot. Rotten eggs and stones were hurled against the building in which the trustees were meeting. The windows were knocked out of the building, and the unruly students called for Shields's scalp. The mob crashed into the building and destroyed files, furniture and other property, while threatening the trustees with physical harm. It is conceivable that if they had found Shields, he could have been killed. The trustees ordered the institution closed until further notice, and the fundamentalist effort at running Des Moines University was finished.[3]

The demise of Des Moines University had a tremendous impact on Bob Ketcham. Though he had not been the recipient of formal training, Ketcham always considered the educational process important. He had a deep desire to see the development of orthodox Biblical institutions where Christian men and women could be trained for service. As an eyewitness to the riots at Des Moines, Ketcham was also aware that fundamentalists needed to guard against further tragedies of that kind.

This incident became an important factor in molding Ketcham's mind to the principle of separation. It became obvious to him that in order to succeed a Christian institution would need a unanimity of purpose. It was absolutely essential that faculty, staff, administration and student body be united on the principles of the Word of God and the application of the Word in faith and practice. Otherwise the institution harbored within its very structure the seeds of destruction.

The obvious question then became, Was the same thing true of a church association? Had the Baptist Bible Union gone far enough? Was it time to alter the very structure of the Union by moving to a position of complete separation? Was there a need on the national level for what Ketcham had seen accomplished on the state level?

Many men of the fundamentalist persuasion began to ask the same questions. The Norris incident, followed by the tragedy of Des Moines University, greatly weakened the allegiance of many Bible-believing pastors to the Baptist Bible Union. The more moderate fundamentalists looked to the conservatives who had remained in the Northern Baptist Convention. At the same time the more aggressive fundamentalists examined carefully the concept of separation. In this context the Baptist Bible Union gradually disintegrated.

Some have blamed the separatist movement for the demise of the

3. For a detailed treatment of the Des Moines University incident, see Delnay's *Union*, pp. 135-176.

Union. "The decision of the Michigan Baptist Bible Union in 1927 to establish the completely independent Union of Regular Baptist Churches shocked others into a realization that a split in the denomination might result from the society's intemperance."[4] Certainly a decision to make a complete break with the Northern Baptists sent the more timid back into the structure of the Convention. However, while this may have contributed to the waning of the Baptist Bible Union, it also signaled the dawn of a new era for fundamentalism.

Perhaps the Baptist Bible Union failed, not due to any specific event or events, but due to a weak foundation.

> It is not greatly over-simplifying the issues to suggest that the fundamental reason was that from the beginning some of the leaders failed to grasp the nature of their undertaking. The men who founded the movement in 1922 and 1923 were driven by their convictions to protest. Their choice was between a token protest and an effectual one; and Massee's group had pre-empted the first alternative. Even before the Kansas City meeting, the Union was committed to a policy of vigorous, effective protest. But its leaders could not agree as to how far to carry their protest. With the perspective of hindsight, the movement was inherently separatistic; but it is clear that few of the early leaders grasped this fact. The problem was not so much the lack of an out-and-out separatist policy as a lack of understanding.[5]

By the time of the 1930 Baptist Bible Union meeting in Grand Rapids, Michigan, it was obvious to everyone involved that the organization was in serious trouble. Bob Ketcham was returned to the executive committee of the group and was speaker at one of the sessions in Grand Rapids. He was named to a committee which was commissioned with the responsibility of structuring a new organization to replace the troubled Union. Subsequently, however, Ketcham resigned from the committee and was replaced by O. W. Van Osdel. Apparently, the Baptist Bible Union did not hold an annual meeting in 1931. But in May 1932, a slim gathering of thirty-four delegates attended a meeting at the Belden Avenue Baptist Church in Chicago.

4. Furniss, *Controversy*, p. 108.
5. Delnay, *Union*, pp. 188, 189.

This proved to be an historic meeting. It was "both the last gathering of the Baptist Bible Union and the first of the General Association of Regular Baptist Churches."[6]

Harry G. Hamilton of Buffalo, New York, was elected president of the new organization, while Earle Griffith of Toledo, Ohio, was named first vice-president. In addition to electing the remainder of the executive committee, the delegates expressed the desire that the new organization be recognized as an outgrowth of the old one. After appointing a committee to prepare a constitution for the new organization, the delegates discussed at some length such problems as missions and membership.[7]

There is no record of Bob Ketcham having attended that initial meeting. However, he was listed as one of the speakers for the second meeting in May 1933. The key role played by Ketcham in the separatist movement was indicated by the fact that the delegates at that second meeting elected him to the position of vice-president. Earle Griffith, who had moved from Toledo to Erie, Pennsylvania, was named president. In January 1933, the fellowship introduced a new paper called *The Bulletin*. First-year president Harry G. Hamilton was editor of the paper when it began. After completing his term as president, he continued as editor of *The Bulletin*.

Prior to leaving the office of president, Hamilton outlined the objectives of the General Association of Regular Baptists in an address delivered to the delegates.

> FIRST—Become an Association of Baptist Churches to maintain a testimony to the supernaturalism of Christianity as opposed to the anti-supernaturalism of modernism.
>
> SECOND—It is an organization determined to do its work independent of, and separate from, the Northern Baptist Convention and all its auxiliaries.
>
> THIRD—It does not in any way propose to preserve a denominational order, but rather to re-affirm the truths of Scripture historically believed by Baptists and expressed by the Baptist Confessions of faith of London 1689 or the New

6. Stowell, *Background and History*, p. 33.
7. Ibid., p. 34.

Hampshire Confession of Faith or the Philadelphia Confession of Faith or the Baptist Bible Union Confession of Faith or any such which enunciates the same truths though in other words.

FOURTH—It is an organization designed to promote a Missionary spirit amongst Baptist Churches for the spread of the Gospel in all the world, and to contend earnestly for the faith once for all delivered to the saints.

FIFTH—It also proposes to assist churches secure safe, sound and satisfactory pastors for the proclamation of the Gospel and the work of the ministry. And to assist churches in needy places as much as in them is.[8]

The new association of Baptist churches was still in a state of flux in its 1933 meeting. Virtually every decision played a strategic role in forming the personality of the General Association of Regular Baptist Churches. Without a question, the most significant event in the 1933 conference was the report of the constitution committee. "When the first draft of the Constitution was presented, it provided for almost all of the machinery of the Old Northern Baptist Convention. It was to be composed of various 'Boards' and 'Agencies' with the usual Convention setup of controlling machinery."[9]

As Bob Ketcham listened to the committee report, he grew increasingly alarmed. His mind flashed back to the repeated losses sustained by the fundamentalists on the floor of the Northern Baptist Convention. He recalled how the boards and agencies of the Convention had become infested with the virus of liberalism. When the Committee on Constitution completed its report, Ketcham immediately stood to his feet.

For over an hour Bob Ketcham campaigned vigorously against the committee's proposal. He reminded the delegates that they were reproducing the organizational pattern of the Northern Baptist Convention. He warned, "You say it's all right because it's fundamental fellows establishing it. Well, fundamentalist fellows were

8. *The Bulletin,* June 1933, as quoted in Stowell's *Background and History,* pp. 36, 37.
9. Ruth Ryburn, "The Outworking of Obedience," *The Baptist Bulletin,* XXXI (March 1966), 11.

running the Northern Baptist Convention at one time!" Ketcham
concluded his argument by saying: "Now I don't want this
machine-like thing; what I want is a free-wheeling fellowship." This
floor battle brought Ketcham into conflict with T. T. Shields, who was a
member of the Committee on Constitution, as Shields defended the
committee report.[10] When the discussion was concluded, the delegates
voted to send the constitution back to the committee for further study.
Because of the strength of his arguments and his obvious insight,
Ketcham was asked to join the committee in revising the initial draft.

The third meeting of the General Association of Regular Baptist
Churches was held in Gary, Indiana. In the year that had passed, the
Committee on Constitution had done its homework. "When we came
to the 1934 meeting in Gary, we presented a constitution which is
practically the same thing we have now."[11] The constitution, bylaws
and a confession of faith were adopted for a period of one year.[12]

This third annual meeting of the General Association of Regular
Baptist Churches proved to be pivotal. In addition to the adoption of a
constitution that structured the Association as a fellowship of churches
rather than a convention, there were two strategic decisions. Bob
Ketcham was vitally involved in both of them.

With Ketcham leading the debate, the Association began to mold
its missionary program. Missions was a vital concern to the
fundamentalist preachers, because the existing denominational
agencies had become so infested with modernism. With Ketcham
leading the way, "this third conference crystallized the organization
and missionary policy toward which many had been looking."[13]

The second key decision involved the prerequisites for
membership in the Association. The full implications of the concept of
separation were not yet understood. Many of the men involved in the
new movement were unsure how far separation should be pushed.
The suggestion was made that dual membership be permitted. Thus, a
church could join the General Association of Regular Baptist Churches

10. R. T. Ketcham, *taped interview,* 1969. Ketcham indicated that this
incident marked the end of Shields's involvement with the GARBC.
    11. Ibid.
    12. Stowell, *Background and History,* p. 40.
    13. Ibid.

without severing its ties from the Northern Baptist Convention. A man for whom Dr. Ketcham had tremendous respect and admiration suggested that it would be an act of love and Christian brotherhood to show concern for those pastors by allowing them into the organization. Under the influence of the Regular Baptists, he suggested, they could be instructed until they became convinced of the value of separating.

Ketcham stood to his feet and in his inimitable, homespun manner said:

> The thing you are suggesting, brother, is that we get out there in the puddle and swim with them and let them come into our puddle and swim with us. If we do that, we may both get drowned. I think what we had better do is stand on the firm solid rocks of the shoreline. When we see these fellows going down the stream, we can throw them a lifeline. We'll throw it out to where they can get it, and we'll stand where we can pull them in to where we are. But we must not let them be members of us until they *are* members![14]

Almost an entire day was spent debating this question. The disagreement was an honest one, and men on both sides of the issue had deep convictions. In the end, however, Ketcham's position prevailed. No church would be permitted membership in the General Association of Regular Baptist Churches without first severing all connections with the Northern Baptist Convention.

Ketcham's strong convictions on this latter issue marked him as a man with unusual insight. His warning that dual membership "would ultimately divide the Association into two warring camps" was proven correct "in the tragic divisions in other movements which have permitted this dual membership."[15]

The delegates to the 1934 annual meeting recognized the leadership qualities of Bob Ketcham. They realized that God had given him an ability to analyze a situation and see both strengths and weaknesses. Their adoption of a constitution that reflected his emphasis on a fellowship as opposed to a convention demonstrated

14. R. T. Ketcham, *taped interview,* 1969.
15. Ryburn, "The Outworking of Obedience," p. 12. Ketcham subsequently urged the Conservative Baptists to follow the same path, but they failed to heed his advice.

their confidence in his judgment. He had argued on that occasion against men who had been in positions of leadership for many years. Some of these men discontinued their involvement with the Association following his victory in relation to the constitution. In the discussion over dual membership, he again was able to carry the day against older and more experienced opposition. Ketcham's insights gained him the respect of the 245 delegates at this third annual meeting. One of the delegates was overheard to say, "Ketcham can see something coming a mile and a half around the corner before the rest of us know it's in existence!"

By the end of the third annual meeting of the GARBC, it was apparent that the new organization had established a solid foundation. Emerging from the ashes of the Baptist Bible Union was a structure that was new. It was designed to be a fellowship of churches in order to avoid the organizational pitfalls of a convention. It was committed to a separatist position in which liberals would have no voice. The issue of separation had been faced, and the commitment to doctrinal purity was firm. According to the Association's historian, "Regular Baptists were in a position now to go forward."[16] And forward they would go—under the direction of their newly elected president, Robert Thomas Ketcham.

16. Stowell, *Background and History*, p. 40.

14

BY THE TIME Robert Ketcham assumed his responsibilities as president of the General Association of Regular Baptist Churches, he had once more changed pastorates. In 1932 he resigned from the First Baptist Church of Elyria, Ohio, to assume the responsibilities as pastor of Central Baptist Church of Gary, Indiana. His predecessor in Gary was William Ward Ayer.

When Ayer resigned the Gary church, the board requested his help in finding a suitable replacement. Without hesitation Ayer recommended Bob Ketcham. Initially the board of Central Baptist Church was reticent to contact Dr. Ketcham.[1] They had invited him to be their pastor prior to Ayer's ministry, but under the Lord's direction, Ketcham chose to go to Elyria instead.

Despite the board's reservations, Ayer continued to urge them to contact Bob Ketcham. The basis of his recommendation was Ketcham's firm separatist stand. Ayer admired what had been accomplished in Ohio in the formation of the independent movement there. He realized that Ketcham had not only had the opportunity to

---

1. Ketcham was awarded a Doctor of Divinity degree by the Los Angeles Baptist Theological Seminary in 1931. Thirty years later he received a second honorary degree, Doctor of Laws, from Bob Jones University.

formulate his own convictions, but had maintained contact with other key separatists, such as H. O. Van Gilder and Earle Griffith. For years Ayer had been loosening all of the connections of Central Baptist Church with the Northern Baptist Convention. They had not yet pulled out of the Convention, but their pastor had been educating them and leading them in this direction. Ayer reminded the Central board that they had been moving in the direction of separation, and argued that Robert Ketcham was the man to finish the job.

When the board contacted Ketcham, he agreed to visit the Indiana city and look at the situation that existed in the Central Baptist Church. Following his visit, the deacons voted to present him to the church membership. They wrote Ketcham a letter, asking his permission to present his name to the church. Ketcham answered that he wanted another engagement with the church. Further, he insisted upon a meeting with church officials: "I want to come to Gary, and I want a Sunday afternoon meeting with the entire official family of the church: all your deacons, all your trustees, all your Sunday school teachers, department heads, youth leaders, advisory board, the entire family in your church that has anything to do in the administration of your school and church. I want a meeting with all of them on Sunday afternoon." The deacons arranged the schedule, and Ketcham came to candidate.

Ketcham preached the morning worship service, and after a short lunch break, returned to the church for the Sunday afternoon meeting. Approximately seventy people attended the afternoon session, and for two hours they sat and listened while Ketcham stood and told them what, in his opinion, was wrong with the Northern Baptist Convention and with its branch in Indiana. He admitted that he had not had personal dealings with the Indiana Baptist Convention. However, he explained, his experiences in Ohio had convinced him that he could not personally have anything to do with an organization that stemmed from the Northern Baptist Convention. He explained to them in detail his reasons for taking such a position.

Ketcham admitted to them that this was his personal position. However, he felt it was important for them to understand that position because their church was still in the Northern Baptist Convention. He wanted them to know that if he came as their pastor one of his principal objectives would be to get them to withdraw from the

Convention. At the same time, he had no desire to force them into a position with which they did not agree. If the leadership of Central Baptist Church felt that a man with his convictions would create a rebellion within the local church, he urged them not to call him. He reminded the church leadership that they had contacted him. He indicated that he was happy and content in Elyria, and stressed to them that unless the church was ready to follow his leadership out of the Convention, he would prefer that they not issue him a call.

Realizing that his remarks had been firm and that some might consider them harsh, Ketcham assured them that he would not lead the church into such a course of action before he got his suitcase unpacked. He admitted that it might take as much as two or three years before he would even ask them to withdraw. He assured them that prior to doing so he would have the congregation thoroughly indoctrinated in the problems of the Convention. Documentary proof, he promised, would be provided on every issue presented. He guaranteed there would be absolutely no reason why they should not withdraw from the apostasy before he asked them to do so. He concluded by urging, "I'll give you every ground of justification for such an action before I ask you to do it. Now if and when I ask you to do it, if you don't think you'll want to come without rebellion, just leave me alone—leave me where I am."

The next Sunday the Central Baptist Church of Gary voted to call Bob Ketcham as its pastor. There were twenty-two dissenting votes. Interestingly enough, the entire seven years Ketcham ministered in Gary, there seldom was a business meeting of any kind that did not register twenty-two negative votes. It became a standing joke in the congregation. In reflecting on this Ketcham said, "The personnel of that twenty-two must have changed, but there was always that crazy twenty-two. Some of the people suggested: 'What's the use of having a business meeting? Just tell us what you want done, and let the deacons and trustees tell us what they want done, and put it down in the books that it carried with twenty-two negative votes.' "

Thus, before Bob Ketcham arrived in Gary, his congregation knew exactly what to expect. Some time after reaching the Indiana city, Ketcham was ready to make his move. His target was the American Baptist Home Mission Society and its million dollar physical plant, the Brooks House, located in Hammond, Indiana. This branch of the Northern Baptist Convention was operated by J. M. Hestenes. Ketcham saw an article in the Hammond newspaper indicating that the auditorium of the Brooks House was to be used by the American Communist Party for a meeting commemorating the death of N. I. Lenin. The same article said regular Friday night classes taught by "socialist leaders" would continue to meet in the Brooks House.

When Ketcham entered the pulpit the following Sunday morning, he had the article in his hand. He read it to his people and announced, "This is it. Eight miles from us, right here under our nose, the money that you folks, back through the years, put into that home mission house over there in Hammond for the proclamation of the gospel is now being rendered every Friday night to the Communist Party to teach their students their devilish stuff. And next Sunday afternoon they're having a great celebration in memory of the death of Lenin. Now next Sunday morning I shall have a resolution of withdrawal from the Convention ready to present to this church. I want you all here."

The next Sunday morning most of the members filed into the auditorium. True to his word, Robert Ketcham had prepared a resolution of withdrawal from the Northern Baptist Convention. A motion was made from the floor to approve the resolution. It was duly seconded, and the church voted to withdraw from the Northern Baptist Convention—with twenty-two negative votes.[2]

In the months ahead, Ketcham grew increasingly concerned about the problem of communism in the Northern Baptist Convention. His concern was stimulated on January 24, 1935, when the *Hammond Times* reported in an article headlined "COMMUNISTS TO HONOR N. LENIN" that the Brooks House seemed to be becoming a center for communist activities. The article announced: "Lydia Oken, director of the Gary Workers' School, will be the principal speaker. Admission will be free, according to the circular printed by the United Workers' organization with headquarters at 6037 Wallace Road, Hammond, sponsor of the function."[3] The title of Oken's presentation was "What Lenin Did for Russia."

2. This account of the withdrawal of Central Baptist Church of Gary from the Northern Baptist Convention is based on a *taped interview* with Dr. Ketcham (1969).

3. *Hammond Times*, January 24, 1935; *Ketcham Papers.*

On Sunday evening, February 2, 1935, Ketcham entitled his message "Communism in Baptist Ranks." In his opening remarks he indicated the focus his message would take: "It is not our purpose tonight to discuss communism from its economic viewpoint, but rather from its religious viewpoint. What is the attitude of communism to Christianity?"[4]

Ketcham then held up a poster for his congregation to see. He indicated that it had been reproduced from an illustrated, anti-religious weekly called *The Godless,* published in Moscow by the Communist Party of Russia. Beneath the cartoon were the words, "Take, eat; this is my body. Matthew 26:26." Ketcham described the cartoon, realizing that many in the congregation could not clearly see the figures on it:

> The center figure in this cartoon is a grotesque caricature of the Lord Jesus Christ. Swarming around and over His body is a horde of men and women. One woman has just pulled a great chunk of flesh from one of the legs of Christ and is gnawing away at it. A man is pictured eating away a foot. Others seem to be tearing an arm from the Savior and greedily running away to eat it. A great hole has been poked in the side of Christ and blood is gushing forth, being caught in a big container preparatory to drinking. The most revolting of all is found when we see the abdomen of the Savior opened, and men and women eating the intestines. This is the Communist view of the broken body and shed blood of the Lord Jesus Christ.[5]

Ketcham went on to deal with communism in various areas of the Northern Baptist Convention, such as the seminaries and social institutions. He pointed to the fact that even Sunday school literature had been infiltrated. Late in his message, Ketcham referred to what he called "the famous brown envelope." The envelope to which he alluded was a "pastor's packet for social action" distributed by the Northern Baptist Convention. The envelope contained several pieces of literature, including a folder which listed publications which could be secured from the National Council for Prevention of War in

4. R. T. Ketcham, *Communism in Baptist Ranks.* Sermon delivered to the Central Baptist Church, Gary, Indiana, February 2, 1935. *Ketcham Papers.*

5. Ibid.

Washington, D.C. Frederick J. Libby was the executive secretary of this council. Ketcham then said:

> The *Washington Post* of January 23, 1925, states: "Frederick J. Libby, super-pacifist, executive secretary of the National Council for the Prevention of War, yesterday was denied the right to speak in the public schools of the District of Columbia. This was done by the action of the Board of Education in adopting a report presented at yesterday's meeting of the special committee to investigate Libby." . . . The fact that Mr. Libby was barred from the public schools of Washington, D.C., did not bar him from the brown envelope.[6]

Ketcham's attack on the Northern Baptist Convention in 1935 culminated in the publication of a pamphlet. This pamphlet had as its main purpose to convince churches to discontinue their association with the Convention. It was more like a legal argument than a tract, carrying the lengthy title "Evidence in Support of the Contention that Baptist Churches Still Holding to the Historic Baptist Faith Can No Longer Fellowship With the Program and Policies of the Northern Baptist Convention and Its Subsidiary Associations and Organizations." Nine lengthy arguments relating to communism and modernism in various areas of the Convention were presented.

Pastor Bob Ketcham was not the only one in northern Indiana to be concerned about communism in the Brooks House. The *Hammond Times* ran an article headlined "Censures Use of Brooks House by Communists." The subheading of the article was "Baptists Held too Friendly to Reds."[7] The article attacked the Northern Baptist Convention, Mr. Hestenes and the management of the Brooks House for their communist activities.

This article drew an immediate response from Rhoda Lundsten, director of house activities at Brooks House. Her complaints were run in the next issue of the *Hammond Times* under the caption "The Reds and Brooks House." She described the *Hammond Times* as "discourteous" and "unjust" and said: "If the Editor of The Times and the American Legion believe this situation to be as serious as the article

6. Ibid.
7. *Hammond Times,* February 1936; *Ketcham Papers.*

implies, the staff of Brooks House welcomes an open investigation of the program and activities of the House at any time. Kindly give this communication space in your paper."[8]

Meanwhile Ketcham continued his crusade against communism. He visited T. J. Parsons, the executive secretary of the Northern Baptist Convention, in Colorado Springs, Colorado, in early June 1935. In a lengthy discussion held in the Convention headquarters there, Ketcham gave Parsons a copy of a handbill that had been distributed in Hammond announcing the meeting of an organization in Brooks House which had communist ties. Parsons demanded that Ketcham prove the organization, the American League Against War and Fascism, had any communist connection whatsoever.

Upon returning to Gary, Ketcham prepared a two-page letter to Dr. Parsons in which he quoted the *Daily Worker* of Friday, May 31, 1935. In this article, the official organ of the Communist Party specifically stated that American communists belonged in the aforementioned league. Ketcham then quoted the *Communist International Magazine* to the same effect. He concluded:

> Now Dr. Parsons, here is the proof. From now on it is up to you and the Home Mission Society. There was a day when the entire responsibility for this disgraceful fiasco could be laid at the door of Dr. J. M. Hestenes, but now that I have presented the un-impeachable evidence, which I am expecting you to take to the Board, the responsibility rests upon the Board, and it will continue to be responsible until the situation is efficiently and effectively dealt with.[9]

While expressing his concern over the "communistic tendencies" within the Northern Baptist Convention, Bob Ketcham's main concern continued to be doctrinal. He summarized the dilemma in the introduction to his pamphlet *Evidence:* "Practically every phase of Convention activity has come under the blighting influence of Modernism, and while there is still much that is good, sound and orthodox to be found in the work of conventions, yet it is so organically tied up with the unsound and unorthodox that it is practically

8. Ibid.
9. R. T. Ketcham to T. J. Parsons, June 21, 1935; *Ketcham Papers.*

impossible to cooperate with it."[10] Consequently, Ketcham viewed with suspicion any organization or institution that had any connection with the Convention. He considered it their responsibility to prove their orthodoxy. Thus when he received a letter requesting permission to send a speaker to his church for Franklin College Day, he immediately wanted to know the doctrinal position of the proposed speaker. It was suggested that Dr. P. L. Powell, dean of the college and professor of religion, be sent to Gary to present the work of Franklin College.[11]

Ketcham responded to the request by writing a letter of inquiry to Dr. Powell: "You are, of course, aware that many of our Baptist Churches are attempting to safeguard their testimony in relation to the historic Baptist faith. Central Church is one of them. Our Baptist schools and seminaries are at the very heart of the present-day controversy touching these matters. In view of that fact I deem it wise to ask that a few questions be answered before we make any decision as to 'Franklin Day' in Central Church. First of all a few personal questions as to your own views."[12] Ketcham listed eight questions relating to basic Bible doctrine. The questions were phrased in such a way that a simple yes or no answer was all that was required. If the eight questions were answered in the affirmative, it would be a clear indication of orthodoxy. Ketcham requested that Powell give his own position, and also the position of Franklin College.

When Powell's reply arrived, none of the questions were answered. Instead Ketcham was told:

> Briefly, my answer to the questions contained in your letter of March 18 is that Franklin College has always stood solidly on the historic principle of "the New Testament as our rule of faith and practice," together with the right of each individual to interpret the teaching of the Bible in the light of his own understanding, aided always by the Divine Spirit. This position, as you may know, has been repeatedly reaffirmed by Baptist Associations and Conventions and by the Northern Baptist Convention in a meeting in recent years in our own State. The time between now

10. R. T. Ketcham, *Evidence* (February 1935); *Ketcham Papers.*
11. W. G. Spencer to R. T. Ketcham, March 7, 1933; *Ketcham Papers.*
12. R. T. Ketcham to P. L. Powell, March 18, 1933; *Ketcham Papers.*

and April 8 would probably be entirely too short for us to satisfy your mind upon the controversial [sic] questions which you raise and which you might subsequently raise, even though we thought it worthwhile to enter upon such an undertaking. In view of these considerations, after consultation with President Spencer, we are withdrawing our request that the college be represented in your church on the date suggested.[13]

In Ketcham's response to Powell, he expressed "distinct disappointment" that no answers were forthcoming. He protested against the tone of Powell's letter, which he felt was discourteous:

A man comes to my door and asks for admittance into my house. I say to him, "Who are you and for what purpose do you wish to enter?" The man replies, "I do not consider it worthwhile to answer, and since you insist upon questioning me, I withdraw my request to enter your house." Such a procedure would hardly have a speaking acquaintance with common courtesy, and the arrogant assumption that one ought to be admitted without questioning is an equal stranger to the exercise of good sense.[14]

Ketcham concluded his letter to Powell by saying: "The scriptural injunction is, 'Be ready to give an answer to everyone that asketh for the hope that lieth in you'; and when a man is asked in all Christian courtesy if he believes that Jesus Christ is God, preexistent with the Father and born of a virgin, and that His death upon the cross bore the wrath of God against our sins, and he refuses to answer, he can not blame his questioner if he assumes that his reason for silence is due to the fact that he does not believe it."[15]

Throughout this conflict, Ketcham was motivated by the desire to be obedient to the Word of God. This was his only basis for a stand, and he steadfastly refused to compromise. His hard-hitting attacks on the issues made him a thorn in the side of the Northern Baptist Convention. At the same time, however, it marked Ketcham as a standard-bearer for the cause of historic Biblical Christianity.

13. P. L. Powell to R. T. Ketcham, n.d.; *Ketcham Papers.*
14. R. T. Ketcham to P. L. Powell, n.d.; *Ketcham Papers.*
15. Ibid.

Dr. Ketcham (third from the left) on the occasion of receiving an honorary Doctor of Laws degree from Bob Jones University (1961)

WHEN KETCHAM WAS elected to the presidency of the General Association of Regular Baptist Churches in 1934, he exemplified on the national level the same intensity for truth that was apparent to his local congregation. He continued to battle against the Convention. He provided leadership for the Association at a time when it was desperately needed. The decisions of those early years were forming the posture which the Association would assume in future years. "The Association's system of approving missions and schools was presented to the GARBC at Gary in 1934 by Dr. Ketcham and his committee."[1] The system was designed to avoid the pitfalls into which the Convention had fallen. No school or agency would have a direct connection with the Association. Instead, each would be a separate and autonomous organization which would be annually approved by the Association. Approval would be immediately withdrawn if an institution or agency departed from the truth of the Word of God.

The fourth annual meeting of the General Association of Regular Baptist Churches was held in Grand Rapids, Michigan. Over 300 delegates were on hand to listen to Ketcham's presidential address. In

1. Ryburn, "The Outworking of Obedience," p. 12.

this message, Ketcham "stated the three-fold purpose of the Association as: (1) To provide a haven of Fundamental Fellowship, (2) To promote Independent, Orthodox, Baptist Missions, and (3) To disseminate authentic information concerning conditions in the Northern Baptist Convention."[2]

These purposes reflect the needs of Bible-believing Baptists in the 1930s. Many churches were disillusioned with life within the Northern Baptist Convention. Many had either officially withdrawn from the Convention or become inactive. Regular Baptists desired to provide a place where all who were willing to disassociate from the Convention could find fellowship. At the time they were ready to provide any interested church or pastor with plenty of information concerning what was happening in the Convention. The Association further recognized the importance of following the Great Commission. Consequently, they were desirous of recommending mission agencies that were thoroughly orthodox, independent of Convention ties and concerned with spreading the gospel. These three purposes provided the dynamic element for the young Association.

Dr. Ketcham was elected to the presidency for a second time in 1935. Under his leadership the Association continued to grow. Consequently in 1936, when the annual meeting of the Association returned to its birthplace at the Belden Avenue Baptist Church in Chicago, the attendance was excellent. Ketcham was elected as president for an unprecedented third term. By this time Bob Ketcham was becoming concerned about his tenure as president of the Association. He was afraid that the stigma of "a one-man affair" would be attached to the organization. He viewed this as a dangerous possibility. Therefore, he indicated to the nominating committee that he would prefer 1936 to be his last term in office.

In 1937 many urged Ketcham to continue as president. Their argument was simple. The General Association of Regular Baptist Churches was still in its formative and critical years. Any change of leadership could have serious implications. Ketcham finally agreed to do so with the following reservation:

2. Stowell, *Background and History*, p. 63.

If I thought for one moment that either the Nominating Committee or this body was naming me to the presidency because they honestly felt that I was the only man that could fill this position, you would have my resignation instantly. There are many who are as worthy and capable as I can ever hope to be. If I thought you were naming me as the president of this Association because you think I am a great man, I would walk from this platform now. I have said, and been honestly sincere in the saying of it, that there are no great men among us. We are all little men with a great God. The moment any one of us in this Association feels that he is a greater man than the rest of his brethren, that moment his services can well be dispensed with. There is only One whom I trust shall ever be honored as great in this Association, and that is the Lord Jesus Christ, the Head of the Church, who died and lives again, Who alone is worthy of greatness. If this is your attitude in asking me to serve another year, I am happy to do my best.[3]

During the years of Ketcham's presidency, the General Association of Regular Baptist Churches experienced growth, both in membership and organization. New churches were added at every annual meeting. Membership was contingent upon the vote of the local congregation to join the Association and the Association's vote to accept the church.

In 1936, at the Belden Avenue Baptist Church of Chicago, Dr. J. Frank Norris appeared. Norris, the famous southern representative of fundamentalism, had been pastor of the First Baptist Church in Fort Worth for many years. By this time, in addition to continuing as pastor in Fort Worth, he was pastor of the Temple Baptist Church in Detroit. He commuted between the two churches.

For years J. Frank Norris had been the center of debate. "A born fighter, he craved and loved controversy. He spent much of his time deliberately stirring up strife, with or without provocation, and became a master of acrimonious and caustic verbal tirades."[4] Ketcham knew Norris personally and was deeply concerned about many aspects of his

3. R. T. Ketcham, "Concerning the Presidency," *The Baptist Bulletin,* II (May-June 1937), 11.
4. C. Allyn Russell, "J. Frank Norris: Violent Fundamentalist," *Southwestern Historical Quarterly,* LXXV, 300.

life. By this time the Texas clergyman already had been "indicted and tried for arson, for perjury, and for murder."[5] Most historians would agree that the personal problems encountered by J. Frank Norris were a significant contributing factor to the demise of the old Baptist Bible Union.

Consequently, when Norris came north to Temple Baptist Church of Detroit and sought affiliation with the General Association of Regular Baptist Churches, Ketcham was alarmed. According to Ketcham, when Norris came north "he found the only nation-wide organized expression of independent Baptist Fundamentalism was that which was expressed in the fellowship of churches known as the General Association of Regular Baptist Churches. Dr. Norris at once sought to make this organization a spring-board from which he could launch his ambition in the North. He attempted to use the General Association of Regular Baptist Churches for personal glory and the building of his paper."[6]

Norris arrived in Chicago in 1936 accompanied by Dr. Louis Entzminger. They brought with them a credentials form which both men had signed, indicating the desire of Temple Baptist Church to be a part of the Association. When Ketcham's assistant, Raymond Hamilton, approached him with the form, Ketcham was suspicious. He requested that Hamilton, who was secretary of the GARBC, withhold Temple's membership application.

The basis of Ketcham's suspicion was the fact that Norris had said nothing in his paper about Temple joining the GARBC. "If the Temple Baptist Church had joined the GARB, it would have been in red letter headlines an inch and a half high on the front page of the *Fundamentalist.*"[7] Therefore, at Ketcham's insistence, Hamilton omitted Temple Baptist Church from the list of churches presented for membership in the Association. Apparently Dr. Norris was out of the room when the vote was taken and did not at that time realize that Temple Baptist had not been included.

5. Ibid., p. 272.
6. R. T. Ketcham, *The Norris Issue Among Fundamental Baptists,* p. 3, (hereafter cited as *Norris Issue*); *Ketcham Papers.*
7. R. T. Ketcham, *taped interview,* 1970.

When Ketcham and Hamilton returned to Gary, Hamilton corresponded with the secretary of the Temple Baptist Church, requesting a copy of the minutes passed by the church when the church voted to join the GARBC. Hamilton indicated that he was in possession of the signed statement of the two pastors that they were the official messengers of the church, but he indicated that there was no application of any kind from the church. Approximately a week later a letter was received from Dr. Entzminger. It included a dated copy of the deacons' minutes in which the board voted to associate with the General Association of Regular Baptist Churches.

Ketcham still was not satisfied. He requested that Hamilton write once more for the proper information, this time insisting that the letter be signed by either the pastor or the church clerk. Over two months passed before a reply was received. This time, Norris answered. In the two-month interim, Entzminger had left the Temple Baptist Church staff. The Norris letter contained a different date and different language for the resolution that had been passed. Ketcham then corresponded with an old friend who had served on his deacon board in Butler and was now a member of Temple Baptist Church. A few weeks later he received a letter in which his friend indicated that most of the deacons had never heard of the GARBC. He also stated that these men had no knowledge of any vote ever having been taken.

Next Ketcham wrote directly to the church clerk. She replied that there was no record of any such action ever having been taken by the church. Ketcham, therefore, was convinced that the credentials were a forgery.

In 1937 the credentials committee met in Johnson City, New York. When the Temple Baptist Church credentials form came to the floor, Ketcham presented the committee with all of his correspondence and evidence. He indicated to them that he was convinced that Temple Baptist Church had never voted to come into fellowship with the General Association of Regular Baptist Churches. "The committee unanimously decided that the evidence supported my conviction, and the application was laid aside and treated as bogus."[8]

During the early months of 1937, Norris continued to seek

8. Ketcham, *Norris Issue*, p. 7.

involvement in the General Association of Regular Baptist Churches. He requested that the Association change the dates of its 1937 conference because those dates conflicted with meetings he had already scheduled in New Orleans. Ketcham informed him that it would be impossible to consider such a change due to the fact that several missionaries had already arranged their schedules to be in Johnson City.

Subsequently, Norris stopped in Gary and requested that Ketcham have breakfast with him at a Gary hotel. In this meeting he once more insisted that the dates for the Johnson City conference be changed. During the conversation, Ketcham remarked that he would be going to Johnson City the next week to make final arrangements for the program. Upon arriving in Johnson City, Ketcham was stunned to discover that Norris had wired Earle Griffith, requesting permission to attend the committee meeting. Griffith, totally unaware of what had transpired, told Norris he would be welcome. Norris then appealed to the entire committee to change the dates. Once more his request was rejected.

Though Norris left Johnson City in anger, approximately two weeks later Ketcham received a letter from the Texan indicating that he had rearranged his schedule and would be in Johnson City and would speak. Ketcham reported: "It then became my painful duty to write Dr. Norris and advise him that while we would be glad for his presence in Johnson City, that I must call his attention to the fact that no one had asked him to speak." Thus a wedge was driven between these two leaders of the fundamentalist movement—a wedge that was destined to bear bitter fruit.

Meanwhile, the decade of the thirties marked a period of tremendous growth in the separatist movement. Churches throughout the nation, increasingly alarmed by the inroads of modernism, were making their break with the Northern Baptist Convention. In the process of doing so, many of them turned to men such as Bob Ketcham for help. As president of the separatist General Association, he became a natural source of information. Ketcham received requests at his Gary church to speak in behalf of the Association and against the Northern Baptist Convention. "These scattered requests became an avalanche when at the annual meeting at Johnson City, the crowd that packed the church to its utmost capacity, voted unanimously to ask the

Gary church to grant its pastor six months leave of absence for field work in behalf of the General Association."[9]

The conference delegates were alarmed over the fact that many of the Baptist churches leaving the Northern Baptist Convention were turning their attention to interdenominational ventures. This was a particular concern in the area of missions. Ketcham's job in the six-month period would be to travel throughout the country, introducing churches to the ministry of the General Association of Regular Baptist Churches. He would acquaint them with Baptist Mid-Missions and the Association of Baptists for Evangelism in the Orient. It was the desire of the Association to see missionary dollars channeled through these thoroughly Baptistic agencies.

The Association's request placed the Gary church in a difficult position. It was a large and flourishing local church with a tremendous outreach program. The concept of Acts 1:8 had been followed by the Gary congregation, and they had started several churches in their area while extending the gospel to the corners of the world through their missionary program. The rapid and sustained growth of the Gary ministry during the four and one-half years Ketcham had been their pastor naturally created tremendous responsibilities.

> We happen to know that there are several major problems confronting Central Church just at this time. During the four and one-half years of *Dr. Ketcham's* pastorate, approximately 675 people have been added to the church; 140 members were lettered out from Central Church to form and organize the Brunswick Baptist Church in another section of Gary. Three other missions have been established by Central Church. . . . Each one of them has developed into a good sized church, and each one of them is in need of a new building to adequately house the fast growing work. The building program confronting the church and its missions will require approximately $25,000.00.[10]

In addition, the church's foreign missionary program had more than tripled, creating important financial responsibilities and commitments.

9. David Otis Fuller, "Central Baptists of Gary Meet Grave Crisis," *The Baptist Bulletin,* II (July 1937), 3.
10. Ibid.

However, Central Baptist Church of Gary was not without resources. Due to the tremendous demands of the ministry, they had called Raymond F. Hamilton as assistant pastor. Hamilton was a dynamic young man. He actively involved himself in the General Association of Regular Baptist Churches and was serving as secretary. He was a man of administrative and pulpit abilities. In addition, the Association promised to help the Gary church by providing their pastors free of charge to supply the pulpit when necessary.

A special business meeting of the Central Baptist Church was called for June 6, 1937. In this session the congregation discussed both their own needs and the needs of the General Association of Regular Baptist Churches. The opportunities on the national level were obvious; but so were the dangers on the local level.

> Yet facing both calmly and prayerfully, the vote was finally taken enthusiastically and almost unanimously, to release the pastor for six months beginning January 1, and to allow him full salary during his absence, in order that the other churches of the Association might carry the burden of remuneration for the men whom *Dr. Ketcham* will have associated with him in these continent-wide conferences who have no church or stated salary back of them.[11]

With only a few months to put his house in order, Ketcham busily attacked his responsibilities. He had to make all the necessary arrangements for his local congregation. In addition, his schedule for the first six months of 1938 had to be arranged to a maximum advantage. At the same time, in his own family an important event was taking place. His oldest daughter, Lois, and her husband, Donald Moffat, were making plans to leave for Manaus, Brazil. As a pastor with a tremendous burden for missions, Ketcham was thrilled that the Moffats were going to the foreign field.

Meanwhile, his continuing conflict with J. Frank Norris troubled Ketcham. By this time Norris was accusing Ketcham of being "power hungry" and wanting to "control" the General Association of Regular Baptist Churches. Ketcham was sensitive to this charge and denied its validity. Instead, he argued, his opposition to Norris was centered on

11. Ibid., p. 7.

two points. First, the notoriety the Texan had received, particularly due to the Chipps shooting, was in Ketcham's mind an albatross around the neck of anyone who associated with Norris. Second, Ketcham believed that the southern preacher had to dominate or destroy any organization with which he was affiliated.

It was in this context that Ketcham took issue with a Norris contention that there was "no organization" and needed "to be none, among fundamental Baptists." Norris argued that organizations became machines. Ketcham felt called upon to defend the General Association of Regular Baptist Churches. He reminded his readers that the Association was "not a machine," and was "so constituted" that it could not become a machine. Instead, he argued, it was "a very simple and modified form of group organization."

While defending the Regular Baptist organizational structure, Ketcham expressed concern that Norris operated "a one man organization." He discussed the Bible schools which were conducted annually in Fort Worth and Detroit, pointing to the great blessings many received from them. He reminded his readers that this type of thing could not be accomplished without some "organization." The tone of Ketcham's article was not harsh. Indeed, he admitted that if by organization Norris meant "ponderous machinery" then he heartily agreed with the Texan. He added:

> Let it be perfectly understood that we are not offering any criticism of Dr. Norris' great work. More power to him, and may his gatherings for fellowship here and there all over the country increase. The point we are making is that these gatherings and fellowships do not just "grow like Topsy." There is a dynamic and moving individual back of them which spells "organization" boiled down to one man. . . .
>
> No doubt there is room in this great country for both kinds of organization—that which is publicized, propagated and perfected by one man, and that which is publicized, propagated and perfected by a responsible group of men chosen by the churches themselves.[12]

12. R. T. Ketcham, "Baptists and Organization," *The Baptist Bulletin,* III (February 1938), 2.

Thus, during his six-month tour in behalf of the General Association of Regular Baptist Churches, Robert Ketcham was called upon to defend the Association against the charges not only of modernists, but even some fundamentalists. At the same time, however, the tour took on a distinctly evangelistic flavor. Many decisions were made for Christ to the delight of all involved.

Dr. Ketcham ready to leave the Chicago office of the GARBC for a preaching engagement (c. 1958)

16

IN THE EARLY FALL of 1937, Dr. Ketcham sat on the platform of the Central Baptist Church with his heart pounding as he listened to his daughter and her husband say farewell to their friends in the Gary church. He heard Lois address the congregation with these words:

> Don and I are going at the call of the Lord to Manaus, Brazil. From there when we have learned the language, the Lord will send us out on one of the many mighty rivers which flow into the Amazon. This is the heart of the jungle district of Brazil. We expect to work eventually on the Rio Negro River. So far as the known records are concerned, a group of seven missionaries went up on this river some twenty years ago. They never returned. They met death at the hands of the savages. No gospel preacher has gone up this river since. It is true that in the building of a great building there must be excavations and there must be broken bits of rock, and cement and stone poured into the foundation before the superstructure can be erected. This is what God has been doing in the jungle district of Brazil. Don and I hope that the foundation process is completed, and that the Lord will take our lives and build them into the beautiful superstructure of a great missionary enterprise in this needy land. But if the Lord still needs some other broken bits in the foundation before He can proceed with the superstructure, both Don and I are ready and willing to be those

broken bits. We are ready to serve Him in Brazil either by life, or
by death, or by broken bodies.[1]

In a few short days the Moffats were on their way to Brazil after a
teary farewell, and Dad Ketcham was once more engrossed in his
responsibilities.

While Ketcham toured the country, he followed with interest the
adventures of Lois and Don Moffat in Brazil. *The Baptist Bulletin*
carried a series of articles containing letters the Ketchams had received
from their "missionary kids." The letters describing the sea voyage
included one written aboard the S.S. *Sheridan* on Thanksgiving Day
1937. Another letter, written just two days after Christmas, told of the
Moffats' arrival in Manaus and the experiences of going through
customs. Ketcham, along with the readers of *The Baptist Bulletin,*
followed the events surrounding the establishment of the mission
station in Brazil.

Under the leadership of Mr. and Mrs. W. A. Ross, Baptist Mid-
Missions had opened a station approximately six hundred miles up the
Rio Negro River. The Rosses were manning that station while Don and
Lois Moffat, along with Mr. and Mrs. Garnet Trimble, studied the
language at Manaus. Mr. and Mrs. Ross provided detailed information
regarding the founding of that station in Iucaby, a two-thousand-acre
plot of ground Ross purchased for the mission. The challenge of the
Brazilian field and the ministry of the Rosses, Trimbles and Moffats
captured the excitement of Regular Baptists.

When Ketcham returned to Gary from his six-month itinerant
ministry, he eagerly anticipated being reunited with his congregation.
The welcome home provided by the Gary church was a joyful one.
They presented Ketcham with a letter dated June 27, 1938, and
addressed "To Our Dear Pastor."

> We, the advisory board of the Central Baptist Church wish to
> take this means to tell you we are happy to have you again in our
> midst.
>
> We feel not unlike the child of the deep-sea fisherman who

---

1. Ketcham quoted Lois Moffat in a typed manuscript entitled
"Wounding Words" written in October 1938; *Ketcham Papers.*

rejoices when his father returns after a long and arduous fishing voyage. You too have returned with fish in the hatch—precious souls for whom Jesus Christ died—so we are twice happy, happy you have safely returned and happy you have come back with a haul.

We also want to pledge again to you our heartiest co-operation and a willingness to go forward in the work of the master. May God's richest blessing abide on you as we labor together.[2]

The letter concluded by quoting Numbers 6:24-26 and was signed by all members of the advisory board.

Ketcham quickly became absorbed in the responsibilities of Central Baptist Church. During the hot summer months he spent many hours in his study. Little did he realize that Lois had become seriously ill. "On the 10th of July, Mrs. Moffat was stricken with pernicious vomitting. That condition continued for more than fifty days, making it utterly impossible for her to retain food or water in any degree so that she could obtain strength or nourishment for her system."[3] Her malady was ultimately diagnosed as beriberi, a tropical disease which deprived her system of vitamin B_1. There were no prior warnings that the illness would strike. At the very time Lois encountered her illness, Ketcham was showing people in his congregation his latest picture of her. It showed that she had gained fifteen pounds since going to Brazil, and he proudly announced, "She had reached a fine weight of 142 pounds."

In a letter written to his family and close friends, Ketcham described the July crisis:

Lois was taken ill in Manaus with some kind of a liver and stomach affliction, evidently caused by the heat and overwork, together with other things. The trouble continued for six weeks. During those six weeks she was unable to retain any food whatsoever, probably not more than a total of a good meal was retained in the entire six weeks. This was accompanied by almost hourly

2. Central Baptist Church to R. T. Ketcham, June 27, 1938; *Ketcham Papers.*

3. R. T. Ketcham, "To the Regions Beyond," *The Baptist Bulletin,* IV (October 1938), 3.

vomitting day and night, and under the terrific heat conditions, it reduced her to a state of practically helplessness.[4]

The Brazilian doctors in Manaus seemed unable to help Lois. On their advice, she was sent to the more favorable climate of Para where better medical facilities were available. Physicians there, however, recommended that she leave Brazil immediately.

Don Moffat began immediate negotiations with Pan American Airways for the trip back to the United States, with Dad Ketcham entering the negotiations from his office in Gary. On August 16, 1938, Evan E. Young offered discount fares to the Moffats for their return to the United States. However, the next day he telegraphed Ketcham that his offer had been rejected: "Our representatives at Rio de Janeiro telegraphed yesterday that the ticket discounts were offered yesterday but that the parties in question were definitely planning to sail last evening by steamship as their doctor feels steamship trip advisable."[5] A day later, Ketcham sent a letter of appreciation to Young. He indicated that the doctors had discovered a heart condition which they felt could be fatal if she traveled by airplane. Consequently, Lois Moffat, on the verge of death, started home.

Don and Lois left Manaus on the steamship *Sheridan*. This vessel was a freighter. It could accommodate about seven passengers, and no medical staff was on board. The Moffats embarked on this crucial voyage to New York trusting in the Great Physician alone.

While the Moffats were at sea, a week passed in which no word concerning Lois's condition was received. Then on Tuesday, August 23, a radiogram arrived from Don. He indicated that Lois would be unable to make it to New York City alive. Therefore, he would be taking her off the *Sheridan* when it docked at Norfolk, Virginia, on Sunday, August 28. In his radiogram Don requested that Dad Ketcham meet them in Norfolk when the boat arrived.

Immediately Ketcham began making arrangements to go. He completed preparations for his Wednesday prayer service, and that

---

4. R. T. Ketcham to friends, August 25, 1938; *Ketcham Papers.* A list of twenty-seven names to whom the letter was sent is attached to letter.
5. Evan E. Young to R. T. Ketcham, August 16, 1938; *Ketcham Papers.*

evening his church spent much time in prayer. On Wednesday Ketcham also dictated a letter, bearing the news of the serious situation to close friends of the family. In this letter he indicated that he would reach Norfolk Friday evening and spend Saturday making arrangements with "the best specialists that the city affords." He was also to arrange ambulance service and hospital reservations prior to the arrival of the *Sheridan.*

The letter he wrote his friends described his and Mary's attitude in this critical hour:

> If Lois is living, and I confidently believe she will be, she probably will have to have some hospital care in Norfolk before she can stand the trip on home. That being the case, we will take care of it at once. However, if she is able to make the Pullman trip from Norfolk to Gary, we will rush her home with all possible speed.

> Both Mrs. Ketcham and I are praising the Lord these days and nights for a sweet and quiet peace in our hearts. Our hearts are, of course, heavy and the future does not have sunshine in it, but it has Him, and when it has Him, it does not need much sunshine. We are preciously conscious these days that Romans 8:28 is still in the Book, and that our half of it is true—that we do love God and that we are called according to His purpose. Therefore, God's half of it must be true—that He will make all things work together for good.

> We are not questioning the why of this experience. Someone said to me yesterday, "Why did God cut this girl off in the midst of such a glorious life of service?" My reply was, "How do you know He has cut her off in the midst of such a glorious life of service? If He should take her to be with Himself, how do you know but what through her death, twenty-five other strong young men and women would be called into that very field through this experience. You certainly cannot call that cutting her off in the midst of a glorious life of service, can you?" After all, it is not ours to question why, it is only ours to obey.[6]

Even with his daughter near death, Ketcham recognized the necessity of obedience. If Lois was to be taken Home, both Bob and Mary knew that she would go in the service of her Lord. Thus, with

6. R. T. Ketcham to friends, August 25, 1938; *Ketcham Papers.*

heavy hearts, but firm and resolute faith, they awaited the will of their Heavenly Father.

On Thursday, August 25, Ketcham's secretary mailed the letter to the families' friends. The same day, Bob left for Norfolk. As he traveled he remembered the many crises he had experienced with his daughters. He reflected on the months when he had of necessity served as both mother and father. Tears welled in his eyes as he recalled the warm and sweet manner in which Mary Smart had quickly assumed the role of mother to his darling girls. He thought about many of the experiences of Lois's childhood. He remembered the excitement of Don's and Lois's courtship, their wedding ceremony, their commissioning service and the farewell service in which Lois had indicated their willingness to be "broken bits" for the foundation of God's work in Brazil. He remembered that Don and Lois were willing to serve God "by life, or by death, or by broken bodies." Those words echoed in his mind, and he wept unashamedly. He was torn by his love for God and his love for his daughter. He was fully willing to accept God's will, whatever it might be; but in an earthly sense, he longed for her restoration to health. The trip to Norfolk seemed to pass quickly for the preacher who was engrossed in his thoughts.

Shortly after arriving in Virginia, Ketcham received a telegram from the steamship line, indicating that the *Sheridan* would be arriving in Norfolk late Saturday night. They warned Ketcham that "his daughter's condition was grave" and required "urgent medical attention on arrival." Ketcham was assured that the steamship agency was doing everything possible.[7] After securing as much information as he could, Ketcham sent the following wire to his wife:

SHERIDAN CAPTAIN RADIOED NORFOLK OFFICIALS LOIS CASE DESPERATE AND ORDERED PLANE OR COAST GUARD TO COME AT ONCE WITH DOCTOR. ABOUT THREE HUNDRED MILES OUT. OFFICIALS TRYING TO GET PERMIT FOR ME TO GO WITH DOCTOR. KEEP LOOKING UP—BOB.[8]

7. Lamport and Holt Line Ltd. to R. T. Ketcham, 3:06 P.M., August 26, 1938; *Ketcham Papers*.

8. R. T. Ketcham to Mary Ketcham, 4:39 P.M., August 26, 1938; *Ketcham Papers*.

Ketcham's use of the word *desperate* to his wife was no exaggeration. The captain of the *Sheridan* was afraid that Lois would not make Norfolk alive. He requested help from either a plane or Coast Guard cutter. The need for a physician was stressed. Though the *Sheridan* was still three hundred miles out of port, Norfolk Coast Guard officials immediately sprang into action. A plane was readied and a physician found, and Ketcham was standing by to accompany them. But the Coast Guard could not fix the location of the *Sheridan*.

Suddenly, radio interference became a problem. No signals were received in Norfolk. Meanwhile, on board the *Sheridan*, the radio man desperately attempted to relay messages through other vessels and other shore stations. But every effort ended in dismal failure. All through the night the Coast Guard frantically sought to establish radio contact with the *Sheridan*, but an occasional partial communication was all they could achieve. They simply could not get enough information to proceed. A Coast Guard cutter had been sent to sea in spite of the interference in the hope that once radio contact had been established it could be directed to the *Sheridan*. It moved to the general area where the *Sheridan* should have been. Clinging to this encouraging note, Bob sent his second wire to Mary at approximately eight o'clock Friday night:

> SECOND REPORT. DOCTORS HAVE RADIOED EMER-
> GENCY INSTRUCTIONS TO SHERIDAN. COAST GUARD
> CUTTER GOING OUT TO MEET SHERIDAN AND TAKE LOIS
> ABOARD TO HURRY ARRIVAL HERE. DOCTORS HOS-
> PITAL AND ALL PREPARATIONS READY HERE. KEEP
> LOOKING UP. HOLD YOURSELF READY TO COME IF I
> CALL—BOB.[9]

On Saturday morning, the Coast Guard sent its planes to search for the *Sheridan*. Ketcham was assured that Lois would be in Norfolk by noon. The weary preacher wired the news to Mary:

> COAST GUARD PLANE ARRIVING IN FORTY FIVE MINUTES
> WITH LOIS—BOB.[10]

---

9. R. T. Ketcham to Mary Ketcham, 7:58 P.M., August 26, 1938; *Ketcham Papers.*
10. R. T. Ketcham to Mary Ketcham, 11:09 A.M., August 27, 1938; *Ketcham Papers.*

When Ketcham returned from sending that wire, bad news
awaited him. Coast Guard officers reported that their plane had been
unable to make contact with the *Sheridan*. Bob Ketcham later
described what happened that Saturday morning:

> At ten o'clock Saturday morning the Coast Guard called the
> United States Navy to come to their assistance, and in exactly one
> hour and two minutes the United States Naval Base had two of
> their most powerful planes, together with the Lt. Comdr. Dr.
> Hazelton, on their way to hunt for the *Sheridan*. Due to the
> uncertainty of the situation, I decided to remain here where we
> could keep more closely in touch with all that was going on. At
> 1:30 P.M. the planes landed alongside the *Sheridan* with a very
> rough sea. One of the planes was dashed against the side of the
> *Sheridan*, taking the cork bumper completely off and smashing
> one corner of a wing. The *Sheridan* lowered its lifeboat and with a
> picked crew started the perilous journey out to the plane carrying
> the doctor. With great difficulty and danger the doctor was finally
> gotten from the plane to the boat. As soon as he boarded the
> *Sheridan* and took one look at Lois, he ordered the planes to
> return without him as it would have been fatal to try and transfer
> her under normal conditions, let alone the rough sea. Dr.
> Hazelton stayed on board and it was his presence there which
> enabled us to finally reach Norfolk with Lois alive. She was
> absolutely at the foot of the hill.[11]

Ketcham stood by the radio through the long Saturday wait.
Finally word was received that the doctor had arrived on board the
Sheridan. Saturday afternoon he sent his beloved Mary still another
report:

> REPORT FOUR. COAST GUARD COULDNT REACH
> SHERIDAN. U S NAVY SENT TWO PLANES WITH DOCTOR
> BUT LOIS TOO ILL TO TRANSFER. NAVY DOCTOR RE-
> MAINED ON BOARD. REACH HERE MIDNIGHT. WORK-
> ING NOW WITH U S OFFICIALS TO LET SHIP COME
> THROUGH WITHOUT STOPPING AT QUARANTINE. THANK
> GOD SHE HAS A DOCTOR AT LAST—BOB.[12]

11. R. T. Ketcham to Mary Ketcham, August 29, 1938. Copies of this
detailed letter were sent to Ketcham's sister, Grace, and three of his close
friends. *Ketcham Papers*.

12. R. T. Ketcham to Mary Ketcham, 3:50 P.M., August 27, 1938;
Ketcham Papers.

It was impossible for Bob Ketcham to grasp fully how terribly ill his daughter had become. She had been unable to retain food or liquid for eight weeks. She was almost completely dehydrated. For almost the entire trip from Brazil she had produced no saliva whatsoever. "Her skin had lost all of its elasticity. In fact she was only a very few hours this side of a complete stroke. Her fingers and toes already beginning to turn in in cramped position. She had been complaining of numbness in her face for several days."[13]

From the moment Dr. Hazelton reached the deck of the *Sheridan,* he took command of the entire situation. In addition to providing immediate treatment for Lois, he ordered the Coast Guard to have a launch standing by to meet the *Sheridan* at sea. He indicated that Mrs. Moffat's condition was so critical it was absolutely essential to get her to shore as quickly as possible. The cooperation of government and Coast Guard officials in cutting red tape enabled Lois to reach shore three hours early. By nine-thirty Saturday evening she was in Norfolk General Hospital and intravenous feeding was under way.

Once Lois arrived, Bob Ketcham became thoroughly absorbed in his daughter. Even with previous warning of the severity of her illness, he was stunned to see her desperate condition. He stood by her bedside hour after hour. He worried over his son-in-law, Don, who was both physically and emotionally exhausted from the long ordeal. Early Sunday morning he wired home once more:

> REPORT FIVE. LOIS IN HOSPITAL BEING FED INTRA-VENEOUSLY [sic]. DOCTOR SAYS SHE IS VERY LOW BUT EXPECTS MARKED RESULTS IN EIGHTEEN HOURS. SHE IS ONLY A SHADOW. DOUBT IF I WOULD HAVE KNOWN HER. HOSPITAL HERE 10 DAYS BEFORE REMOVAL HOME. DON IS FINE AS CAN BE BUT AWFUL TIRED. HAVE ALL REPORTS READ AT SERVICES—BOB.[14]

After staying with Lois almost constantly through Sunday, Ketcham finally sat down at noon Monday to summarize his thoughts

---

13. R. T. Ketcham to Mary Ketcham, August 29, 1938; *Ketcham Papers.*
14. R. T. Ketcham to Mary Ketcham, 7:46 A.M., August 28, 1938; *Ketcham Papers.*

of the previous two days. Through most of this time period, Lois had been unconscious. Sunday she had regained consciousness for "about two minutes," and in that time she had recognized Ketcham and tried to say "Daddy." Ketcham described her effort at speaking and smiling as "pathetic." But in spite of her comatose state, he reported that she was responding "beautifully" to treatment: "We have every reason to believe that within the next 24 hours we will have a different girl. It is going to be a long, hard pull, but there is nothing now which would indicate any possibility of danger to her life."[15]

With the crisis past, he thought, Ketcham was able to take measure of what had happened. He reflected ruefully on the tremendous expense involved: the hospital was $30 a day; three special duty nurses working around the clock, $15 a day; plus the doctors' fees, medication, hotel and board for both him and Don. Meanwhile Don was providing further information on the voyage: "Don has been telling me something of the desperate fight which Lois herself put up in order to reach home. Her one object which she kept before her during the last three days of the voyage was 'Daddy will be there.' Whenever sinking spells and difficult moments confronted her she seemed to reach out with a new determination to hold on until she reached here."[16]

Ketcham then demonstrated his concern for his son-in-law. The impact of this dreadful ordeal had left its mark on the young missionary. Ketcham was not so concerned for his own flesh and blood that he failed to look lovingly at his "adopted" son:

> Don's condition is giving me a bit of concern, although he is apparently coming through in fine shape. You can well imagine what it has meant to him to sit by during these weeks and see the bungling of those doctors in Brazil, and then those 15 days on the ocean with no doctor on board the ship and everyone so utterly helpless to do anything. He is evidencing some nervousness, due, I think, now to a let down that the tension is over. He is not resting nights as well as he ought to, and one of his eyes is giving him

15. R. T. Ketcham to Mary Ketcham, August 29, 1938; *Ketcham Papers.*
16. Ibid.

considerable difficulty, but we have a specialist working with that today and we hope that it will clear up soon.[17]

Ketcham concluded his lengthy letter with a brief description of Lois. By this time, she had lost over sixty pounds.

It is impossible to describe to you Lois' appearance. Frankly, and without exaggeration I would not have known her had I not been looking for her. There isn't a single solitary thing of the old Lois left. It is just a bit of dried skin stretched over the bones. The eyes have lost their snap, and, of course, the old cheery smile is gone. We are, however, deeply grateful to our Heavenly Father for bringing her thru, and we are confident that she will be her old self within a few months.[18]

Monday at noon, when Ketcham wrote the letter quoted above, his mind remained deeply troubled. His thoughts were too frightening and too intimate to share even with his wife. Though he was confident Lois would live, he dreaded the possibility that her mind might be permanently damaged. This thought was too horrifying, too dreadful to share with others. Only in the lonely solitude of his own thoughts could he consider this agonizing possiblity.

With tension binding his heart like a constricting cord, Ketcham returned to the hospital. He once more stood vigil by Lois's bedside, awaiting an answer to his dreaded question. Finally, his daughter's eyelids fluttered. She looked blankly into the face of her beloved father standing by her bed. He looked at the vacant stare in her eyes, and tears came to his eyes as he realized that she did not know him. In silent agony Bob poured out his heart to his God. He pleaded for his daughter's sanity.

As he gazed intently at her, those vacant eyes began to focus in recognition. A forced smile crept to her lips as she recognized her father. She feebly reached for him, and with tears streaming down his face he bent over her emaciated body. The weakened arms reached around his neck, and she clung to him. Though Lois was still too weak to communicate, Ketcham knew that his prayer had been answered.

Late that evening he returned to his room with more spring in his step than he had experienced for several days. He reached into his

17. Ibid.
18. Ibid.

briefcase and pulled out a couple sheets of GARBC stationery. Across the top of the first sheet he scrawled "Monday night eleven P.M." He then shared his most intimate fears with his beloved Mary.

> Dearest Girl—
>
> Just back from the hospital tonight. Lois really knew me and oh did she hang on!! Darling, I'm glad in one way you have not been here. I would give a world if I could erase from my mind the horror of the last 48 hours. I did not put this in my letter today but I am telling *you* and you must not breathe it to a soul, but I was afraid (and so the doctor) that Lois' mind was affected by this fearful dehydration. Her attempts to speak my name were not the efforts of physical weakness so much as *mental* weakness. It sounded just like an imbecile trying to talk. And that *awful stare*. What pathetic efforts she made to come out from behind that veil cannot be described—nor forgotten! But, oh sweetheart, she was out tonight. And that fear is removed. My how she hugged and kissed me. She can only speak a word or two at a time because of weakness but it is *clear* and distinct. I sat down in a chair and dropped off to sleep and while I was sleeping she saw me and said to Don "Daddy—sleep—I'm glad." The precious dear—thinking of others even then.[19]

Thus the crisis was past. There would be many months of recovery and lingering aftereffects of the illness, but Lois Ketcham Moffat had been spared by her God. Her husband, her parents and all their friends throughout the nation rejoiced. The prayers of thousands had been answered.

19. R. T. Ketcham to Mary Ketcham, August 29, 1938. Second letter of the day handwritten at 11:00 P.M. *Ketcham Papers.*

17

THE ROAD TO recovery was a long one for Lois Ketcham Moffat. Her father's initial optimism when her mind cleared on Monday, August 29, was short-lived. In the next several days she made only slight improvement, and her condition remained grave. On Saturday, September 3, Ketcham wired a progress report to his assistant, Raymond Hamilton:

> LOIS MADE SLIGHT IMPROVEMENT EACH DAY UNTIL FRIDAY NO IMPROVEMENT SINCE BUT HOLDING HER OWN. MIND IS CLEAR EACH MORNING BUT DELIRIOUS REST OF DAY. INTRAVENIOUS [sic] FEEDINGS RESUMED YESTERDAY. FUTURE MIGHTY UNCERTAIN SO KEEP PRAYING. HOPE WE MAY START HOME END OF WEEK BUT LOIS MUST IMPROVE LOT IF WE DO. LOVE TO MY DEAR AND GLORIOUS CHURCH—RT KETCHAM.[1]

The physicians continued to watch Lois closely. Her condition improved slightly, and by late the following week it was decided that

---

1. R. T. Ketcham to R. F. Hamilton, September 3, 1938; *Ketcham Papers.*

167

she could return to Gary and the home of her family. Ketcham wired Ray Hamilton, requesting that his assistant meet him with a car.[2]

Plans for the return to Gary took shape quickly. Though Mary had joined him in Norfolk, Ketcham was nonetheless anxious to return home. He had been out of his pulpit for three consecutive Sundays, and for a preacher that was no small burden! He was not merely concerned for his church—for he knew it was in good hands with Ray Hamilton—but he was anxious to be back in the pulpit. Details were quickly expedited, and shortly after the noon meal on Friday, the orderlies came to prepare Lois for the trip. She was carefully wrapped in blankets and placed on a stretcher. The stretcher was carried to a waiting ambulance which took her to the Norfolk train depot. The trip from Norfolk to Gary would take over twenty-four hours, so a special bed was prepared for her on the train.

When the train arrived in Chicago on Saturday afternoon, an ambulance was waiting. Lois was immediately taken to the Harris Clinic and Hospital in Gary. The trip was a success in that her condition did not degenerate because of it.

Following his joyful return to his pulpit on Sunday, Ketcham prepared a letter to send to his close friends and associates reporting his daughter's condition. The letter reflected the complexity of the entire situation. Though Lois had been eating consistently and retaining her food, she did not seem to be gaining strength. Her memory did not appear to be returning—a matter of great concern. Her physician in Gary, Dr. Harris, decided that one or two blood transfusions might cause her to turn the corner. Ketcham urged his friends to continue to pray: "She is still a desperately sick girl however, and we must not leave the Throne a minute day or night on her behalf, because Satan is ready to pounce the moment this servant of the Lord is left unguarded. Satan has certainly put up a terrific battle for possession of this dear girl."[3]

One week later Ketcham penned another letter to his friends. He was clearly perplexed by some aspects of his daughter's recovery. Lois

2. R. T. Ketcham to R. F. Hamilton, September 8, 1938; *Ketcham Papers.*

3. R. T. Ketcham to friends, September 12, 1938; *Ketcham Papers.*

was "eating ravenously" and retaining her food. She seemed to be gaining strength in that she could turn over in bed, turn on her bed light and handle her fork. But in spite of those encouraging signs, two areas caused major concern. One related to a kidney infection, but Ketcham reported that the doctor seemed to have that well in hand. The other was her mental condition.

> She is not delirious, her mind does not wander around in that respect, but she is utterly unable to retain anything in her memory. If one of us goes into the room and has a visit with her, she will carry on conversation in the same old Lois fashion, wisecracking and laughing, and indeed keeping us guessing to keep up with her. We leave the room and come back in an hour, and she has forgotten that we have been there. She does not remember that Don was with her in Brazil. I am broadcasting every noon over WMBI from Moody, and we have a radio at her bedside. She listens to me every day at noon, and at 2:30 when I return and come to her room, and ask her if she enjoyed the broadcast, she has utterly forgotten that she heard it.[4]

This loss of memory was of grave concern to the Ketchams. At the family's request, an eminent neurologist and nerve specialist, Dr. Cohr, traveled from Chicago to Gary to examine Lois. The family was concerned that her memory loss might be a permanent result of her dibilitating illness. After a thorough examination, the specialist provided encouraging news:

> Dr. Cohr gave us every assurance, even to a practical guarantee, that Lois would be perfectly O.K. within a few weeks or months. He did indicate that she had a long, hard pull ahead of her, and that she would be months making a complete recovery, but that the memory would absolutely come back as soon as body strength was rebuilt. We were tremendously encouraged and are grateful to our Heavenly Father this morning for the encouragement, and we believe that it is just a case of waiting until nature itself can overcome the terrific onslaught which was turned loose upon her.[5]

In spite of the doctor's report, little improvement was seen.

---

4. R. T. Ketcham to friends, September 18, 1938; *Ketcham Papers*.
5. Ibid.

Ketcham's next news bulletin was very brief. He reported that she remained in Harris Hospital "gaining in weight slowly, eating well, resting much better, getting to look a little more like her old self." He indicated she complained of "severe numbness in face and throat." He concluded by saying, "Her memory is not much better, although there are marks of improvement." He closed with the simple request, "Keep praying!"[6]

His October 7 bulletin was much more positive. He reported that Lois had been brought home from the hospital and had achieved the improved weight of ninety-nine pounds. Though her memory was improving only slowly, Ketcham was obviously thrilled that his daughter was coming home.[7]

But Ketcham's exuberance was short-lived. Following her return home, Lois did not respond. Within a week she was returned to the Harris Hospital. For the next several days, her condition remained at a standstill. Little if any improvement was seen. Finally, Dr. Harris ordered that no one except Don and Mr. and Mrs. Ketcham would be permitted to see her. The doctor sought to remove every possible cause of draining her strength. Ketcham was deeply troubled:

> The case still continues to baffle us. We are not sure of the ultimate outcome. All we are sure of is that God will certainly work out His will in the case. Some days we feel that the memory is returning with renewed vigor, but possibly the very next day, we will have indications that the memory is no better than it has been. And so the case goes up and down, up and down, and it is rather difficult to make a definite statement concerning it. We can say definitely that Lois is a very, very sick girl, and that there is a long, long hard battle ahead for recovery of both body and mind.[8]

During the early days of Lois Moffat's illness, word spread rapidly throughout the country. Expressions of concern began to pour in to the Ketcham residence. When Lois was returned to Gary, one of the first things Bob Ketcham did was begin answering each letter

6. R. T. Ketcham to friends, September 28, 1938; *Ketcham Papers.*
7. R. T. Ketcham to friends, October 7, 1938; *Ketcham Papers.*
8. R. T. Ketcham to friends, October 18, 1938; *Ketcham Papers.*

personally, whether it was from a member of a former congregation or the president of a large institution, such as the letter received from Will H. Houghton, president of Moody Bible Institute.

Some correspondence posed the question, Why would God let this happen? Countless numbers of people, from the Coast Guard officers to church members he encountered throughout the country, asked the same question.

When Bob Ketcham wrote the account of Lois's illness in *The Baptist Bulletin,* he addressed himself to this question. He offered three explanations, though only the first one was necessary:

> Well, the first answer to that question is a rather blunt one. It is none of our business. God is marvelously capable of taking care of His own cause, and He is doing things that are so far above us that we cannot hope to understand them until we see the completed pattern in that blessed eternity just ahead of us, and happy the soul that can rest and wait God's unveiling.[9]

Bob Ketcham knew full well that a sovereign and righteous God owed no explanations to man. He knew that God's ways were not always man's ways, but he also knew that it was natural for men to try to understand. So he gave a second explanation.

He told of a young woman in nurse's training who was moved by his daughter's illness to pledge her life to go to the Rio Negro region when she completed her training. He pleaded for a doctor or nurse who could go immediately, pointing out the tremendous physical needs of the missionaries who remained on the field. Ketcham was convinced that if American medical aid had been available on the mission field, Lois would not have become so seriously ill. It was his desire that someone respond to the tremendous need when they heard the sad case of the Moffats. If that occurred, it would be enough. "If it has taken all of this sad experience to arouse the youth of our home land who have medical and nursing talent to the awful need out yonder, then who are we to say that this is all so useless."[10]

Ketcham's third possible explanation was that the native Christians in Brazil had grown tremendously through the time of Mrs.

9. Ketcham, "To the Regions Beyond," p. 6.
10. Ibid., p. 7.

Moffat's illness. They had seen faith in action. This, he believed, was a rich fruit of his daughter's trial.

During the months prior to his daughter's illness, Ketcham had been increasingly impressed by the great opportunity available to the General Association of Regular Baptist Churches. While on his six-month tour of the United States, he had conducted many evangelistic crusades. He had seen many accept the Lord Jesus Christ as their personal Savior; others had dedicated their lives to Christian service. He had met with literally dozens of pastors who shared his concerns about liberalism and communism in the Northern Baptist Convention. The potential for a fundamentalist, separatist association was almost beyond his comprehension.

Increasingly aware of his own limitations and convinced of the necessity of "more hands" being involved in the effort, Ketcham developed a new plan of action. He reflected on the manner in which the brethren had prevailed upon him to accept the presidency of the General Association of Regular Baptist Churches for a fourth term in 1937. As his thoughts turned to the next annual meeting, he became increasingly convinced that a fifth term would be unwise. He had been critical of J. Frank Norris for having a "one-man organization." He did not want the GARBC to gain the reputation of being a one-man operation—especially if he was the one man!

Ketcham knew that his six-month tour as the representative of the Association had contributed to such rumors. In fact, the rumors went back even before that, but the tour had greatly added to them. Consequently, when the executive committee of the Association met prior to the annual conference, Ketcham presented to the men an organizational proposal designed to eliminate the existing executive structure. The changes proposed were sweeping. His own office as president was to be abolished, along with the offices of vice-president and the various state vice-presidents. In their place he proposed a council composed of fourteen men. After the first year, each man would serve a two-year term; thus, seven would be elected annually.

The executive committee approved Ketcham's proposal. While being grateful for Ketcham's leadership, they, too, had heard the criticism of their leader. They recognized the wisdom of his plan and presented it to the Association at the annual meeting in Waterloo, Iowa, April 18-21, 1938.

The executive committee asked Bob Ketcham to present the proposal to the delegates in Waterloo. When Ketcham looked at the delegates, he knew that what he was about to propose would mean a "letting go" of the reins of leadership. But he was convinced it was the thing to do. It was God's organization, not Bob Ketcham's.

> There has been widespread criticism that this organization is a one-man outfit. While this is not true and could not be true, due to the method of election which we have always constitutionally observed, whereby the members of the nominating committee are selected by the individual churches themselves, (each church naming one of its messengers to serve on such a committee prior to the annual gathering)—yet the general public still regards the president of this organization—whoever he may be, as the director and controller of all its activities; and the acts of the president in the public mind have become the acts of the Association; and his statements, however definitely personal they may be, are attributed to be the considered and collective thought of the entire Association.[11]

Ketcham's tone captured the attention of his entire audience. They sensed the importance of the moment. As they leaned forward attentively, Ketcham continued:

> While this should not be, it nevertheless exists and will continue to exist regardless of who is made president of the Association, as long as the public is unable to differentiate between the personal views of the president of the Association and the stated policies of the Association itself. Hence the Executive Committee feels that if the constitution of the Association is changed to eliminate the lifting up of one man to the headship of the organization as president, and instead provides for the establishment of a properly elected council of fourteen men, independently nominated by the individual churches prior to the convening of any annual gathering of the Association, that the public will begin to realize what we have long contended, namely, that there are no big men in the General Association but only many little men with a big God.[12]

11. Ketcham's remarks were quoted in an article entitled "Truly a Glorious Fellowship," *The Baptist Bulletin,* III (May-June 1938), 3, 4.
12. Ibid.

The closing sentence of Bob Ketcham's speech to the delegates at Waterloo was possible only in one context. At the very time that statement was made, Ketcham was in the midst of the tour which had led many of his friends to describe him as "Mr. GARB." But instead of that name making him hungry for power, it had the opposite effect. It sent him to the drawing board for an organizational structure which would play down his leadership role, spread the burden over many, and give the glory to God. God was holding Bob Ketcham to his word. The commitment made by the young preacher years before to Colossians 1:18 was still firm: "That in all things he might have the preeminence."

The delegates were moved by Ketcham's presentation. His arguments were direct and convincing. "The recommendation of the Executive Committee was unanimously passed and was adopted as part and parcel of the Association's constitution." [13]

In the subsequent elections, Ketcham was reunited with his friends Earle Griffith and H. O. Van Gilder. The three men, who had been so vital to the separatist movement in Ohio, were now all on the Council of Fourteen, although separated by many miles in their respective ministries. Griffith by this time was pastoring in Johnson City, New York, Van Gilder in Portsmouth, Ohio, and Ketcham in Gary. Griffith was chosen as chairman of the Council and Ketcham as secretary-treasurer. The latter position had previously been filled by Ketcham's assistant, Raymond F. Hamilton, who was also elected to the Council of Fourteen.

When Ketcham proposed the reorganization of the General Association of Regular Baptist Churches, his purpose had not been to eliminate himself from the fight. On the contrary, he planned to continue with all his energies. While in Waterloo, the newly elected council asked Ketcham to assume the responsibilities of editor of *The Baptist Bulletin*. David Otis Fuller had been the editor since June 1935. He continued in that capacity through the May-June issue of 1938. He prepared an introduction of the new editor which was printed in the May-June issue.

13. Ibid., p. 4.

It was mutually agreed upon at Waterloo that Dr. Robert T. Ketcham should become editor of the Baptist Bulletin for the coming year. We could think of no better choice for this difficult position.

For our own part, we have enjoyed the editorship of the Bulletin the past three years, but we are quite certain that a far better piece of work can be done and will be done by "Bob". And we are not in any way stooping to that lowest and most obnoxious form of all speech—flattery—when we say this. It comes from our heart and we mean it.

The reason we believe that "Bob" will carry the Bulletin to greater heights and wider circulation, is because he is not at all interested in seeing his picture in every issue and on every page. Those of us who heard the masterful sermon delivered at Waterloo on Tuesday night on "The Preeminence of Christ" know that "Bob" Ketcham is concerned mainly with exalting his Saviour and *not* himself.[14]

The next issue of *The Baptist Bulletin* contained "Greetings From the New Editor." In his introductory remarks, Ketcham thanked David Otis Fuller for his faithful ministry in editing *The Baptist Bulletin* in previous years. He then outlined his editorial policy for the magazine. He promised to prepare at least one expository message for each issue. Next he committed himself to "several pages of missionary material" each month. Finally, he promised to continue the battle against liberalism and modernism.

One of the vehicles for accomplishing this final objective was a column named after the pamphlet Ketcham had written two years before, "Facts for Baptists to Face." In this column, Ketcham promised, ". . . We shall bring forward without bitterness, but nevertheless with the uttmost [sic] frankness, and supported by the uncontrovertible proof, some fact [sic] which Baptists ought to know."[15] Attitude was important to Ketcham:

14. David Otis Fuller, "Our New Editor," *The Baptist Bulletin,* III (May-June 1938), 2.

15. R. T. Ketcham, "Greetings From the New Editor," *The Baptist Bulletin,* IV (July-August 1938), 1.

We shall not seek to make the Bulletin a contentious periodical. We shall bend every effort to make it constructive and a blessing, but we shall nevertheless be mindful of our obligation to let Baptists everywhere know the facts concerning the destructive work which Modernism is accomplishing in the ranks of the people called Baptists.[16]

By the fall of 1938, Bob Ketcham was "almost beside himself" with the burden of his responsibilities. His daughter's illness had consumed huge quantities of time. The responsibilities at Central Baptist Church continued to grow. The added task of editing *The Baptist Bulletin* was proving to be an even greater burden than he had anticipated. All of this placed an ever increasing burden on his study and prayer time. Ketcham knew that to be successful in his ministry he had to have time for that! And it was good that Bob Ketcham guarded his personal relationship with his Lord very carefully. For on the horizon was a test of obedience greater than anything previously experienced by this warrior of the faith—a trial that would threaten to ruin his ministry and his life.

16. Ibid.

ONE CRISP AUTUMN morning in the first week of October, Bob Ketcham sat in his office, sorting his mail. One of the letters in the pile was from J. Frank Norris. The Texas preacher was incensed that Ketcham had criticized him for having "a one-man organization." This, aparently, was the straw that broke the camel's back in the mind of Norris. Ketcham caught his breath as he looked down at the page. Phrases seemed to jump off the page at Ketcham, and his throat became dry as he read:

> Your feet will be held to the fire on this one issue.
>
> You have been hollering and squawking about me trying to crucify you. You have crucified yourself.
>
> Everybody is laughing at you—lifelong friends—men who have known you are pitying you.
>
> You were fired at Waterloo (from the G.A.R.B.) and they let you down easy by discontinuing the office. They did like I saw a crowd do to a smart alec [sic] at a country dance when I was a boy. They slipped the chair out from under him and his caboose hit the floor.
>
> In your asinine conceit—and most big bellied men are conceited—you thought I needed a favor from you. Why should a man want any favor from a man whose work is on four flats.

You remind me of a little flea-bitten dog jumping up in a wheat field to see which way the rabbit ran.

You are mad and you are going to get madder, and you might just as well understand you will have to stand up and take it.

You have ruined the G.A.R.B.

You think you are a great preacher, and there are a thousand others just as good, many of them better.

You run your hands down in your pockets, strut up and down the stage, and folks laugh at you.

Everybody knows that your jealousy is measured by your large waistband, and they are all laughing about it.

If you knew some of the wonderful things that have come into my work of the men who are backing me, you would just bust your bellyband with the worst case of envy, even worse than the envy that caused Saul to go to the witch of Endor.[1]

Ketcham read the letter a second time. His eyes went back to one section that caused rage to well within his breast. Again and again he read the words: "Dr. Hawkins has not exploited the fact that his daughter went to Africa. Dear Brother Hawkins has not exploited his daughter, nor has he sought to get cheap sympathy. Men don't have to do that unless they want to alibi for either their failures or their lying."[2] This obvious reference to his daughter's illness was almost too much for Bob Ketcham. He could not believe his eyes. Standing to his feet, he paced back and forth in his office. He returned to his desk once more and read the letter again. Then his eyes fell on a statement he had missed earlier: "When a man is conceited, he should have something to be conceited about. I am writing you with the hope that I can make you mad enough to send out some letters."[3] Ketcham decided right then that no letters would be written. But this was only the opening volley for Norris, and as time went on Ketcham weakened in his resolution not to respond.

1. All these quotations are taken from one letter. J. Frank Norris to R. T. Ketcham, October 1, 1938; *Ketcham Papers.*
2. Ibid.
3. Ibid.

J. Frank Norris was a strange enigma. His flare for the dramatic and his ability to handle an audience were unquestionable. Literally thousands of people flocked to hear him in Texas and Michigan. His congregations at the First Baptist Church of Fort Worth and the Temple Baptist Church of Detroit were among the largest in the entire nation. He battled liberalism and modernism in the Southern Baptist Convention with resolution. But he always seemed to be embroiled in controversy. It was as though he could not function without it. He was impatient with anyone who disagreed with him and absolutely incensed if anyone contradicted him. Consequently, many godly men felt the acid of his pen. One of his former associates said with both humor and contempt: "He used to always say, 'I fight dirty,' and that's one time he slipped up and told the truth. Oh, yes, he was ruthless."[4]

Longtime associate Beauchamp Vick recognized the enigmatic character of Norris:

> Now he has helped a great many preachers. I mean, I thank the Lord for the association that I had with him. I learned a lot of things to do, and I learned a great many things not to do. But he did help a lot of young preachers, and he was almost the idol of many young preachers in the south. But on the other hand, he left behind him a trail of broken preachers, some of whom left the ministry because of his treatment of them.[5]

Vick believed Norris had two sides. In his early years, he was tremendously used of God. "But then as he got older, he wist not that the Lord had departed from him. I think even with charity I could say that."[6]

Within a week of his letter, Norris attacked Ketcham in the pages of his weekly newspaper the *Fundamentalist*. As the basis of his attack he used an apparent disagreement between Dr. M. E. Hawkins, the godly president of Baptist Mid-Missions, and Ketcham concerning the administration of Baptist Mid-Missions. At the time, Ketcham served on the board of Mid-Missions. In the article Norris referred to Ketcham

4. G. Beauchamp Vick, *taped interview*, 1970.
5. Ibid.
6. Ibid. In response to the author's question, "Would you say this had taken place by the time of the conflict with Dr. Ketcham?" Vick replied, "Yes, yes, I think so."

as a "Judas." Of Ketcham he said, "This brother has made a fine protest, but in taking himself too seriously—measuring himself by his waistband—he has sought to regulate and dictate."[7]

Norris did not mention Ketcham by name. This was not his style. However, several references and incidents in the article left no doubt that Ketcham was the target of his attack.

> The trouble with this dear brother, if he would reduce his waistband and conceit, he would be happier, and perhaps would let other people's affairs alone.

> He reminds me of a flock of crows. When I was a boy the crows were plugging my watermelons before they were ripe, and a neighbor told me how to get rid of them. I shelled a long ear of yellow corn, split the grains and put an inch-long horse hair through each split grain and put a double handful in a pan of water, and let them soak all night, and the next morning they were twice their normal size. I went out the next day and scattered the grains with the horse hairs in them all over the watermelon patch, and soon a flock of black crows swooped down and they gobbled up the corn, but in a few minutes I saw every one of these crows ripping his craw open, and the ground was soon covered with the dead crows.

> My watermelons were left alone and they grew great big thirty, forty, fifty, sixty, seventy pounders, and how delicious they were! The crows made a mistake![8]

Then Norris made a reference to Hawkins that was to haunt Ketcham. He indicated that you could measure the "mission soul" of a preacher by his children. With a stroke of devious genius, Norris attacked one godly man while praising another. "Their daughter . . . is a truly great missionary. She and her fine husband didn't go to Africa on a 'romance.' . . . [He] has never exploited or made any appeal for himself because of his daughter."[9]

When these words appeared in the *Fundamentalist,* Lois

---

7. J. Frank Norris, "Dr. M. E. Hawkins in Mid-Missions—What a Testimony," *Fundamentalist* (October 7, 1938), p. 7.
   8. Ibid.
   9. Ibid.

Ketcham Moffat remained hospitalized and critically ill. Bob Ketcham fought the anger that welled within him. But his fight was not always successful. He was accustomed to lashing out at liberals, modernists and communists. He was a direct and forthright man, and in his anger he reacted to J. Frank Norris. He defended himself against the Norris charges and lashed out at his adversary's tactics. He forgot in the heat of the moment that this was exactly what Norris wanted.

When Ketcham returned from a Grand Rapids meeting, in which he had addressed himself to the Norris attack, a telegram from Norris was waiting:

> RECEIVED FULL REPORT OF ANOTHER ONE OF YOUR MEETINGS HELD IN GRAND RAPIDS LAST WEDNESDAY NIGHT. YOU MADE ME FRIENDS, SETTLED THE DOUBT OF SOME, AND ONE WHO WAS PRESENT WRITES, 'POOR FELLOWS THEY ARE BLIND.' YOUR PITIFUL ANGER IS THE LAUGHINGSTOCK OF THE LIMITED NUMBER WHO KNOW YOU AND YOUR COTERIE. YOU WILL FAINT WHEN YOU SEE FULL WRITE UP OF MY CONTINENT WIDE TOUR, RADIOS, NEWSPAPERS, AUDITORIUMS AND BACKING . . . THREE HUNDRED THOUSAND READERS WILL SEE REPORT OF LAST WEDNESDAY NIGHT'S MEETING—J FRANK NORRIS[10]

Ketcham was not the only Regular Baptist to come under the fire of Norris in the *Fundamentalist*. "Dr. Norris published in the Fundamentalist that Dr. Strathearn had opened Fundamentalist subscription envelopes in a back room of a church at Richburg, New York; had taken out the money, and had not forwarded it on to the Fundamentalist office."[11] Strathearn refuted this and other charges in a document entitled "Lies Versus Truth." Dr. David Otis Fuller, former editor of *The Baptist Bulletin,* also came under attack.

Dr. Earle G. Griffith, chairman of the Council of Fourteen of the General Association of Regular Baptist Churches, was outraged by the attack on Bob Ketcham. With a conviction that further silence would be "intolerable and cowardly," Griffith prepared a document in

10. J. Frank Norris to R. T. Ketcham, October 9, 1938; *Ketcham Papers.*
11. Ketcham, *Norris Issue,* p. 15.

defense of Ketcham entitled "Facts or Figments." He was concerned that Norris was damaging both individuals and the cause of fundamentalism. A typical Norris practice that alarmed him was that of sending the *Fundamentalist* to many people who had never subscribed. If he were attacking a particular pastor, for example, Norris would see to it that the entire congregation of the man's church began receiving copies of his paper.

Hence, Griffith set about to answer five specific charges that Norris had leveled against Ketcham. First, he thoroughly refuted the Norris allegation that Ketcham's church was "on four flats." He quoted statistics that revealed the impact of Central Baptist Church on the Gary community. The numerical and financial statistics revealed a growing and flourishing local testimony with a solid missionary budget and program.

Second, Griffith dealt with the Norris argument that Ketcham had "ruined the G.A.R.B." Griffith felt ideally suited to answer this argument. He had been the second president of the Association and intimately involved in the inner workings from the outset. He pointed to the rapid growth of the Association. New churches were being added every month, missionary giving was increasing, and accredited agencies were ministering throughout the world.

Third, Griffith turned his attention to the charge made by Norris that Ketcham was "a Judas with a 'scheme' to fire a great and good man like M. E. Hawkins." He reminded his readers that Norris had also described Ketcham as a "policy dictator" of Mid-Missions. In reference to this charge Griffith said:

> The facts are easily stated. Dr. Ketcham has long been an esteemed member of the Mid-Missions Council. He is now vice-president. In the Johnson City meeting of the G.A.R.B. as president he gave large recognition to Mid-Mission representatives; the same was repeated at Waterloo, April, 1938. The *Central Baptist Church of Gary is the strongest contributor to the support of the home office of Mid-Missions.* It was Dr. Ketcham who made the motion which put Dr. Hawkins in his present position, which he well deserves and fills.

> But note a quotation from Dr. Hawkins, dated October 21st, 1938, "Dr. Ketcham and I have always had the *sweetest fellowship* and we still have. *There is absolutely no friction in Mid-Missions.*"

If Dr. Ketcham is giving time, energy, money, his daughter and son-in-law to Mid-Missions; if he and the president are "still" having the "sweetest fellowship;" if Mid-Missions is frictionless; by what evidence or process of reasoning could Dr. Ketcham be branded as dictatorial or traitorous? Is not the charge a figment of a designing mind? *Is not Mid-Missions to somebody the ready made coveted Naboth Vinyard to be secured at any forfeiture of honor?*[12]

The fourth charge made by Norris was that Dr. Ketcham was "fired at Waterloo" by the General Association of Regular Baptist Churches. It was at Waterloo that Ketcham proposed his reorganization of the Association. When his concept was initially presented to the executive council of the Association, several urged him to retain the office of president. Griffith indicated that he knew of no one who desired a change.

It was Dr. Ketcham's spirit of self-effacement and determination to keep the control of the Association in the hands of the churches, small and large, that terminated his presidency. The present constitution which paves the way for the most democratic plan of action ever was devised by Dr. Ketcham himself, and unanimously approved by the old executive committee and unanimously adopted by the host of messengers present. The old executive, present council and convention assembly would have returned Dr. Ketcham to the chair had he agreed to it.[13]

Fifth and finally, Griffith turned his attention to the charge that Lois Moffat's missionary work was a "romance" and that her father had exploited her illness for "cheap sympathy." Griffith was appalled at this charge. He had stood by the bedside of Lois Moffat and knew full well how desperately ill she was. He had been the recipient of every bulletin Bob Ketcham had sent concerning his daughter's health. It was inconceivable to him that a Christian brother could make such a charge.

Were this not in the paper of which Dr. Norris is editor, as well as in a personal letter over his signature, we should question the

12. Earle G. Griffith, "Facts or Figments," n.d., pp. 4, 5.
13. Ibid., pp. 5, 6.

actuality of the statements. We hardly find it in us to believe that any Christian, much less one with the commitment of proclaiming the Gospel of Grace, could be capable of such cruel allusions and insinuations toward a suffering servant of his Lord.[14]

But Norris had made the charge, and literally thousands had read it. Ketcham knew he could become bitter, but he also knew he must not. When feelings of bitterness welled in his breast, he went back to his special verse, Colossians 1:18. If preeminence was to go to Christ, he reasoned, it mattered little what people thought of Bob Ketcham. Then why was he so upset? Why did he have to fight the feelings of anger? Was it human frailty? At times Ketcham was not sure. But he was sure of one thing. He was sure that the cause of Jesus Christ could not possibly benefit from this type of conflict among Christians. He was sure that this controversy was not of God. He expressed his concern to Norris:

> I tell you again, Dr. Norris, I am sorry beyond words to express, that such a man as yourself with tremendous talents for leadership and ability to organize and carry on great pieces of work, should in his insane desire to crush men who disagree with him in the slightest, make such a sorry spectacle of Fundamentalism. Truly, Dr. Norris, I care not one bit for myself, what you may say about me, or what you do about me. The Lord's blessing is upon me and upon my work in power and that is all I need to be concerned about so far as I am personally concerned. But my heart is truly broken as I see this awful spectacle of slam and bang, mud-slinging, innuendo, insinuation, vituperation, throatcutting and crucifying, going on in your Fundamentalist with men whom you have set out to ruin because they would not consent to bow down before your image.[15]

While all this controversy raged around her, Lois Moffat remained gravely ill. Subsequently, Ketcham published his first report in several weeks. Though it was not dated, it apparently was drafted in late December 1938 or early January 1939. He apologized to his friends

14. Ibid., p. 6.
15. R. T. Ketcham to J. Frank Norris, n.d.; *Ketcham Papers.* It would appear this letter was written in October 1938.

for not writing sooner. His schedule, he explained, had been overcrowded and he had not known what to say, for little improvement had been seen. Lois was still unable to sit up or be out of bed. Though she had initially gained some weight, she no longer was doing so. Her attitude was good, but her progress was slow—very, very slow.

During the long weeks and months of his daughter's illness, Ketcham had been a faithful father. When Lois was in the hospital, his visits were regular. When they were able to bring her home, he would sit with her by the hour. His spare moments were devoted to his daughter's needs.

After returning home late one afternoon and visiting briefly with his wife, Bob made his way to his daughter's bedroom. He paused by the door and braced himself. The long weeks had not made it any easier to look upon her weakened body. As he entered the room and stood by her bed, he gave her a brave smile which she tried to return. In his mind he thought, "Look at her just lying there—a bundle of bones. She's just a shadow of her former self. Her body and mind are practically shot, and she looks so tired." He glanced around the room, realizing that he could not share his thoughts with his daughter. He saw the overstuffed chair near the bed. He put his hand to Lois's cheek and said softly, "Lois, would you like to sit in this big chair?" She squeaked out a weak little yes, and then, as if afraid it was not heard, she slowly nodded her head.

Bob moved the few steps to the big chair and drew it to the side of the bed. He then lifted his daughter as easily as you would lift a small child. He placed her in the chair and turned back to the bed to pick up a pillow. As he did so, he heard a dull thump! He quickly looked back and discovered his daughter flat on her face on the floor. She was unable even to sit up in the chair. In a moment he was kneeling beside her. He quickly lifted her in his arms and returned her to her bed. Tears streamed down his cheeks as he saw the disappointment and pain etched on her face. He wrapped his beloved daughter in his arms and wept unashamedly.

As he drew back from the bed and looked down upon his daughter once more, the sorrow in Bob Ketcham's heart was replaced by a new emotion. He remembered what J. Frank Norris had said about the Moffats' missionary "honeymoon." As he recalled those words, it felt like someone had placed a metal band around his chest and was drawing it tight. A wave of hatred swept through his entire being. His eyes glazed, his hands clenched, and a low gutteral sound came from his throat, as wave after wave of white, hot, burning, fiery hatred swept through his heart for J. Frank Norris. Describing that moment to his niece years laters he said, "If I could have gotten hold of J. Frank Norris that day, . . . I would have torn him limb from limb.' I was caught up in a blinding fury of such hatred as I suppose few people have ever known."[16]

As beads of perspiration formed on his forehead, Ketcham realized his thoughts were unimaginable. He staggered to the door of his daughter's room saying, "Lord, this must not be; this must not be." Leaning against the door frame for support, he called his wife. Alarm registered on Mary's face as she approached the room. She could see the tortured agony in her husband's face. She looked questioningly to him for an explanation and looked quickly into the room to check on Lois. Waves of anger continued to engulf Bob. He did not want his daughter to be alone, but he knew that he had to be alone. He was concerned that Lois had seen his feelings on his face. Because of this and because of her fall moments before, he asked Mary to stay with her while he was gone. Then he left the room.

He staggered through the house, looking for a place where he could be completely alone. "A room," he muttered, "a room to lock." The only room with a lock was the bathroom, so Ketcham entered that room and secured the door. He looked at himself in the mirror and saw the hatred in his eyes. He dropped to his knees and confessed his sin to his God. He pleaded with God for forgiveness and strength. He could not believe that after twenty-five years of serving his God as a pastor, and after seeking throughout those years to give God the

---

16. R. T. Ketcham to Mrs. Don Rice, January 5, 1965; *Ketcham Papers.* Ketcham made a similar statement in a *taped interview* in 1970.

Ketcham was not the only Christian leader to feel this way about Norris. Beauchamp Vick expressed the identical spiritual crisis in his life. In a taped interview (1970), Vick said: "I'll tell you, the only time in the world that I would say I ever hated anybody, I believe. And I wanted to kill him, and I could have. I thought the world would be better off without him." Vick admitted this was an area over which he had to gain spiritual victory. Thus, two men of God, both richly used, faced spiritual crises in their lives because of J. Frank Norris.

preeminence in all things, he could fall so completely out of fellowship. He actually hated a man.

In his twenty-five years in the ministry, Bob Ketcham had become thoroughly familiar with the Word of God. He recalled the apostle John's many admonitions to love in the Epistle of 1 John. He remembered the familiar words: "If you cannot love your brother whom ye have seen, how can you love God whom ye have not seen?" He lifted his eyes heavenward and said, "Lord, I'm not coming out of this room until I can pray in love for J. Frank Norris."

The minutes slipped by slowly, but the silence was broken only by sobs. Ketcham remained in that bathroom for over an hour. He would kneel and pray. He would lie flat on his back and pray. He would stand, sit, lie on his stomach, begging God for the power to pray in love for Frank Norris. "I would struggle up the mountain; when it seemed I was almost ready to reach the apex where I could formulate some kind of words that would be a prayer for J. Frank Norris, I would drop clear back down to the foot of the mountain again, only to try to do it all over again. Up and down. I would get *almost* to the place, then I would realize that if I said the words they would just be words—words with no real love in them; and down I would go again."[17]

Ketcham was pacing back and forth in the tiny bathroom when he finally realized he had failed. The weight of that realization was more than his legs could stand. He dropped with a thud to the floor and groaned, "Lord, I can't." Sobs racked his weary body as he realized his absolute defeat. But even as he wept the Lord spoke to his heart, saying: "Son, I know you can't, but I can; and if you really want Me to do it, I will do it through you." In that moment, Bob Ketcham grasped the sufficiency of God's grace. Before he knew what was happening, he was pouring out his heart "in a passion of love for J. Frank Norris, asking God to bring him to himself and straighten him out."[18] Ketcham knew that it was only God's love that enabled him to so pray.

When Bob Ketcham unlocked the door and walked back into the presence of his family, he had been transformed by the power of God. The hatred was gone. His face bore shining testimony to the victory in his life. A ministry that could have been destroyed by bitterness was preserved that God might have the glory.

17. Ibid.
18. Ibid.

"Dr. Bob" at Gull Lake Bible Conference,
Hickory Corners, Michigan (1942)

Dr. Ketcham in his study

IN THE MONTHS following his great spiritual battle, Bob Ketcham learned as never before to draw his strength from God. His work load continued to expand. In addition to the responsibilities of his own congregation, other areas made ever-increasing demands for his time. Churches needed help in withdrawing from the Convention. Pastors needed encouragement because of trials in their ministries. Each month a sermon had to be prepared for *The Baptist Bulletin,* and other editorial chores had to be expedited. Ketcham drew heavily on the men who were his associate editors and used their talents to the greatest possible advantage, but the burden remained heavy.

Meanwhile Lois continued her battle to regain strength. One day when her dad walked into the room, she shocked him with the announcement that she was going to have a baby. The child had been conceived just days prior to her illness. Ketcham looked down at his daughter. His mind raced . . . a grandchild! . . . a grandchild? Would it be possible for Lois to give birth to a child?

When this question was posed to her doctors, their answers were not encouraging. It was very probable, the physicians reported, that the child would experience some birth defects—if it survived at all. The vitamin deficiency that she had experienced gave no cause for hope of a normal birth.

Ketcham's newsletter of late 1938 carried the first report of the impending birth: "Some time in late February or early March, it is expected that she will be called upon to undergo the ordeal of childbirth. The doctors have not yet decided whether it should be normal or be Caesarean operation. Certainly, unless she gains a great deal of strength between now and then, the Caesarean operation will be resorted to."[1] Ketcham closed his letter to his friends with an urgent plea for all to unite with him "at the throne in prayer" during the days and weeks ahead.

Word spread rapidly throughout the country of Lois Moffat's condition. It was announced in pulpits nationwide, and literally thousands of Christians united their hearts in prayer in behalf of Don and Lois Moffat. As the weeks slipped slowly by, Mrs. Moffat's condition improved little. Ketcham issued his final note to his friends on March 2. He indicated that Lois was experiencing "considerable trouble with nerves and a general upset condition." However, she never complained about her situation, and many drew strength from her. But time was gone. There was no longer opportunity for her to gain strength. The baby had to be delivered. The whole matter was in God's hands. Ketcham shared the situation with his friends, urging them to continue to pray:

> As you know, the arrival of the baby has been expected around the 11th of March. The family has felt right along that a Caesarean delivery was the only safe or possible method. The physician, however, has been unwilling to commit himself on this point until today. He had hoped that she would gain more rapidly in strength than she has. In fact, she has not gained in strength at all. She has not been able to sit up even twenty minutes a day for the past six or eight weeks.
>
> Today Dr. Verplank made his final decision and unless present plans are changed, Lois will be taken to the Methodist Memorial Hospital in Gary next Thursday, March 9, and will have a Caesarean operation performed Friday the 10th.
>
> We will deeply appreciate it if you will unite with us at the throne in prayer during these days.[2]

When Lois entered the delivery room for her surgery, Mary

---

1. R. T. Ketcham to friends, n.d.; *Ketcham Papers.*
2. R. T. Ketcham to friends, March 2, 1939; *Ketcham Papers.*

Ketcham faced a great challenge. It was her responsibility to keep Daddy Don and Grandpa Bob from wearing a hole in the hospital floor! Though the situation had been thoroughly committed to the Lord and all involved trusted completely in God's will and His divine plan, they experienced all the normal crises of awaiting parenthood.

When the doctor emerged from the delivery room, he announced that Lois had given birth to a son. Though tests would have to be run to be certain, it appeared that the child was normal. The doctor's prognosis proved to be correct. John Wendell Moffat became known as the miracle baby; the prayers of thousands had been answered.

Meanwhile, Grandpa Bob was about to burst his buttons! He chortled, he boasted, and he raved. He even devoted two pages in *The Baptist Bulletin*, complete with pictures, to announce his grandson's birth:

> Through all these weeks and months, thousands of friends across the United States and in foreign lands, have been holding on to God in prayer for the recovery of Mrs. Moffat and also for God's special providence over her in the birth of her baby. Thousands were also concerned about the baby itself. Humanly speaking, there was absolutely no possible way for this baby to be born physically perfect. But there are no impossibilities with God. The result of that proposition is that on the 10th day of March, by Caesarian delivery, a baby boy weighing 7 pounds 12½ ounces, was presented to the Moffats, and the attending physicians said, they had never seen a more perfect specimen of babyhood.[3]

Just days after their grandson was born, an event occurred in Dallas that was destined to alter the lives of Robert and Mary Ketcham. P. B. Chenault, pastor of the largest Regular Baptist church in the state of Iowa, the Walnut Street Baptist Church of Waterloo, was in Texas for meetings with Dr. John R. Rice. As Chenault drove north, a drunken driver approached in the southbound lanes, veered left of center and sideswiped Chenault's automobile. Chenault's car was forced off the highway into a deep ravine, and the preacher was thrown out of the vehicle and killed instantly.

3. R. T. Ketcham, "To the Regions Beyond," *The Baptist Bulletin*, IV (May 1939), 7.

Almost three thousand people crowded the Walnut Street Baptist Church on April 4 for the pastor's funeral. Because Pastor Chenault was a member of the Council of Fourteen and the Walnut Street Baptist Church was actively involved in the GARBC, Ketcham traveled to Waterloo to represent the Association at the funeral. Ketcham reported the death of the thirty-five-year-old preacher in the same issue of *The Baptist Bulletin* that carried the news of the birth of his grandchild. He closed his report with these words: "The love and sympathy and prayers of thousands of Baptists across this continent go out to the Walnut Street Church and to the bereaved family with a sincere hope and trust that God will lead and guide in no unmistakable way during these days of crisis."[4] Little did Ketcham realize when he penned those words that God's leading for Walnut Street Baptist Church would involve him.

That same May issue of *The Baptist Bulletin* carried as Ketcham's message for the month a sermon entitled "The Preeminance [sic] of Christ." It was built around his life verse, Colossians 1:18. In the message he demonstrated the preeminence Christ had with God the Father, with God the Holy Spirit, and with the Word of God. The message reflected the extent to which Ketcham had studied his life verse. Under the third point of his outline, he demonstrated how Jesus Christ was given the preeminence in every single book of the Bible. The sixty-six books of Scripture were named and a reference showing Christ's preeminence was listed for every book. In conclusion Ketcham said: "Jesus Christ fills the *eye* of God the Father, the *lips* of the Holy Spirit, the *pages* of the Book, therefore, He has a right to the preeminence in every believer's life."[5]

In the following weeks God began to work in the heart of Bob Ketcham. The Walnut Street Baptist Church asked him to consider becoming its pastor. In the midst of his discussions with Walnut Street, his long-time assistant, Raymond F. Hamilton, resigned from the staff of Central Baptist Church to become pastor of the First Baptist Church

---

4. R. T. Ketcham, "P. B. Chenault—At Home With the Lord," *The Baptist Bulletin*, IV (May 1939), 3.
5. R. T. Ketcham, "The Preeminance [sic] of Christ," *The Baptist Bulletin*, IV (May 1939), 23.

of Pana, Illinois.[6] On June 16 the Walnut Street Baptist Church extended a call to Ketcham to become its pastor. His acceptance letter was dated June 22, and he read his resignation to the membership of the Central Baptist Church in Gary on June 25.

In his letter to the people of Central Baptist, he reviewed the accomplishments of his seven-year ministry, highlighted by more than 1,000 public confessions of salvation. Over 950 people had been added to the church roll, and several had entered Christian service.

> All of this blessed accomplishment could never have been realized apart from the fine, beautiful and wonderful cooperation of you dear ones. We want definitely and sincerely this morning, to acknowledge to you, my beloved people, the debt of gratitude I owe you for making this all possible under our pastoral leadership.
>
> Into this blessed and happy relationship, has come what we believe to be the call of God to accept the pastorate of the Walnut Street Baptist Church of Waterloo, Iowa. Through the waking hours of the days since the call came, and for that matter, through the sleepless hours of many nights, we have been earnestly and honestly endeavoring to find God's will for us in this matter. It has been no easy thing to do.
>
> We have constantly found our opinions being colored by personal desire. I am personally reluctant to sever the sweet and blessed ties which bind us together here, but I have preached to you dear ones too long and too often that personal interests must never enter into consideration of whether or not we shall do the will of God. We have therefore, sought to put into practice that which we have preached to you, and have honestly endeavored to disassociate our personal interests from this whole matter, and seek to determine our answer on the basis of God's will for our life.
>
> Following that procedure, we have arrived at a definite conviction that it is God's will for us to minister henceforth in the Walnut Street Baptist Church of Waterloo, Iowa.
>
> We are, therefore, presenting to you this morning, our resignation as the pastor of Central Baptist Church of Gary, Indiana to take effect August 31, next.[7]

6. R. T. Ketcham, "Rev. R. F. Hamilton Called to Pana, Illinois," *The Baptist Bulletin*, V (June 1939), 4.

7. R. T. Ketcham, "Dr. Ketcham Accepts Call to Waterloo," *The Baptist Bulletin*, V (July 1939), 2.

Shortly after Ketcham arrived in Iowa, the members of the Walnut Street Baptist Church became keenly aware of their new pastor's intense interest in missions. He proposed that they immediately implement an annual missionary conference during the month of November. This conference was to involve a week of missionary services, plus the establishment of a high financial goal, not only to care for the expenses of the missionaries, but also to provide a solid honorarium for each one. When he announced his goal for that first conference, the deacons were reticent to accept it. They felt that many other expenses—especially related to the physical plant—needed immediate attention. But under Ketcham's persuasion, they acquiesced. The church not only made their hefty financial goal in that first conference, but the needed physical plant repairs were also paid for within a month! In subsequent years, though major problems frequently stood in the way of their missionary goals, they continued to meet those goals as God's blessing richly reposed on the people of the church.[8]

The move to Waterloo did not change Bob Ketcham's involvement with the General Association of Regular Baptist Churches. The Walnut Street Baptist Church had been led out of the Convention and into the GARBC under the ministry of Pastor Chenault. They were a solid, separatist congregation. Consequently, they encouraged their pastor to continue his leadership role in the national organization.

In his continuing capacity as editor of *The Baptist Bulletin,* Ketcham kept hammering away at the Northern Baptist Convention. Virtually every issue carried articles denouncing modernism at every level. Liberal preachers were quoted, and their theological heresies were described in detail. In spite of his failing vision, Ketcham was an avid reader, and his reading was not limited to that with which he agreed. He thoroughly examined the writing of every modernist theologian he could find, and he sought to refute their arguments. The enemy was real. Men who denied the virgin birth of Jesus Christ and the inspiration of Scripture were quoted and rebuked.

When the Northern Baptist Convention attempted to subvert the

8. Donn B. Ketcham, *taped recollections,* n.d.

will of the majority of the membership of the First Baptist Church of Princeton, Indiana, Ketcham quickly publicized the case. The Princeton church voted 92 to 18 to withdraw from the local, state and national organizations of the Northern Baptist Convention. The 18 individuals who had voted against this action finally gathered an additional 9 opponents to join their protest against the majority decision. (It was a church of about 450 members.) This small minority tried to take over the church and its property by electing trustees for "the First Baptist Church of Princeton, Indiana."

The pastor and the main body of the congregation were forced to go into court to secure an injunction against the minority's use of the church name. Through this injunction they also precluded the minority from assuming control of church property. But the minority group continued its crusade with the constant encouragement from the state and national representatives of the Northern Baptist Convention. The Convention leaders were determined to pursue the matter as far as possible. There ensued a protracted court battle which saw the Reverend Levi Spurgeon Sanders, a witness for the Convention, describe any non-Convention church as a "bastard Baptist Church." The pastor of the Princeton Baptist Church, Ford Porter, took the witness stand in behalf of the majority, while the Convention pulled in several witnesses to defend its position. After two and one-half days of testimony, Judge Eby ruled in favor of the majority group.

The fundamentalist majority had little time to enjoy its victory. The minority group immediately announced that they would return to the courtroom, request a change of venue and bring the matter to trial once more, using a different argument. The second trial ended with the judge again ruling in favor of the majority group. After listening to the Convention testimony for a day and a half, "Judge Youngblood handed down a decision, *making the injunction permanent, and restraining the minority group forever,* from acting in the name of the First Baptist Church or electing trustees thereof."[9]

The Convention group planned to appeal to the Supreme Court

9. R. T. Ketcham, "The Princeton Case," *The Baptist Bulletin,* V (May 1940), 10.

of Indiana. However, as the weeks passed, they allowed the time limit to lapse in which they were required to make such an appeal. This was a signal fundamentalist victory. Ketcham devoted almost one-half of *The Baptist Bulletin* of May 1940 to a summary of this test case. Throughout the months of battle, he had kept his readers posted on the progress in the courtrooms. When he received word that victory was assured by default, he was somewhat disappointed that the case had not gone to the Supreme Court.

> Personally, this editor wishes that they had gone through with the appeal, for we are as certain as we are that we are living, that they would have lost their case and having lost it in a State Supreme Court, it could then be used as the standard of judgment in any other case in any other State. As it is now it is just another circuit court decision, which of course, cannot be used as a guide for other cases. However, we do rejoice that the pastor and members of the First Baptist Church of Princeton may now go on with the glorious work of the Lord as they have been doing but no longer under the pressure of this useless and senseless persecution.[10]

The years that followed saw the General Association of Regular Baptist Churches continue a steady growth. In May 1942, when the conference met in the Walnut Street Baptist Church of Waterloo, the Association voted to enter into "active cooperation" with the recently organized American Council of Christian Churches. The ACCC was an interdenominational organization composed exclusively of groups which had separated from the mainline denominations over the issue of modernism. The ACCC was viewed as a vehicle through which Regular Baptists would be able to gain the ear of government in such areas as receiving commissions in the chaplaincy. Though the Association voted this point of contact with the ACCC, every church in the Fellowship maintained its autonomy and had to determine individually whether or not it wished to be involved.[11]

Bob Ketcham had worked with the American Council of Christian Churches from its inception. He was deeply convinced of its programs and approaches. Another organization with similar programs, the

10. Ibid., p. 11.
11. Stowell, *Background and History,* p. 68.

National Association of Evangelicals for United Action, had attracted the attention of some Regular Baptists. Consequently, Ketcham decided to analyze the two organizations for readers of *The Baptist Bulletin.* He explained: "THE AMERICAN COUNCIL *has had, from its inception, a positive* program of action embodying all of the constructive elements later adopted by the National Association. The primary issue is, therefore, not programs nor personalities *but* the Federal Council!"[12] Ketcham reminded his readers that the ACCC had been organized seven months before the National Association of Evangelicals. He indicated that the ACCC leadership had "offered to withdraw from office if that was the hindering factor in uniting our forces against the Federal Council."[13]

But leadership was not the problem—philosophy was! Ketcham noted the basic philosophical difference from three angles. First, the ACCC openly opposed "the Federal Council of the Churches of Christ in America," while the NAE refused "*to take a definite stand* against the modernistic Federal Council." Second, the ACCC restricted "*membership* to those churches (and individuals)" who had "repudiated the Federal Council," while the NAE included "*in its membership* many Churches still related to the Federal Council (through their denominational affiliations)." Third, the ACCC "was organized to provide a *united evangelical front against* the *Federal Council,* and other apostate organizations," while the NAE "was organized *in definite opposition to the American Council's* repudiation of the Federal Council."[14]

Thus, the key issue in the development of a nationwide, interdenominational fellowship was separation from modernism. It would have been absolutely unthinkable, in Ketcham's mind and the minds of his Regular Baptist brethren, to separate from modernism in their denomination and then join with them in an interdenominational structure. Obedience to the Word of God demanded separation from apostasy at every level.

12. R. T. Ketcham, "Why the General Association of Regular Baptists Declared Itself In Fellowship With The American Council of Christian Churches," *The Baptist Bulletin,* VIII (October 1942), l.
13. Ibid.
14. Ibid.

Don Moffat with his miracle son (1939)

THE GROWTH OF THE General Association of Regular Baptist Churches led to the calling of a full-time field representative in 1944. Ketcham saw the need for such a man, though he had no desire whatsoever to fill the position. He described that need in an editorial in *The Baptist Bulletin:*

> The need of a national representative for the G.A.R.B. has been abundantly evident for the past two years or more. This need was greatly emphasized by the situation now existing in hundreds of Northern Baptist Convention churches. The recent crack-up in the Northern Convention over the foreign mission situation has caused scores, if not hundreds of those churches to re-examine their relationship to the whole Northern Baptist Convention machine and program. The mails of G.A.R.B. men have been flooded with letters of inquiry and requests of information concerning the work of our Association. We have done the best we could by printed literature and correspondence, but the outstanding need has been for some man who knows the situation from the ground up and who has a keen mind and level head, coupled with a sympathetic and understanding spirit, to actually sit down with these pastors and boards and churches and discuss the whole situation with them.[1]

1. R. T. Ketcham, "National Representative," *The Baptist Bulletin,* X (October 1944), 1.

The man chosen for this tremendous responsibility was Dr. H. O. Van Gilder, who assumed his new position in the fall of 1944. Ketcham gave the new National Representative his unequivocal endorsement:

> It has been this editor's high privilege to know Dr. Van Gilder and to work intimately with him for the past twenty years. It was Dr. Van Gilder, along with Dr. Griffith, who was associated with us in the founding and organizing of what is now known as the Ohio Independent Association of Baptist Churches. Aside from the Grand Rapids Association founded by Dr. Van Osdel, the Ohio group was one of the first to really set an organized expression of the fellowship of churches which had withdrawn from the Northern Baptist Convention.[2]

The General Association of Regular Baptist Churches rented a three-room suite in downtown Chicago for its offices. (The rent was $50 per month!) Dr. Van Gilder was joined by Miss Ruth Ryburn of Waterloo, Iowa, who served as his secretary. These two made up the staff of the Association at that time. Ketcham reminded his readers that the churches of the Fellowship were financially responsible for this new venture, though given the nature of the organization, all gifts were voluntary.

In a front page editorial in the January 1945 issue of *The Baptist Bulletin,* Dr. Ketcham announced his resignation as editor. He indicated that earlier he had asked to be relieved by May 1945. However, with the acquisition of a national home office and a national representative, he suggested to the Council of Fourteen that the transfer of responsibility to Dr. Van Gilder could take place sooner. Ketcham's reasons for resigning were twofold: the heavy work load that he was encountering, and "the fact of a very slow but nevertheless real decrease in the acuity of vision."

In reviewing his years as editor, Ketcham confessed that the task had not been an easy one. His hard-hitting, uncompromising editorial policy had aroused the ire of some of his brethren. Some in the Association did not feel that conditions within the Northern Baptist Convention should even be mentioned. But Ketcham continued to name names in his direct, clear-cut way. He listed three reasons for

2. Ibid.

ignoring the criticism in this direction. "The first is that the reading public has a right to know the situation as it relates to the apostasy."[3]

His second reason was "because it is imperative that our Baptist people in their separation do not forget what it's all about." Ketcham was deeply concerned for young preachers graduating from the seminaries or new preachers coming into the movement for the first time. Many of these younger clerics were unfamiliar with the struggles of the Convention days. They had not encountered firsthand men who openly mocked the great doctrines of the Word of God. Thus, Ketcham reasoned, "Lest there should grow up in separationist Baptist circles, a longing for the onions, leeks, and garlic of old Convention days, the Baptist Bulletin has, when occasion demanded, pointed out the sin of the Convention, the folly and foolishness of its leaders, as well as of those who could seek to *change* Egypt instead of *come* out of it."[4]

Ketcham's third reason for ignoring the criticisms was found in his "conviction that while having escaped out of Egypt ourselves, we have an obligation to others who are still there."[5] This reason certainly reflected the tone of Robert Ketcham's ministry. In his mind it was not enough to separate himself from the Northern Baptist Convention. He viewed it as a spiritual responsibility to provide information and aid for any and all others who might wish to take the same step. The struggle with modernism was, in his mind, a holy war which had to be waged to the utmost at every opportunity.

Leaving the editorship of *The Baptist Bulletin* enabled Ketcham to devote more time to his most recent responsibility. In September 1944 he had been asked to become president of the American Council of Christian Churches. This organization was of tremendous importance to Ketcham. He viewed it as a separatist movement which could withstand liberalism in the national theater. As the modernistic movement coalesced in the Federal Council of Churches of Christ in America, it professed to speak for all of Christianity on the national

3. R. T. Ketcham, "Changing Editors," *The Baptist Bulletin,* X (January 1945), 1.
4. Ibid., pp. 1, 16.
5. Ibid., p. 16.

level. Ketcham was convinced that this was the ultimate modernist power ploy. The ACCC, in his mind, represented the fundamentalist counteraction. Therefore, he faced the challenge of the ACCC with his customary vigor.

Meanwhile, Ketcham's move to Waterloo did not enable him to escape the vicious attacks of J. Frank Norris. In spite of the obvious reality of Lois Moffat's illness, Norris continued to refer to the missionaries who went on a "honeymoon romance." He castigated Ketcham on a variety of other issues, but the "honeymoon romance" was his favorite theme. Below is a typical piece of Norris's rhetoric:

> Nothing hurts the mission cause more than for two overzealous young people to go to the foreign field for their "honeymoon" and when the "honey" gives out and the "moon" goes down—get homesick and return—sometimes the climate is too severe and the health of the young missionaries breaks and they have to return.
>
> Their faith is weak and when they see the "perils" in a strange land, they flee like the ten spies from the sons of Anak.
>
> But, whatever the cause for young missionaries returning, it doesn't help, but hurts, it discourages and breaks down the mission spirit at home.[6]

In the fall of 1943, Norris began a new form of attack. When the Walnut Street Baptist Church withdrew its support of a veteran missionary, Norris chose to rebuke both the pastor and the church for its decision. On September 26, 1943, he fired a lengthy telegram to Ketcham, chastising him for the action and promising to attack Ketcham in the pages of the *Fundamentalist.* Norris demanded that Ketcham allow him to appear before the deacons to defend the missionary.[7]

This was not the first telegram Ketcham received from Norris on this issue, nor would it be the last. In subsequent broadsides, he pelted Ketcham with such mocking phrases as: "Your members pity and laugh when you cry. . . . You and your crowd are mad. . . .

6. J. Frank Norris, "Special Prayer for Dr. M. E. Hawkins and Mid-Missions," *Fundamentalist* (February 28, 1941), p. 6. See also issues of September 23, 1938; February 17, 1939; and April 21, 1939.

7. J. Frank Norris to R. T. Ketcham, September 26, 1943; *Ketcham Papers.*

Tremendous circulation Fundamentalist revealed you to whole world and worse coming. . . . You are causing laughter and pity. You are cornered, and why not quit your folly."[8] All these telegrams were timed to arrive at the Walnut Street Baptist Church shortly before Ketcham was to enter the pulpit on Sunday morning!

In addition to this direct, personal assault, Norris constantly lashed out at Ketcham in the pages of the *Fundamentalist*. Further, he somehow managed to get a copy of the Walnut Street Baptist Church membership list. Norris then saw to it that every member of Ketcham's church received each copy of the *Fundamentalist* with his vicious attacks on Ketcham. Finally Ketcham refused to accept delivery of the telegrams Norris was sending on Sunday mornings. The telegrams continued to appear; the tone was the same; but the signatory on the telegrams had been changed. Now they were signed by "Wilson" or "John" or "Gordon," but they came from the same place, and everyone, including Western Union, knew it.

Eventually a Western Union representative called Dr. Ketcham. It was the same man who earlier had informed Ketcham that he could refuse the telegrams that were coming from Norris. This time he said, "Dr. Ketcham, we know who is sending these. We know it is J. Frank Norris. Now I can lose my job for what I am going to tell you to do, but if you say so, any telegram of that kind that comes to you on our ticker, we will mark it refused and send it back to him collect." Ketcham thanked him and asked him to do just that.

In addition to the telegrams, Norris made innumerable phone calls to Ketcham on Sunday mornings. The content of those phone calls will never be known, but a member of his staff reported: "Dr. Ketcham would receive them just before he was to preach. The messages were beamed at upsetting him."[9] The continued assault by his adversary created a serious crisis in the life of Robert Thomas Ketcham and his congregation. By the fall of 1943, the Norris charges

8. J. Frank Norris to R. T. Ketcham, October 23, 1943; December 2, 1943; December 31, 1943; *Ketcham Papers*.
9. Helen Floden, "Thank you, Dr. Ketcham," November 2, 1977. A brief, typed tribute to Dr. Ketcham sent to Dr. Merle R. Hull, editor of *The Baptist Bulletin; Ketcham Papers.*

were completely out of hand. In the pages of the *Fundamentalist*, Norris accused Ketcham of burglarizing a home and spending a night with a Sunday school teacher from one of his former churches. This assault on his integrity and morality could have destroyed Ketcham's ministry were it not for the fact that the article contained the dates of the alleged incidents and the Walnut Street Baptist Church congregation knew the charges had to be inaccurate because Ketcham was home in Waterloo at the times involved.

But what of the thousands of other people in churches throughout the land who did not know? The people of Ketcham's congregation realized that the false charges could destroy their pastor. Therefore, on September 23, 1943, the advisory board of his church took action, and Ketcham received the following communication:

TO OUR BELOVED PASTOR,
'Valiant for truth'—
Dr. Robert T. Ketcham

  We, the undersigned, as the official board of Walnut Street Baptist Church of Waterloo, Iowa, take this opportunity of saluting you, and affirming our enthusiastic confidence in you in these days.
  Of necessity, the battle for truth brings wounds—brings, too, the smoke-pall and the cloud 'neath which there can be bred misunderstanding. Friends may mistake truest friends in the haze—and enemies may use such a fact to promote their ends.
  We want you to know, pastor, that we are by your side, and that battle-scars make you but the dearer to our hearts. This is our pledge of whole-hearted and loving cooperation in the work of this church and in the larger ministry to which God has called you.
  "Beloved, I wish above all things that thou mayest prosper and be in health, even as thy soul prospereth. For I rejoiced greatly, when the brethren came and testified of the truth that is in thee, even as thou walkest in the truth."—3 John 2-3.[10]

Robert Ketcham was deeply moved by his congregation's willingness to stand with him. But through the final months of 1943

10. Advisory Board to R. T. Ketcham, September 23, 1943; *Ketcham Papers.*

and into the early months of 1944, the attacks of Norris continued. When he could no longer contact Ketcham on the telephone, and when telegrams were sent back collect, Norris turned to the penny postcard for his assault. In March he mailed four cards, consecutively numbered, to Ketcham. On these cards he quoted letters he had received from members of the Walnut Street church. One of the letters told of how stunned Ketcham had been when he discovered, during a Sunday service, that virtually every member of his congregation received the *Fundamentalist.* Norris next reported that another member of the congregation wrote: "It is all our folks do, is talk about the Fundamentalist, and many are wondering when will all this mess come to an end. We love our pastor; he is a man of ability, but we feel so sorry that he has gotten all tangled up in this mess." Norris went on to say, "Even your own fellows, some of your own appointed counselors, are laughing at you and this whole business." He concluded: "It costs nothing to write you up in the FUNDAMENTALIST; we don't have to pay one cent of extra postage, and it is amusing reading for everybody to laugh at 'Brother Diotrephes.' "[11]

Mary Ketcham watched helplessly as Bob struggled with this crisis. She sustained him in prayer and offered encouragement at every opportunity. She knew he had no vehicle for defending himself against the onslaught that threatened to destroy both his church and his reputation. Together they prayed for God's help and awaited divine direction. Ketcham continued with his many responsibilities, but it was hard to concentrate. Often, while alone, he prayed to God for preservation against the bitterness that he had felt against J. Frank Norris years before. He pleaded with God to keep him faithful to the promise of Colossians 1:18. Indeed, if all preeminence was to go to Christ, and if that had been the goal of his ministry all these years, then he would leave his personal reputation in the hands of his Savior.

Perhaps one of the finest measures of a man is how people respond when he is accused. One Sunday morning as he entered the church auditorium, Ketcham was stopped by the chairman of his deacons, who requested that the pastor come to an evening meeting

11. J. Frank Norris to R. T. Ketcham, March 24, 1944; *Ketcham Papers.*

of the advisory board. That night when Ketcham walked into the room, the entire group of eighty-two men and women were waiting for him. With a knot in the pit of his stomach, he walked to the front and stood before that company of people. The chairman of the board opened the meeting with prayer and then turned to his pastor. He indicated that the board had met the previous week, and as he said this Ketcham's heart sank. Never before had a church board held a meeting without his knowledge! In a moment the whole history of the conflict flashed before his eyes. Had they had enough? Would they demand his resignation? Could he really blame them if they did?

His ears focused once more on what the moderator was saying. A resolution had been passed . . . and the chairman began to read it: "Dear Pastor, Resolved that the Walnut Street Baptist Church of Waterloo, Iowa, places at your disposal all of its facilities and its financial ability to take Dr. J. Frank Norris into court and sue him for slander and libel." Tears streamed down Ketcham's face, and he openly and unashamedly sobbed. When he finally regained his composure, he stood to his feet. He thanked the board for their action and said: "I cannot take a man into court whom I have been taking to the court of high Heaven now for several years, asking the Lord if he isn't saved to save him, and if he's crazy to heal him." Ketcham then explained to his church how one night years before he had locked himself in his bathroom to commit to God his hatred for his adversary.

Shortly after this experience in his local church, Ketcham received a vote of confidence from the Council of Fourteen of the General Association of Regular Baptist Churches. The Council, composed of men from all over the United States, was fully aware of the attack of Norris on Ketcham. It was their desire to express their confidence in their friend and colleague, and they did so with the following letter:

> To the members of the Walnut Street Baptist Church of Waterloo, Iowa:
>
> Greetings in the name of our great God and Savior, Jesus Christ!
>
> The undersigned, members of the Council of Fourteen of the General Association of Regular Baptist Churches, are sincerely desirous of writing you concerning your beloved pastor, Dr. Robert T. Ketcham, one of the members of this Council.
>
> Your honored pastor and our true friend in Christ has recently been subjected once again to a vicious and slanderous

attack upon his name and character. This attack has not one single word of truth to support it.

For twenty years Dr. Ketcham has been vitally related to every major doctrinal and ecclesiological controversy among Northern Baptists, and in no instance has he deviated from fact, truth or a high sense of honor, friends and foes being the judges.

We earnestly wish that you, as members of the Walnut Street Baptist Church, would know that every member of this council has the fullest confidence in, and the highest regard for your beloved pastor, Dr. Ketcham. We believe him to be a man of God, whose sincerity, integrity and earnest passion for souls has never once been questioned among us. We unitedly praise God for the fellowship of Dr. Ketcham in the Council, and for his untiring efforts in the cause of our Lord Jesus Christ. May God mightily bless you and him in your labors together for Christ and the salvation of souls.[12]

This letter was signed by every member of the Council of Fourteen! Thus, Bob Ketcham had the support of the people in his church as well as the men with whom he had served in his beloved Association. His faithfulness to God and his obedience to God provided a character reference that enabled him to withstand the onslaught of his self-appointed enemy.[13] This was, indeed, a reward of obedience.

12. Council of Fourteen of the GARBC to the Walnut Street Baptist Church, n.d.; *Ketcham Papers*.

13. For all practical purposes, this ended the exchanges between Ketcham and Norris. On May 16, 1952, Rev. Bob Ingles and Dr. Luther Peak wrote an article for the *Fundamentalist* under Norris's byline (with his approval). In this article Norris dismissed the conflicts between himself and other leaders as "a clash of personalities" and said he "bore no ill will" to Ketcham and several others whom he named. This was as close as Norris ever came to apologizing for his actions. By the time Norris died later in 1952, Temple Baptist Church in Detroit had broken all connections with him, and his fellowship of churches had splintered, with many breaking away to form the Bible Baptist Fellowship.

Dr. Ketcham at his desk

21

THROUGHOUT HIS ministry, Robert Thomas
Ketcham faced the problem of deteriorating vision. By the mid 1940s
the problem had advanced to the state that it appeared he might lose
his sight altogether. He and Mary spent much time in prayer
concerning this difficult burden, and they finally determined that it was
the leading of the Lord for him to undergo a difficult operation, a
corneal transplant. Word of his decision was announced in *The Baptist
Bulletin* in order that his friends throughout the country might pray.

> The operation consists of transplanting a section of clear cornea
> from the eye of a dead person to the eye of a living person. It is
> certainly the most delicate operation possible on the human body,
> and probably one of the most painful. The operation will be
> performed in New York City, by the worldknown Dr. Ramon
> Castroviejo, sometime early in January.[1]

It was anticipated that Dr. Ketcham would be away from his
congregation approximately three months following the surgery. But
the church encouraged their pastor to go ahead with the operation.
There seemed to be no alternative if his vision was to be saved.

1. H. O. Van Gilder, "Dr. Ketcham to Undergo Serious Operation,"
The Baptist Bulletin, XI (November 1945), 4.

The surgery was performed on schedule, and the initial medical reports which followed were very encouraging. Ketcham sent a night letter to his church, indicating that the doctors were optimistic, although he admitted that it would be several weeks before they could be sure.

These were difficult days for Bob and Mary Ketcham. It seemed Bob's ministry depended so much on his ability to see! By the time the surgery was performed he was holding books right against the tip of his nose in order to read them. Having traveled to New York City, the Ketchams were away from the friends and loved ones in the Walnut Street Baptist Church. During those days, Mary faithfully stood by her husband's side.

In the quietness of his hospital room, Bob Ketcham had time for the kind of reflection that a busy man usually cannot enjoy. He thought of the thirty-four years he had spent in the ministry and rejoiced in how faithful God had been to him. He remembered the loyalty of his wife, Mary, who had stood with him for almost twenty-five years; how she had filled the void in his life created by the loss of his first wife. He rejoiced in God's blessing in providing this precious woman for him. His schedule had been a busy one. She had often been alone to raise their only child, Donn, but she did not complain. Indeed, she urged him to continue in the great ministry to which he was called.

After weeks of waiting, the day approached when the bandages would be removed. As the time grew close, Ketcham experienced a natural feeling of anxiety over the success of the surgery. In the flesh a man would worry. But Bob Ketcham did not want to approach the removal of the bandages in the flesh. He wanted to do it in the power of the Spirit.

As the "day of reckoning" approached, it became more and more difficult for Bob to be calm. The tension was almost unbearable. He was completely committed to the will of God in his heart, but he could hardly wait to know what God's will for his *eyes* would be! On occasions when he could not sleep, Ketcham would review again and again the hand of God as it had worked in his life. On the evening of March 5 his mind was particularly active. Mary sensed this and stayed in the chair by his side. They shared their thoughts together in quiet tones, and then lapsed into a lengthy silence. Mary dozed in the chair, but Bob's mind was racing, thinking of the hand of God . . . no . . . the hands of God.

A huge clock with a big hand and a little hand appeared before the "unbandaged" eyes of his imagination. A smile crept to his lips as he thought of the hands of God being like the hands of a clock. Slowly his mind formed phrases. He reviewed those phrases again and again until they expressed the feelings of his heart. He called: "Mary! Mary!"

Mary aroused from her slumber with a start. "What is it, Bob?" she asked.

"Mary, quick, Mary, get a pen and paper."

Mary Ketcham had lived with Bob long enough to realize that he wanted to say something that would not wait until morning. She took a sheet of stationery from the table and a pencil, which was all she could find. At 12:10 on the morning of March 6, 1946, Bob Ketcham began to dictate:

> Our lives are like the dial of a clock with its "big hand" and "little hand." The hands are those of a Heavenly Father too good to be unkind and too wise to make mistakes. The little hand is His hand of chastening and discipline; the big hand is His hand of mercy and compassion. The hand of chastening and discipline moves slowly but surely across the life of the child of God. But for *every* time it thus moves, the hand of mercy and compassion moves over and over again, twelve times for *every* time of discipline. The heart of the child of God rests in the sweet assurance that *both* hands are fastened to and moved by the same central mechanism—the loving heart of our Heavenly Father.[2]

Thus, in those hours just prior to the removal of the bandages from his eyes, hours of trial and testing, Bob Ketcham recognized his God as a God of love and compassion. In the hour of his crisis he voiced the words which were to be reproduced on cards, decoupages and plaques for hundreds to appreciate and enjoy in years to come: "Your Heavenly Father is too good to be unkind and too wise to make mistakes."[3]

---

2. The original pencil copy of this beautiful saying together with a typed copy are in the *Ketcham Papers*.

3. It is often said there is nothing new under the sun. Thus it is with this saying. It did not originate with Dr. Ketcham, although he probably did not

A few days later the bandages were removed from Ketcham's eyes. But the success of the operation remained unknown. The doctors warned him that it would take fifteen to twenty days for his eyes to begin to adjust to the light. Four days after the bandages were removed, he reported that he could only keep his eye opened for a moment against the light. But since the eye had been covered for forty-six days, he was not at all alarmed by this prospect. Dr. Van Gilder printed a letter from Dr. Ketcham:

> It seems that most everyone had the idea that as soon as the eye was uncovered, I would be able to really see. This, of course, is not the case. It will be another three or four weeks before we will know very much, if anything, as to the amount of vision I will have. It has been a long time in the exercise of patience and faith. I can't claim a perfect score on either one, but moments of discouragement have only been for the moment. I have had only to remember the multiplied thousands who are praying for me daily, and I have "thanked God and took courage."[4]

In the weeks ahead, the transplant seemed to be successful. Ketcham left the hospital and was recuperating nicely. Suddenly the eye became cloudy, thus shutting off his vision. On March 28 he returned to the hospital, and the surgeon performed two additional operations on the eye in an attempt to stop further deterioration. It was originally anticipated that only a few days would be spent in the hospital on this occasion, but the stay extended much longer. In reporting this to *The Baptist Bulletin,* Mrs. Ketcham concluded:

> One assurance has been given. If this cloudiness does not clear up, another cornea transplant can be attempted in a few months. Mr. Ketcham cheerfully remarks, "I still have several yards of cloth in the bolt." It has been a time of testing and nerve strain, but as ever, the Lord has given needed Grace and Patience.[5]

know where or when he had heard or read anything similar. But it is found in a variant form in the works of Charles H. Spurgeon.

4. H. O. Van Gilder, "Concerning Dr. Ketcham," *The Baptist Bulletin,* XI (April 1946), 9.

5. H. O. Van Gilder, "Continue to Pray for Dr. Ketcham," *The Baptist Bulletin,* XI (May 1946), 8.

Following his second release from the hospital, Ketcham returned to Waterloo. However, on May 18, he was forced to go back to New York City to undergo a third operation in an effort to save the original corneal transplant. This operation also failed, and in the fall of 1946, Ketcham returned to New York City yet another time. The doctors decided to start the entire process again. A second corneal transplant would be attempted in a final medical effort to restore his vision.

Again Ketcham's system began to reject the transplant. In December 1946 *The Baptist Bulletin* carried this urgent message:

> We urge special prayer for Dr. Ketcham. Word received prior to going to press is that there is a great deal of irritation in his eye. The blood vessels of the eyeball are attaching themselves to the cornea. Already four X-ray treatments have been given, in an endeavor to keep these blood vessels away from the cornea. The human eye can stand only four such treatments. If this does not prove successful then there may be need of scraping the eyeball. Many are standing by watching to see God's hand in this. Pray that the Lord will accomplish His will in the matter.[6]

The sovereign God of eternity heard the prayers of His people in behalf of Robert Thomas Ketcham. Thousands pleaded with God, "Thy will be done." And God's will was done. The Waterloo church released word of the will of God early the next year: "Dr. Earle G. Griffith will be supplying the pulpit the last two Sundays in January, after which time Dr. Ketcham hopes to be sufficiently recovered from his corneal transplant operation to resume his duties as pastor. *The operation was not successful"* [italics mine].[7]

Not successful? How could this be? Bob Ketcham and his thousands of friends throughout the nation could not answer that question. They recognized that the wisdom of God was beyond their

6. H. O. Van Gilder, "Concerning Dr. Ketcham," *The Baptist Bulletin,* XII (December 1946), 2.
7. This statement appeared in a regular news column in *The Baptist Bulletin,* edited by Ruth Ryburn, entitled "The GARBC Across the Country." It was an item submitted by the Walnut Street Baptist Church, *The Baptist Bulletin,* XII (January 1947), 14.

understanding. But Bob Ketcham knew and reposed with absolute
confidence in the fact that his Heavenly Father was too good to be
unkind and too wise to make mistakes.

Dr. Ketcham preached from sermon notes written with a
white grease pencil (in large letters) on black paper.

22

BY THE MID 1940S, members of the General
Association of Regular Baptist Churches had detected a strong drift
within the Fundamental Fellowship of the Northern Baptist
Convention toward separation from the Convention. "As early as
1945, Dr. Ketcham had written such leaders of the Convention
Fundamentalists as Dr. R. S. Beal of Tucson, Arizona and Dr. Albert
Johnson of Portland, Oregon urging that if the Fundamentalist
Fellowship came out of the Convention that there ought to be an
attempt to get the two groups together."[1]

While Ketcham fought for his sight, Convention fundamentalists
fought for their faith. Their battle was a losing one. In the Northern
Baptist Convention sessions of 1946, the fundamentalists went down
to defeat on every issue they proposed. The fundamentalists in the
Convention had been growing more and more militant over the
previous two years, although some still clamored for moderation. But
their overwhelming defeat in the 1946 convention, particularly their
attempt to disenfranchise the paid staff of the Convention, was viewed
as the death knell of fundamentalism in the Convention. Many
clamored for separation, and the Council of Fourteen of the GARBC
considered the possibility of the two groups merging.

1. Stowell, *Background and History,* p. 70.

By 1946 Ketcham's longtime friend, Dr. W. B. Riley, had come to the point of no return with the Convention. When the General Association of Regular Baptist Churches was formed in 1932, Riley continued to cling to the hope that the Northern Baptist Convention could be purged from within. By 1946 Riley had been trying to purge the Convention for a half century! He was too ill to attend the Fundamentalist Fellowship meetings prior to the 1946 convention, but he prepared the address he was to deliver, and it was read by Dr. John W. Bradbury, the editor of the *Watchman-Examiner.* In his address, Riley posed the question, "What will conservatives do?" In answer, he indicated only two alternatives. Either liberalism had to be purged out of the Convention, or fundamentalists had to leave! This was a new concept for Riley. The alternative of separation had not been acceptable to him in the late 20s. He had begged Bob Ketcham not to give up the ship in 1927. Now, almost twenty years later, he not only moved to the separatist position—but endorsed the action the GARBC had taken years before:

> Should correction fail, there is but one other course that could be acceptable to Christ and that's the course that has already been taken by Southern Illinois, by the GARB, by the Swedish Baptist Conference, by the C.B.F.M.S.; namely, separation! It has taken me fifty years to reach this conclusion. In that time I have tried in every way possible to save fellows for the Northern Baptist Convention, because to me the true old-time Baptist position and the position of Scripture were sound, but their faith has long been flouted and the leopard does not change his spots nor the Ethiopian his skin. To serve longer under the management of those who make much of our name but who have no respect for our faith, or for the noble history incident to our ancestor endeavors, is to prove ourselves unworthy of freedom.[2]

Following the publication of Riley's endorsement of the separatist position, Regular Baptists openly courted the Convention fundamentalists. In a five-page editorial, H. O. Van Gilder posed the

2. W. B. Riley, "What Will Conservatives Do?" Reprinted in *The Baptist Bulletin,* XII (September 1946), 1, 28, 29. This appears under the heading "Doctor Riley Endorses Separationist Position." Editor Van Gilder prefaced the reprint with a brief introduction. The entire section quoted here was originally printed in italics.

question "Convention Conservatives—Can We Get Together?" In his article Van Gilder reviewed what had been accomplished the previous two years, including Ketcham's letter to Doctors Beal and Johnson. He pointed out that Ketcham's action had received the full approval and endorsement of the Council of Fourteen just two months later. Van Gilder's editorial also included correspondence that he had had with key fundamentalists within the Convention. It was the clear hope of the General Association of Regular Baptist Churches that a merger with Convention fundamentalists would effectuate one strong separatist organization to stand against modernism and liberalism.[3]

With that objective in mind, the General Association of Regular Baptist Churches planned its 1947 meeting for Atlantic City, New Jersey. They convened just before the Fundamentalist Fellowship of the Northern Baptist Convention was to meet in the same city. While the GARBC was in session, Dr. H. O. Van Gilder received a copy of a letter that had been written by W. B. Riley. The letter was addressed to the president of the Northern Baptist Convention, Edwin Dahlberg. In this letter Dr. Riley requested the cancellation of his life membership in the Northern Baptist Convention. After sixty years of involvement with Northern Baptists, Riley could continue no longer! He listed four reasons for leaving the Convention, then concluded his letter with these words:

> I am no longer a young man, having seen my eighty-sixth birthday, and I should be ashamed to die in the fellowship that seemed to me un-Biblical, and consequently un-Baptistic.
>
> John, in his second epistle, verses 9 to 11, writes, "Whosoever transgresseth, and abideth not in the doctrine of Christ, hath not God. He that abideth in the doctrine of Christ, he hath both the Father and the Son. If there come any unto you, and bring not this doctrine, receive him not into your house, neither bid him God speed: For he that biddeth him God speed is partaker of his evil deeds." I accept those words as divinely inspired.
>
> Paul, writing to the Corinthians in the second epistle, sixth chapter, verse 14, says, "Be ye not unequally yoked together with unbelievers;" and in verse 17 he adds, "Wherefore come out

3. H. O. Van Gilder, "Convention Conservatives—Can We Get Together?" *The Baptist Bulletin,* XII (April 1947), 4-8.

from among them, and be ye separate, saith the Lord." Again I believe this to be divinely inspired direction; hence, my request. I am expecting, of course, that it will be granted willingly.

Respectfully yours,
Signed: W. B. Riley[4]

As the letter was read, Bob Ketcham listened intently. Tears trickled down his face as he recalled his friendship with Dr. Riley, who had stood faithful to the Word of God inside the Convention for so many years. He knew that by this time Riley was too ill to attend Convention sessions. He admired Riley for wanting to go on record as a separatist before he died. When Van Gilder finished reading Riley's letter, Ketcham sat for a moment with his mind racing back through the years. He recalled the hurt expression on Riley's face when he had announced to him twenty years earlier that he would never again attend the Convention sessions. As the significance of Riley's break with the Convention penetrated Ketcham's soul, he stood and ran out of the convention hall. He looked for a place of solitude and finally made his way into the cloakroom where he openly sobbed, overwhelmed by the tremendous impact of Riley's withdrawal.

Shortly thereafter, Ketcham penned the following words to his friend:

It is impossible to describe the thrill which came to my heart in Atlantic City the other day when your letter to the President of the Northern Baptist Convention was read. Through the years I have thanked God over and over again for your testimony and witness against the evils of the Convention. Along with this thanksgiving there has always gone a fervent prayer that some day you would not only witness against it, but utterly repudiate your connection with it.[5]

Ketcham went on to ask Riley if, by his letter, he had hoped to see other fundamentalists join him in separating from the Convention. He

4. W. B. Riley to Edwin Dahlberg, May 10, 1947, as reprinted in *The Baptist Bulletin*, XIII (June 1947), 8. This appears under the heading "Dr. Riley Quits Convention," with a brief introduction by editor H. O. Van Gilder.
5. R. T. Ketcham to W. B. Riley, June 9, 1947, as reprinted in *The Baptist Bulletin*, XIII (August 1947), 7. This appears in an article entitled "The Riley Withdrawal," by R. T. Ketcham.

then promised Dr. Riley: ". . . Some of us who are not too advanced in age as yet, will have to carry on where such great soldiers as yourself have had to rest a while from the battle." Finally, he indicated to Riley: "Your letter just as it stands is one of the most powerful contributions to the present warfare that has been made in the last ten years."[6]

Ketcham had written Riley for two purposes: to commend his friend on the stand he had taken and to see if Riley was encouraging other Convention fundamentalists to do the same. Some within the Convention were arguing that Riley's letter was only a personal thing and in no way contained a recommendation to other fundamentalists. This was not Ketcham's interpretation; hence, the inquiry to Riley.

Riley's reply was immediate, in spite of the fact that by this time he was too ill to be on his feet. The old warrior phoned his secretary and dictated a letter of reply to Ketcham. Riley explained to Ketcham why the separatist position had been so long in coming in his life. He then concluded:

> You interpret me correctly. I very much desired to see the entire company of Baptist conservatives pull out of the Convention at Atlantic City, and so advised them. That shall be my advice henceforth.
> Praying much blessing upon your great movement, and thanking God you took it when and as you did, I remain
> Fraternally yours,
(Signed) W. B. Riley[7]

For several months in 1947 the Regular Baptists and the Convention fundamentalists explored the possibility of a union. A meeting was held in January 1947, in which "a wonderful spirit of fellowship was established. Little was actually accomplished except that the Conservatives for the most part voiced the opinion that they were on the way out of the Convention and promised to adopt a resolution indicating the impossibility of continued cooperation within the Convention."[8]

In Atlantic City a committee of Regular Baptists and Conservatives was formed, but they were unable to reach a common

6. Ibid.
7. Ibid., W. B. Riley to R. T. Ketcham, June 11, 1947.
8. Stowell, *Background and History,* p. 70.

ground on the issue of separation. Regular Baptists insisted that any association with their organization be on the basis of absolute and total separation from the Northern Baptist Convention. Conservative Baptists, in contrast, were determined to accept any fundamental church regardless of its other affiliations. Hence, the Conservatives wanted to form an association which would permit dual membership in their organization and the Northern Baptist Convention. Historian Bruce Shelley stated:

> In 1947 this difference more than anything else kept the two groups apart. Conservatives preferred to distinguish a Conservative Baptist by what he believed and to leave the matter of affiliation to autonomous churches while the GARBC limited their fellowship to churches subscribing to their doctrinal statement and to their view of organizational affiliations.[9]

While Conservative Baptists and Regular Baptists continued to have enjoyable fellowship at the local level, this difference on the issue of separation was to preclude the possibility of their working in the same structure. Conservative Baptists formed their own organization, supporting the principle of the right of the local church to choose its own affiliations and even to remain in the Northern Baptist Convention if it wished. Meanwhile, the General Association of Regular Baptist Churches reaffirmed its historic position on separation:

> The Constitution and spirit of the General Association of Regular Baptist Churches calls for and demands that any church desiring the fellowship shall be completely separated from any and all apostate organizations. Therefore, while recognizing the right of a Baptist Church to fellowship with whom it pleases, we deem it a distinct violation of both the Constitution and spirit of the G.A.R.B. for any church in our fellowship to unite itself with any organization which permits within its membership churches still in apostate organizations.[10]

9. Shelley, *Conservative Baptists*, p. 56.
10. H. O. Van Gilder, "Greatest Meeting in G.A.R.B. History." *The Baptist Bulletin*, XIV (June 1948), 8. This issue carried a full report of the 1948 GARBC conference. The entire section quoted here was originally printed in bold type.

In the 1948 meeting of the Association, Dr. H. O. Van Gilder announced his resignation as National Representative in order to become president of Western Baptist Bible College. After accepting Dr. Van Gilder's resignation with regrets, the Council of Fourteen unanimously voted to ask Dr. Robert Ketcham to become the second National Representative of the Association. Ketcham did not reply immediately.

During the following weeks, Bob and Mary Ketcham prayed concerning the leading of God. Their objective was to move in obedience to the command of the preeminent Christ Whom they had served together down through the years. After much prayer, they decided to answer in the affirmative.

Ketcham's decision to accept the position reached Dr. David Otis Fuller, chairman of the Council of Fourteen, in time to appear in the August issue of *The Baptist Bulletin.* In his acceptance letter Ketcham indicated his desire to see fundamental Baptists united: "I believe that ultimate union of all separationist forces in the fundamental wing of the people called Baptists is not an idle dream." But at the same time, he remained firm in the conviction that the only way to effectuate such a union was to disassociate completely all fundamentalists from the Convention. He knew it would be no easy task, but it was a principle he did not feel could be compromised.

In closing his acceptance letter, Ketcham said: "I recognize that the pathway in a thousand other directions is fraught with difficulty and danger. This is no easy task to which you have called me, but under God and with the help of the indwelling Holy Spirit, together with the sympathetic understanding and loyal support of our pastors and churches, I will endeavor to do my best."[11] Thus, the fifty-nine-year-old Ketcham, by this time virtually blind, prepared to lead the General Association of Regular Baptist Churches through a "pathway . . . fraught with difficulty and danger" in obedience to the call of God.

11. R. T. Ketcham to Dr. Fuller and the Council of Fourteen, n.d., as reprinted in *The Baptist Bulletin,* XIV (August 1948), 4. This letter appears under the heading "Dr. Ketcham Accepts" with introductory remarks by editor H. O. Van Gilder.

Dr. Theodore Epp and Dr. Ketcham at a Moody Founder's Week conference, Chicago

23

THE DECISION TO become the National Representative for the General Association of Regular Baptist Churches was not an easy one for Bob Ketcham. He had been pastoring local congregations for thirty-six years. To leave the responsibilities of the local church was most difficult. Exchanging the intimacy of a local congregation for an itinerant ministry and a seat behind a desk was quite a transition.

When the concept of a National Representative had been conceived a few years earlier, members of the Council of Fourteen had explored the possibility of Ketcham filling the position. But he had rejected that early interest because his son was still living at home. "I'll accept no position that will take me away from home very much until my boy is through school and in college somewhere," was Ketcham's response to the suggestion that he might be the first National Representative. The same year H. O. Van Gilder resigned as National Representative, Ketcham's son, Donn, finished high school and left for Baptist Bible Seminary in Johnson City, New York. This fact was vital in Ketcham's ultimate decision to accept the call of the Council.

Ketcham's farewell at the Walnut Street Baptist Church was a moving experience. His last Sunday was September 26, 1948. In the church bulletin for that day, Ketcham expressed his gratitude to the people of his congregation with the following words:

I could covet for every pastor the world over, the same blessed and happy relationship which I have enjoyed with you, my people, as well as with the various boards and committees of the church. I could covet for them also the same response to leadership and cooperation in Christian service which this Church has so graciously accorded me. I am sorry that there were even a very few in this great membership whose love and loyalty it was impossible for me to win. I am deeply grateful that the great host and great heart of this Church has been mine in love and confidence and helpfulness. It has been only through such cooperation on the part of you dear ones that has made possible the progress and constructive work of these past nine years.[1]

The statistic that gave Ketcham the greatest personal satisfaction was the fact that forty-nine members of his congregation had gone into Christian service.

The people of the Walnut Street Baptist Church were brokenhearted at the loss of their pastor, but they rejoiced in the challenging ministry to which he had been called. Following the service on September 26, Dr. and Mrs. Ketcham were the recipients of a large number of gifts, many of them very expensive. When all the gifts had been showered on the Ketchams, "the Chairman of the Board of Trustees came to the platform and after calling the official family of the church to join Dr. and Mrs. Ketcham on the rostrum, presented them with a check in the amount of $1,325 as a love offering."[2]

The Ketchams made the move to Chicago during the last week of September 1948, in order that Ketcham might assume his responsibilities as National Representative on October 1. They rented a six-room apartment in the city, which gained Mrs. Ketcham's approval in spite of the fact that it did not have a garage for the car. Dr. Ketcham had found the apartment with the aid of his secretary, Ruth Ryburn. In light of the fact that their son was in college, the Ketchams invited Ruth to reside with them. This proved to be an ideal arrangement for all involved. Dr. Ketcham's inability to see clearly

1. H. O. Van Gilder, "Dr. Ketcham Finishes Ministry at Waterloo," *The Baptist Bulletin*, XIV (October-November 1948), 4.
2. Ibid.

made it inconvenient for him to find his way to work on crowded public transportation. Ruth helped him to the office via the elevated train. In addition, when Dr. Ketcham was on the road, his wife, Mary, had someone to keep her company.

The reality of his new situation came home with a sudden burst of understanding to Bob Ketcham on Sunday, October 3. He described it in these words:

> I had a new experience yesterday. If my memory serves me correctly, I can recall only three or four occasions during the last 36 years when it was my privilege to slip quietly into a worshipful Sunday morning service, and listen to the man of God preach. Except for the "time out" in hospitals, I have been busy preaching myself.
>
> I had another new experience yesterday. For the first time since Sunday, September 22, 1912, I did not have a church "of my own." One week ago I had said goodbye to one of the greatest churches on earth, old Walnut Street, in Waterloo. As I walked along the street toward Belden Avenue Baptist Church in Chicago yesterday morning, a sense of peculiar loneliness came over me. I do not mind admitting that I was sort of "down" when I entered the sanctuary. I slipped quietly into the second seat from the rear, and prepared to listen to my old friend, Dr. Howard Fulton. I do not know about the rest of the worshippers, but I know there was one fellow, second seat from the rear, who needed a "lift."[3]

Ketcham then described Fulton's message, which was on the theme "The Forgiveness of Sins." After reviewing the message, Ketcham concluded:

> The fellow in the second seat from the rear forgot his loneliness, forgot that he didn't have a church "of his own," he forgot a lot of things, and was lost and lifted by the blessed and overwhelming conviction of the reality of "the Man in the Book." When the benediction was pronounced, the man in the second seat from the rear also breathed a fervent thanksgiving for the man in the pulpit.[4]

3. R. T. Ketcham, "The Editor Goes to Church," *The Baptist Bulletin*, XIV (December 1948), 2.
4. Ibid., p. 6.

When Ketcham became the National Representative of the General Association of Regular Baptist Churches, he once more assumed the responsibilities of editor of *The Baptist Bulletin*. The former National Representative and editor, H. O. Van Gilder, remained on the *Bulletin* staff as associate editor in charge of books. Ruth Ryburn continued her responsibilities as associate editor in charge of news, and Inez Norlin became associate editor in charge of missions.

The battle against modernism in the Convention was a burning burden in Dr. Ketcham's life. Late in 1947, Ivan M. Shreve, pastor of the First Baptist Church, North East, Pennsylvania, prepared for his congregation a twenty-seven-page pamphlet entitled *The Baptist Denomination: Who We Are, What We Are, Why We Are.* This pamphlet attempted to defend the Convention as a conservative body. Shreve addressed the charges made by Regular Baptists that the Convention had departed from the faith: "The Northern Baptist Convention, as a whole, believes *every* fundamental Christian doctrine. There are, of course, individual exceptions."[5]

Shreve assumed the position that conditions had improved since the 1920s and accused Ketcham and his Association of overlooking this fact.

> The General Association of Regular Baptist Churches still depend on the condition which existed during the 1920's for their accusations! Conditions are greatly changed now from what they were twenty years ago. The prayerful effort which the Convention put forth during these past years has resulted in great and wise changes. Let us face the problem on the basis of present-day conditions.[6]

It was clearly Shreve's desire to see Baptists unite. He viewed the GARBC as divisive and therefore evil. "Let us give our best to make things as they should be and not wreck the house to do it!" The Northern Baptist defender then concluded: "The historic Baptist faith is a great one, but that the Northern Baptist Convention does not

---

5. Ivan M. Shreve, *The Baptist Denomination: Who We Are, What We Are, Why We Are* (1947), p. 8. A mimeographed pamphlet prepared for the members of the First Baptist Church of North East, Pennsylvania.
6. Ibid.

possess it any longer is a most untrue statement. The Baptist faith has never changed. It is the same faith that it ever was."[7]

Shreve's defense of the Northern Baptist Convention was considered by the Convention executives to be a good one. They reproduced his pamphlet and circulated it among their churches. Because it purported to be the Convention's answer to the fundamentalists' charges, Ketcham made sure that he got a copy of the paper.[8]

In response to Shreve's presentation, Ketcham wrote a hard-hitting booklet called The Answer. Ketcham answered Shreve's concept of "doctrinal purity" within the Convention point by point. Quoting clergymen, missionaries and administrators within the Northern Baptist Convention to buttress his statements, Ketcham refuted with current examples every argument offered by Shreve. In vivid detail he demonstrated the degree to which modernism had infested the Convention. Though the pamphlet was updated for its third edition in 1956, it retained much of the original information which demonstrated beyond the shadow of a doubt that the Convention was thoroughly infested with liberalism in the late 40s.[9]

In 1949 Ketcham again locked horns with the Convention. The First Baptist Church of Smethport, Pennsylvania, voted to withdraw, not only from the Northern Baptist Convention, but also from all its affiliates: the Pennsylvania Baptist State Convention, the Allegheny River Baptist Association, and the Federal Council of the Churches of Christ in America. There were only five negative votes, as the pastor and people of Smethport determined to sever their relationship with these organizations due to the modernism that characterized them.

Several years prior to this action, the church had received some monies from the Convention. In 1913 the Pennsylvania Baptist State Convention had given them $500 for physical plant repairs. In so doing, the state convention demanded the deed to the property and

7. Ibid.
8. Ketcham's original copy of the pamphlet, complete with his hand penned notations, is in the Ketcham Papers.
9. R. T. Ketcham, The Answer (Chicago: General Association of Regular Baptist Churches, 1956).

continued to hold that deed through the years. When the church built a parsonage in 1940, the Pennsylvania Baptist State Convention "donated" $1,000 toward the project. "However, for this favor the Convention insisted that there be written into the deed a reversionary clause which provided that if the Smethport church should ever cease to be a cooperating church within the limits of the definition of that term, as set forth in the by-laws of the Pennsylvania Baptist State Convention, then the entire property should revert to the Pennsylvania Baptist State Convention."[10]

When the church voted to withdraw from the Convention, they had their attorney draft a letter, asking the state convention for a clear title to their church property. They agreed to return the donation of $1,000 which the Convention had given them in exchange for the clear title. Instead of doing so, the Pennsylvania Baptist State Convention "began a series of attempts to dig in behind the sovereign action of a sovereign church, and through the creation of dissension [sic] among its members, seek to undo the action of the church, and reverse the will of the church, and the leadership of its pastor."[11] The Convention even went so far as to have their state evangelist, Paul Raycroft, send a letter to the entire membership of the Smethport church, calling for a meeting at the residence of a dissident member. The official church board immediately circulated their own letter to counteract the Convention action. "For nearly a year the Pennsylvania Baptist State Convention, through its officials, did everything in its power to disturb and break up the harmony and happy fellowship of a Baptist church, rather than to proceed to an orderly and honest settlement of the claims of the church."[12]

In this context, L. C. Wilcox, pastor of the Smethport church, contacted Dr. Ketcham. Ketcham agreed to come to Smethport to confront Convention representative G. A. Gabelman. Ketcham outlined certain conditions that were to be met. On October 31, 1949, the First Baptist Church of Smethport sent a letter to Gabelman,

10. R. T. Ketcham, *When a State Convention Secretary Walked Out* (Hayward, CA: J. F. May Press, n.d.), p. 1.

11. Ibid., p. 2.

12. Ibid.

inviting him to attend a meeting in the church to present the Convention's position. He was told that R. T. Ketcham would be there to present the position of the local church and engage in "open discussion." Gabelman accepted, and the meeting was arranged for Monday, December 5, 1949.[13]

On the appointed night, Ketcham and Gabelman met to confer prior to the public meeting. As a result of that confrontation, Gabelman and the men that accompanied him refused to appear in the public meeting. With the congregation of the Smethport church waiting, the Convention representatives walked away. Following their departure, Dr. Ketcham, accompanied by Pastor Wilcox and Dean Banta (who had been appointed moderator) entered the auditorium to face approximately four hundred people who had been waiting forty-five minutes for the meeting to begin:

> Mr. Banta made a simple announcement stating that Dr. Gabelman and his colleagues had not agreed as to the matters to be discussed in the public meeting, but that finally when Pastor Wilcox had given his consent to let the State Convention men say anything they wanted to say, and discuss anything they wanted to discuss, on the condition that they would first listen to Dr. Ketcham's documented disclosure of modernism in the Conventions, they had refused to accept this condition, and had walked out. Dr. Ketcham was then introduced and he expressed his regret that Dr. Gabelman had not been willing to stay, but that he would proceed to give the same address which he had planned to give with Dr. Gabelman present.[14]

Ketcham then delivered a forceful address in which he exposed modernism at every level of the Convention. He attacked the Convention for interfering with the autonomy of a local congregation and demonstrated, by quoting several sources on Baptist polity, that every local Baptist congregation should have the right of self-determination. Stressing this Baptist distinctive of the autonomy of a local church, Ketcham said: "A Baptist church can withdraw from a local association, a State Association or Convention, or a National Convention, even though that Convention is composed of angels and

13. Ibid., pp. 2, 3.
14. Ibid., p. 3.

the Arch-angel Gabriel is the President, and Michael is his assistant. . . . You can withdraw for any reason sufficient to yourself, and you could do it if they were all angels."[15]

The remainder of Ketcham's address, however, made it clear that he did not believe the Convention was composed of angels! He called attention to the statements of such liberal members of the Northern Baptist Convention as Dr. Harry Emerson Fosdick, whom he demonstrated did not believe in the virgin birth of Jesus Christ. Example after example of members of the Northern Baptist Convention who denied the basic principles of Christianity were cited for the people of the congregation. At the close of his address Ketcham led the congregation in prayer. This prayer demonstrated the great burden of his heart:

> Our Father, we thank Thee for these men and women who have sat tonight and listened. We've only scratched the surface; we've just taken a cross section and a little cut here and a little sample there. Our hearts go out in love and sympathy for the countless thousands who are back in these Convention churches who are really born of God—oh how we wish that everybody who loves Jesus Christ would just walk out of this thing, or stand together for 24 months without any argument or without any compromise, or without pulling any punches—just walk out and stand together for 24 months. The battle would be over. The Convention couldn't continue under its own power if God's own people would refuse to support it. It hasn't power enough, it hasn't spirit enough, it hasn't vision enough, to stand for 24 months without the money of the fundamentalists. Lord, help God's people to see this and come out, and stand together, ready for the day when You put back in our hands these glorious opportunities to get the Gospel to the ends of the earth. God bless this preacher with all of the slander and opposition. Help him and his church to forget it all, and to love those who speak against them, to deal with them with patience, and brotherly love, and to turn their faces to the Lord Jesus Christ, and go on in this town to work for Him. God in heaven, fill this church with Sunday School children, and put people in these pews to hear the Gospel, and to get saved. Warm the heart of this pastor and his wife, and of those in this church who want to see this thing separated from apostasy

15. Ibid., p. 12.

and modernism. We pray for those, who may not see it that way, who sincerely don't see it that way, and yet members of the church. We pray that Thou wilt give them patience, too, and a willingness to see and to investigate and to look at facts, and God grant that all of them, regardless of past experiences, might unite around the throne of prayer, and here in this church, by themselves one of these days, melt down before God, and with their hearts abounding in love for each other and for God, turn their faces to winning Smethport for Christ. We ask it in Thy Name, Amen.[16]

When Ketcham returned to his Chicago office from Smethport, he prepared a booklet about the entire experience, including the full text of his message to that local congregation. He was convinced that the Northern Baptist Convention was planning to use the reversionary clauses which accompanied their "donations" to control local congregations—a concern which proved to be correct. It was Ketcham's hope that the pamphlet on the Smethport case would prove helpful to other churches facing a similar crisis.

Throughout Ketcham's years as National Representative, he traveled from place to place across the country, battling the Convention. He loved helping local congregations withdraw from the Convention and preserve their autonomy as well as their integrity to the Word of God.

For their part, the leadership of the Northern Baptist Convention set about to discredit Bob Ketcham. They described him as a contentious troublemaker, and sought to undermine his integrity by accusing him of shoddy research and deliberate deception. They claimed that his presentations were filled with errors. The Pennsylvania Baptist State Convention organized a committee of three individuals who prepared a document on the Smethport situation. The product of their investigation was a twenty-four-page booklet, *The Truth About the Smethport Church—An Unmasking of Charges Made by R. T. Ketcham.* They sought to minimize the charges of modernism made by Ketcham. But they also attacked Ketcham personally: "We would recommend that Rev. Ketcham read Luke 6:41-42 *after which his eye*

16. Ibid., pp. 23, 24.

affliction may be so improved that he may be able to read Burma Surgeon correctly" [italics mine].[17]

Ketcham was obviously piqued by their insensitivity to his physical condition. In his response to their booklet, he protested: "Any group of persons, especially Christians, whose sense of ethical standards and fair play has sunk to such a low level as will permit them to speak tauntingly or flippantly of another's physical afflictions and handicaps, should be pitied indeed, and treated with the contempt of silence, but since this would be an easy way for me to meet their so-called 'unmasking' of my charges I prefer to take the longer way, and deal with several items in the book."[18] After refuting the charges made by his opponents, Ketcham closed his reply by posing a series of eighteen questions for the Convention group to answer. There is no record of any answers ever being given.

Thus, when Robert Thomas Ketcham became the National Representative of the General Association of Regular Baptist Churches, he envisioned his role as both a preacher of the gospel and a protector of the Faith. He accepted the exhortation of Jude 3: ". . . That ye should earnestly contend for the faith which was once delivered unto the saints." A holy war was to be waged in behalf of the cause of Biblical Christianity. Obedience demanded an unwavering defense of the Word of God.

17. Floyd C. B. Aldrich, Lester C. Barton, Mary E. Welfling, *The Truth About the Smethport Church—An Unmasking of Charges Made by R. T. Ketcham* (n.d.), p. 13.

18. R. T. Ketcham, *A Reply to the So-called "Un-Masking" of Charges in the Case of the First Regular Baptist Church of Smethport, Pennsylvania* (Chicago: General Association of Regular Baptist Churches, n.d.), p. 1.

24

BECAUSE OF HIS vigorous support of the Smethport congregation, Ketcham was in great demand. Congregations seeking to sever their relationships with the Northern Baptist Convention frequently turned to him for aid. While he enjoyed this vital part of his ministry as National Representative of the General Association of Regular Baptist Churches, it increased his work load tremendously.

But in spite of the fact that Bob Ketcham was in his sixtieth year, "work load" seemed to be no problem. Ketcham was an avid reader, though books had to be held to his nose and read with a magnifying glass. He seemed to have the knack of remembering most of what he read. His secretary confided: "What would really be embarrassing would be when I would type a letter and think it was perfect or type an article or something and he would find a mistake; and that happened more than one time, I can assure you! I really admire him for all the reading he's done and the retention of it. I wish I had half as good a memory!"[1]

When he returned to the office from his trips, Ketcham frequently had a briefcase full of work for his secretary. Before she could get a good start on it, he would be dictating answers to the stack of

1. Ruth Ryburn, *taped reflections,* n.d.

correspondence that had accumulated during his absence. One day Ruth Ryburn looked at four different stacks of work on her desk. She appeared to be a little discouraged. Ketcham peered over and said, "What's the matter, Ruth?" She replied, "Well, I just was sitting here wondering what it would be like if you had two good eyes instead of only one!"[2]

But Ketcham did not sit in the Chicago office very often or very long. Throughout the 1950s he spent most of his time on the road. After a brief stay in the office, he would gather all his belongings and be off on another trip. "I can see him yet, starting out on his trips with a wire recorder that weighed something like eighteen pounds in one hand and a heavy briefcase in another, plus his suitcase. And that's the way he traveled."[3]

Ketcham loved his wire recorder, although it was difficult for him to operate because of his poor eyesight. Often, when he was dictating, the wire would break, and the spool would continue to turn without his knowledge. Before long he would be surrounded by wire. He would have to sort through that wire and start anew. Frequently, this would create an embarrassing situation. Once while visiting in LaPorte, Indiana, he was in the living room of the pastor's home, dictating letters. The wire on the recorder broke. The pastor and his wife found Ketcham sitting in the middle of the living room floor, surrounded by a pile of wire he was trying to untangle!

Ketcham faced a variety of experiences in his ministry. He traveled to churches to encourage local congregations, to preach Bible conferences or to aid a church in withdrawing from a convention dominated by modernism. Though most of his experiences involved the Northern Baptist Convention, occasionally he would go into the South to help a church do battle with the Southern Baptist Convention.

One trip took him to Rocky Mount, North Carolina, to be a witness in behalf of a Baptist church seeking to withdraw from the Southern Baptist Convention. The Convention had taken the church

2. Ibid. Ruth added: "And, of course, you know he didn't even have one real good one."
3. Ibid.

to court, and the local congregation asked Ketcham to be a witness for the defense. The trial lasted somewhat longer than anticipated, and Ketcham was there three days instead of the two he had originally planned. The evening of the third day, Ketcham took the last train out of town because he had an engagement elsewhere the following evening. He had to travel by train to Washington, D.C., to make connections to Chicago. By the time his train reached Richmond, Ketcham realized the train was late. The conductor assured him that he would make his connection; but the train reached Washington just minutes before the Chicago train was scheduled to leave.

As Ketcham descended from the coach, he saw a porter standing nearby. Rushing over to him, Ketcham said, "Do you want to earn five dollars?"

The porter quickly replied, "Yes, sir!"

"Well," Ketcham asked, "has the train for Chicago left yet?"

The porter glanced at his watch and said, "It should be leaving any minute."

"Well," Ketcham rejoined, "I've got to get on it!"

The porter ordered Ketcham to get on his long, flat-bottom baggage truck. Ketcham knelt on the truck with his baggage around him. He grabbed hold of the two front posts, and the porter began pushing him. As the porter pushed the cart, he yelled, "Here I come! Out of the way! Here I come! Out of the way!"

Thus the "dignified" National Representative of the General Association of Regular Baptist Churches was pushed lickety-split through the main foyer of the Washington, D.C., train terminal on a porter's cart! People stood in amazement as Ketcham knelt, clinging to the sides of that flatbed cart while the porter pushed him from one train to the other. But Ketcham caught his train, and the porter made five dollars!

Though an itinerant ministry provided occasional humorous incidents such as this, for the most part it was a taxing and demanding responsibility. It placed a burden not only on the traveler, but also on his family or mate. But Bob Ketcham had an ideal mate for such a ministry. In spite of the days and weeks she spent alone, Mary Ketcham did not complain. She stood with her husband like a tower of strength in crisis after crisis. The sustaining power of her prayer life went with him as he traveled throughout the country, and in times of trial he always knew he could depend on her. Ruth Ryburn was Mrs. Ketcham's companion during the many weeks when he was away. She could make the bold statement, "I never once heard her [Mrs. Ketcham] complain when he would be gone for a week or two weeks or even longer."[4]

Ketcham was scheduled to leave for a series of meetings in California, Oregon and Washington when he received word that Mrs. Ketcham's sister Blanche was dying. Blanche was a widow, and when her condition became such that she could no longer live alone, she had moved in with Bob and Mary. As her condition steadily deteriorated, it became evident that she would go to be with the Lord while Bob was away.

Ketcham was prepared to cancel his meetings so he could help his wife and be with Blanche. But Mrs. Ketcham would not hear of it. She reminded him that the meetings had been scheduled for well over a year and that the churches involved needed his ministry. She assured him that she could manage affairs at home, including the funeral. Ketcham was torn between love for his sister-in-law and the important ministry to which he was called. Bob and Mary prayed and together finally decided that he should go.

Before he left for the West, he went to the hospital to see Blanche. She was so sick and so weak she could hardly speak. They both realized they would not see each other again on this earth. Bob stood by her bed and held her hand. He looked down on her frail frame, dissipated by the effects of cancer. He explained to her that he was going to California to serve the Lord they both dearly loved. Then bending over her, he kissed her and said, "Well, good-by, Sis; I'll see you in Heaven."

Looking into his somber face, Blanche demonstrated that she still had her sense of humor. A smile touched her lips and a faint twinkle appeared in her eye. With a feeble voice—not much more than a whisper—she replied, "Yes, and you'll be so much better looking then!"

With that fond memory in his heart, Ketcham returned to the itinerate ministry to which God had called him.

4. Ibid.

Ketcham's travels brought him into contact with pastors from churches of all sizes. Bob Ketcham had a pastor's heart, and he loved to fellowship with other servants of God. He had pastored large and small congregations and was familiar with both situations. He knew the ministry could be very lonely at times. One of the major burdens of his heart was to provide counsel and encouragement for others in the ministry. Literally hundreds of pastors through the years benefited from his practical wisdom and his fellowship.

Ketcham refused to involve himself in any local church struggle which related to the personality of the pastor. If a church wanted to get out of the Convention, he would be right there. But if they wrote him asking how to get rid of their preacher—and churches often did—he had a standard reply. He requested that the complainant write him again through the pastor or that he give the pastor a copy of the letter. Ketcham then indicated he would answer the correspondence in the same fashion, sending a copy to the pastor. In all the years that he was National Representative, only one person agreed to correspond on that basis. Ketcham's action in this regard was not the result of a conviction that pastors could make no mistakes. He simply did not feel it was his place as the National Representative of the General Association of Regular Baptist Churches to get involved in local matters. To him, that would have made the Association too much like the Convention, and that was the last thing he wanted.

On one occasion Dr. Ketcham arranged a series of thirteen regional conferences. In each three-day conference he dealt with the issue of ecclesiastical separation. In his messages he quoted several modernists to demonstrate the evils of liberalism. When he was at Boise Baptist Temple, he quoted Nels Ferré to the effect that Jesus Christ was born of Mary and fathered by a blond German soldier. As he said this, an old gray-haired man about four seats from the front stood up like a ramrod and screamed at the top of his lungs, "You sit down, mister! You sit down, mister! You sit down! You can't deny my Lord's virgin birth in this church!"

Ketcham replied, "Well, I didn't deny it. I was just reading about some. . . ."

"No, I heard you say it! You read it right out of your own book there!" the man interrupted.

Someone seated beside the old man tugged on his coat and

pulled him down, whispering something in his ear. The pastor leaned forward and informed Ketcham that the old gentleman was partially deaf. Ketcham reiterated his point and concluded his sermon without further interruption.

At the close of the service, Dr. Ketcham was in the back of the auditorium, shaking hands with members of the congregation. The old gentleman appeared before him. As Ketcham extended his hand, this elderly saint of God threw his arms around Ketcham's neck and wept openly. "Dr. Ketcham, please forgive me. I don't hear well, and I thought you were denying the virgin birth of our Lord Jesus and saying that His father was a blond German soldier. That's what I thought you said; but now I know you didn't! You were telling us that one of those modernists said that." He continued to cry and beg Dr. Ketcham's forgiveness.

Ketcham looked the old gentleman squarely in the eye as he put his hands on his shoulders. With a smile he said, "Listen, my dear brother, if what you did this morning had been done fifty, sixty, seventy years ago by men like yourself when this modernist business began to sweep through our churches, we wouldn't have to be here this morning. We wouldn't have to have a conference against this stuff! When these men came into the pulpits and said what they wanted to say about the virgin birth of Jesus Christ and about the blood of Christ not meaning anything, if only someone in the churches had stood up like you did this morning and put a stop to it and said you can't preach like that in my church, things would be different. Oh, dear brother, if they had done like you did this morning when you thought you had a case, we never would have had to have the General Association of Regular Baptist Churches!"

As Ketcham traveled across the country in these regional conferences for the GARBC, he found himself again and again in the homes of pastors who were living on almost nothing. "I found a pastor living in a little dugout shack in the middle of a sand dune with the sand blowing in every nook and corner and water having to be drawn and carried to his house. Here he was with his wife and two little children, determined that he was going to start a Baptist church in that area. Here he was, just merely existing. I found something similar to this in several places."

As he traveled Ketcham asked the Lord to give him some idea of what the Association could do for these stalwart soldiers of the cross who were willing to live on almost starvation support in order to start a Baptist church. As he shared his burden with another preacher, the man gave Ketcham an idea.

Dr. Ketcham presented the idea to the next meeting of the Council of Fourteen. The Council approved the simple plan that was to become the cornerstone of the Baptist Builders' Club. The plan was that individuals in the Association would agree to send two dollars to the Builders' Club when requested. However, there would never be more than five requests a year. The money donated by these individual members would then be dispensed by the Baptist Builders' Club to help small churches get on their feet. For the most part, the money was to be used to help erect church buildings.

In February 1950 Ketcham presented the Baptist Builders' Club, with the approval of the Council of Fourteen, to the membership of the Association in the pages of *The Baptist Bulletin*. He described the small pastor who struggled to make ends meet, working a job on the side while trying to build a local church. Ketcham reminded his readers that the idea for a Builders' Club was not new. He indicated that several Christian organizations were already using some form of the concept with success. He pointed out that "the group is to be composed of individuals throughout our Fellowship who will sign a membership card, and promise to pay during the course of a calendar year not more than $10, payments to be made $2.00 at a time upon call of the committee in charge."[5]

In addition, Ketcham explained, "The committee of three from the Council of 14, together with two laymen, appointed by the Council, are to constitute the administrative committee of the Baptist Builders' Club."[6] This committee would be charged with the responsibility of investigating requests for aid. These requests would be for building projects, projects to develop the work, or emergencies. The only stipulation was that a church had to be in fellowship with the General Association of Regular Baptist Churches.

Almost immediately the question was raised as to whether the

5. R. T. Ketcham, "The Baptist Builders' Club," *The Baptist Bulletin*, XV (February 1950), 3.
6. Ibid.

Builders' Club donations would have any strings attached. Would it be like the Convention with reversionary clauses which required the church to turn over its deed to the Association? Ketcham's answer came quickly:

> Everyone may be perfectly at rest on this matter. No such procedure will be tolerated or permitted. The Lord knows we have had enough of that kind of business. Any agreement surrounding any gift to any church will have written into it as a part of the agreement itself that the minute the church is ready to proceed "on its own," that minute any claim because of the gift ceases. It will be the same procedure which our approved home mission agencies have been using in the help they have extended to new churches.[7]

When Ketcham wrote the original pamphlet for the Baptist Builders' Club, he again stressed that there would be no strings attached to the club gifts:

> It should be borne in mind that no grant made from the funds of THE BAPTIST BUILDERS' CLUB will carry with it any reversionary clauses or mortgages—these grants are outright gifts. Naturally, if when the church, in later years, gets on its feet and becomes prosperous and wants to repay to the Club any of the money that was given to it, in order to help other needy churches, that will be the privilege of the church, but there will be no legal attachments which can be forced into courts and collected by the cruel operation of lawsuits.[8]

Since the inception of the Builders' Club, thousands upon thousands of dollars have been invested in helping hundreds of churches. This ministry was very dear to the heart of Bob Ketcham.

The years during which Robert Thomas Ketcham served as the National Representative of the General Association of Regular Baptist Churches were years of unprecedented growth. Churches were added annually to the Association, and Ketcham was kept busy informing

---

7. R. T. Ketcham, "The Baptist Builders' Club," *The Baptist Bulletin,* XV (March 1950), 10.

8. R. T. Ketcham, "The Baptist Builders' Club: What It Is, What It Does," p. 5. This was an eight-page pamphlet with a membership card to be completed by those wishing to join.

local churches concerning the position of the GARBC. In addition to the tremendous amount of travel that was done, many responsibilities were related to administration. Through the years both the office and the staff grew. The development of Regular Baptist Press was such that it was not possible for Ketcham to manage such an operation. Consequently, Mr. Larry Ward was brought to the Chicago office to be managing editor of *The Baptist Bulletin* and to direct other publications.

It became the desire of the Association to present the separatist position in a variety of published sources. One obvious and important area was Sunday school literature. This also was Ward's responsibility. As with any new program, the development of Regular Baptist Press ran into its share of difficulties. Finally it was announced that as of April 1, 1952, Regular Baptist Press would be transferred to Hayward, California. The home office of the Association remained in Chicago. The reason for transferring Regular Baptist Press was to locate it near the printer who was doing *The Baptist Bulletin.* Consequently, Regular Baptist Press offices were located on the second floor of the J. F. May Press in Hayward.

Ketcham expressed the hope that Sunday school lessons would be delivered on time as a result of this move. He warned, however, that most of the difficulty to that point in the newly developing program of Regular Baptist Press had been with the writers of the lessons, not with the printers.[9] Even with the move of Regular Baptist Press, Ketcham continued as editor of *The Baptist Bulletin.*

The California location was adequate for the rapidly expanding publications department of the GARBC only for a short time. By 1954 it was necessary to move once more.

> The nation-wide response to the Regular Baptist Press materials . . . the burgeoning sales in a few short quarters . . . the tremendous potential represented by the thousands of other-than-GARBC Baptist churches across the land—all these combine to make the move here announced absolutely essential for RBP in carrying out the sacred responsibilities entrusted to it.

9. R. T. Ketcham, "Regular Baptist Press to Open in Hayward, California, April 1," *The Baptist Bulletin,* XVII (April 1952), 3.

Effective with the printing of the July materials, all *orders* will be handled through a Dayton, Ohio office. The RBP materials will be printed for us by a leading publishing house in Ohio.[10]

While Regular Baptist Press moved to Ohio, Mr. Ward and Miss Ruth Herriman maintained the editorial offices on the west coast. They also were available for Sunday school conferences and related ministries in that area. Meanwhile, the Ohio office was staffed by Mr. and Mrs. Merle R. Hull. Hull, after prayerfully considering the move for approximately one year, agreed to leave the pastorate and join the Regular Baptist Press staff.[11]

Within less than a year, it became obvious that this new arrangement was inadequate. Therefore, in March 1955, the Association announced: "Effective April 15, 1955, the activities of the present Chicago, Dayton and Hayward offices of the GARBC will all be transferred to a new location in Chicago."[12] The move to Chicago was made without Larry Ward, who had resigned the newly created position as editor-in-chief of all publications. Ward's work was described by the chairman of the publications committee as "magnificent," so the responsibility of replacing him was a heavy one. After prayerful consideration, Merle Hull was named executive editor of publications.[13]

Still, Ketcham continued his responsibilities as editor of *The Baptist Bulletin.* However, it became increasingly clear that this arrangement was no longer acceptable. The burden of travel and other duties was far too great. Consequently, when the Council of Fourteen met prior to the 1955 annual meeting, Merle R. Hull was named not only executive editor of publications, but also acting editor of *The Baptist Bulletin.* In this new structure Ketcham became an associate editor. The Council recognized the expanding needs of their

10. Larry Ward, "RBP Moves to Ohio," *The Baptist Bulletin,* XIX (April 1954), 3.

11. Larry Ward, "RBP Names S.S. Consultants," *The Baptist Bulletin,* XIX (April 1954), 6.

12. R. T. Ketcham, "GARBC Takes Another Step of Faith," *The Baptist Bulletin,* XX (March 1955), 3.

13. Robert L. Powell, "A Special Report," *The Baptist Bulletin,* XX (May 1955), 3.

Association in this reorganization: "For many years it has been apparent to all of us that the prime need of the BAPTIST BULLETIN is a full-time editor. The Council faced up to this need, and took definite action toward the securing of such a full-time editor."[14] In June 1957 the "acting" was removed from Hull's title, and from that time until the present he has been editor of *The Baptist Bulletin.*

These moves were important to the General Association of Regular Baptist Churches. They reflected the growing ministry of the Fellowship. It was no longer possible for one man to serve as National Representative and editor of *The Baptist Bulletin.* In addition, with the development of Regular Baptist Press, the influence of the GARBC was reaching into literally thousands of churches with solid, Biblical, Baptistic literature. Bob Ketcham took great satisfaction in these developments. It was a thrill for him to see the Sunday school literature develop and to see the program of the Association move forward.

Down through the years Ketcham's pen proved to be important. He prepared twelve GARBC literature items. To date, almost three million copies of these have been circulated to churches throughout the nation. In addition, he wrote a dozen books, ranging in subject matter from the battle against modernism, *The Answer,* to the beautiful study of the Twenty-third Psalm, *I Shall Not Want.* Approximately three hundred thousand of his books have been placed in circulation. Of the many pamphlets that he wrote, five have been printed, and over two hundred thousand copies have been distributed. One pamphlet, the sensitive and tender *Christ the Comforter in Sorrow,* accounted for over half of that total. This was truly an amazing accomplishment for a man who had to do all the research for his writing with the books rubbing the end of his nose!

Thus, in addition to his traveling and preaching, Ketcham provided the General Association of Regular Baptist Churches with solid administrative leadership. The implementation of the Baptist Builders' Club and the development of Regular Baptist Press were

14. Merle R. Hull, "We Bless God," *The Baptist Bulletin,* XX (June 1955), 3.

singularly important contributions to the long-range development of the Association.[15]

15. As the ministries of the Association grew, additional office space was needed; so an office building was purchased in Des Plaines, a suburb northwest of Chicago. The move was made in 1965, and Dr. Ketcham had an office in the building until his retirement. To accommodate further expansion, this building was eventually sold and another building purchased and occupied in 1976 in Schaumburg, ten miles northwest of the Des Plaines location. Dr. Ketcham visited the new offices and rejoiced in this further evidence of the Lord's blessing.

GARBC and Regular Baptist Press office building, Des Plaines, Illinois

Present facilities, Schaumburg, Illinois

THROUGHOUT THE years Dr. Ketcham continued to
speak directly and dynamically to the issues. His forthright style of
naming names created some enemies, but it was the only way he knew
to deal with apostasy. Whenever someone undermined the Word of
God, Ketcham was ready to attack. If a brother in the Lord suggested
anything other than total withdrawal from modernism, Ketcham was
ready to dissent. His program had no room for compromise. Only
absolute and total separation from anyone or any program denying
the validity of the Scripture or the deity of Christ was adequate.

When the *Chicago Daily News* reported that Alan Redpath,
pastor of the Moody Memorial Church, suggested the union of
fundamentalists and liberals in the cause of Christ, Ketcham
immediately made contact with Redpath. Redpath had said:
"Religious liberals and fundamentalists should unite in one great army
for Christ." Redpath had described the social gospel as bankrupt and
fundamentalism as broken. He went on to say, "There is a battle to be
won, and we must do it together."[1]

Ketcham was stunned by what he read in the newspaper. Four

---

1. "Church Groups Told to Unite For God," *Chicago Daily News,*
(February 5, 1954); *Ketcham Papers.*

days later, he sent a six-page letter to Pastor Redpath. He expressed his concern for the willingness of this brother in Christ to compromise with the modernists. Ketcham quoted American modernists, particularly their statements concerning the authority of Scripture and the deity of Christ. He thought that perhaps Redpath, a Britisher, was unfamiliar with the nature of liberalism in the United States. Ketcham concluded his letter by saying: "I trust you will forgive me for this long, long letter, but it has come out of my heart to you. While some of it may sound a bit hard, please believe me when I say again that I believe your unfortunate statements grew out of an unawareness of the actual situation. I dare to hope that when you have studied the situation more carefully, you will publicly rescind your statements of last Friday."[2] This comment demonstrated the attitude Ketcham assumed toward a brother in Christ with whom he disagreed.

Redpath replied on February 12, indicating that he had been misunderstood. Ketcham responded that if this was the case, it was vital for Redpath to issue a retraction. In two separate letters he urged, yes begged, Redpath to "do something" to clarify the situation.[3] The correspondence continued for several weeks. During those weeks it became apparent that Ketcham and Redpath had strong disagreements on the concept of the relationship between a Bible-believing Christian and a modernist. Ketcham continued to urge Redpath to take the separatist position, but the latter steadfastly refused. In April 1954 Redpath admitted the two were deadlocked in divergent interpretations: "I shall continue to respect your standpoint though I may not agree with it, and I hope that such an attitude will be mutual."[4] When the correspondence concluded almost five years later, Ketcham continued to express the hope that Redpath would make a clean break with the modernists: "Forget me as a critic, Brother Redpath, and think of me only as a brother in Christ pleading

    2. R. T. Ketcham to Alan Redpath, February 9, 1954; *Ketcham Papers.*
    3. Alan Redpath to R. T. Ketcham, February 12, 1954; R. T. Ketcham to Alan Redpath, February 15, 1954 and February 24, 1954; *Ketcham Papers.*
    4. Alan Redpath to R. T. Ketcham, April 27, 1954; *Ketcham Papers.*

with you to pull away from these entangling alliances before you wind up with Jehoshaphat."[5]

While assuming this hard-nosed unwillingness to in *any* way have *any* connection with *any* religious liberals, Ketcham nonetheless maintained a position of love in relation to his fellow believers. He battled modernism with such vigor because he felt the modernists deprecated his Savior. An insult to his Savior was something that he took personally, for in his life the Lord Jesus Christ was everything. Christ was the preeminent One, and any who denied His virgin birth, His miraculous resurrection or the redemptive quality of His ministry on the cross became the focal point of Ketcham's attack.

Bob Ketcham realized that the battle against modernism had played an important and dynamic role in his life. He had grown to manhood in that era of human history when the church was experiencing a theological convulsion. Apostasy had crept into every denomination and threatened to destroy the very fabric of the church. When Bob Ketcham offered to give absolute obedience to his Heavenly Father, God led him into the path of defending the Faith. The enemy was real, and so was the battle. From the time he wrote his first pamphlet concerning the Convention's inclusive missionary program, down through the years of his ministry in Pennsylvania, Ohio, Indiana and Iowa, Ketcham again and again was called upon to defend the Faith. As the National Representative of the General Association of Regular Baptist Churches, he became one of the nation's leading spokesmen for the separatist position. From 1927, when he walked away from his last Northern Baptist Convention meeting, until his death, Ketcham defended the position: "Be ye not unequally yoked together with unbelievers" (2 Cor. 6:14).

Because of this fearless defense of the Faith, Ketcham was frequently known to his opponents, and sometimes to his friends, as "fighting Bob." This was a title which he disliked intensely. He fought only because he believed he had to fight. He fought in defense of the principles of the Word of God, not for personal acclaim. "It bothers him when people think of him as a fighter. They don't appreciate the fact that *every* time he had to fight something like that [modernism]

5. R. T. Ketcham to Alan Redpath, January 21, 1959; *Ketcham Papers.*

there was many an hour that he spent crying himself to sleep over having to fight."[6]

In reality, Ketcham was a man of compassion and tenderness. Those who listened to his messages heard not only his solid defense of the truth, but also his passionate adoration of his Savior. No one who listened to his series of messages on the Twenty-third Psalm could help but see how much he loved his Lord. Oftentimes, however, people were too busy anticipating a fight to listen to either the Word of God or the servant of God. Several years ago when Ketcham was scheduled to preach at Grand Rapids Baptist Theological Seminary, some of the students went to Dr. Welch, president of the seminary, and asked to be excused from the chapel sessions. When asked why, they indicated that they did not want to hear "fighting Bob," a fighter and troublemaker. Dr. Welch asked them if they had ever actually heard Bob Ketcham preach, and they confessed that they had not. Welch wisely suggested that they go hear Ketcham one time. If, after hearing him once, they wanted to stay away for the rest of the meetings, they would be permitted to do so. Following Ketcham's initial message, the students returned and apologized to the president for having judged hastily.[7]

Though Bob Ketcham had no formal training in seminary, he studied the Word of God avidly. Most of his sermons involved meticulous research and preparation. He spent hours reading everything he could find on a subject, studying and reflecting on the Word of God and praying for the direction of the Holy Spirit. Occasionally he could come up with a whole new sermon in a matter of minutes. For example, when he was pastoring the Walnut Street Baptist Church in Waterloo, he once jotted down a sermon outline based on the choral anthem—as the choir sang. When the choir finished, he preached from that outline instead of his prepared message. But, for the most part, Ketcham spent long hours in preparation before a sermon was delivered.

He had no system of sermon building. He did not know the rules and regulations of homiletics, once confessing, "I wouldn't know

6. Donn Ketcham, *taped reflections,* n.d.
7. Ibid.

homiletics if I met it coming down the street!" But he did have one hard-and-fast rule when it came to preparing a sermon. That rule was rooted in his firm principle of giving Christ the preeminence: "I just look and I think, 'Will that help me tell somebody about Christ?' That's my first and only rule in building a sermon. It must, it absolutely *must* present the Lord Jesus Christ in all His glory. The sermon that does not do that never ought to be preached. I don't care what we're dealing with. Theological matters of the deepest order should be so dealt with that they glorify the Person of Jesus Christ."

Late in his life, Dr. Ketcham received a letter from a pastor who had heard him speak at an annual meeting. The pastor confessed that he had never seen Dr. Ketcham in person until that time. He then said, "I went to see Dr. Ketcham. I saw Jesus Christ." When the letter was read to Ketcham, tears streamed down his face as he said, "I'll never have a higher compliment than that in all my ministry."

Curiosity sometimes gave Ketcham a starting place in building his sermons. He would see something in the Scripture, get an idea and not be able to let go of it. Sometimes it would take a few hours to find the answer. On other occasions, it would take a few weeks, a few months or even a few years. But however long it took, when his curiosity was settled, he usually had a sermon.

One day he received an advertisement for a book entitled *Why Was Christ a Carpenter?* He could not afford the book at the time, but the title aroused his curiosity. Why *was* Christ a carpenter? He worked and worked on that, but he could not come up with an answer. He wondered why Christ had not been born into a shepherd's family. The shepherd goes out and brings home every single one of his sheep. If it had been up to Ketcham, he would have had Jesus born in a shepherd's home. Christ was the Good Shepherd, but He was never near a sheepfold as far as Ketcham knew. Then he wondered why Christ had not been made a fisherman. "He told the boys where to drop their nets and all the rest of it, but He himself never had a net in His hand so far as I know. He was the master shepherd, but He wasn't a shepherd. He was the master fisherman, but He wasn't a fisherman. He was a carpenter. Why a carpenter?"

After grappling with this question for many months, Ketcham suddenly realized that even before the Incarnation, Christ had been a carpenter. Indeed, all through eternity Christ was a carpenter. "He was

God's eternal carpenter. He was God's carpenter, and He created the universe. Why is that mountain like that over there, that star like that? Because He built it that way. He is the carpenter that built the universe. Second, He is the carpenter Who is building the Church. He is a carpenter because He is building a city. He has gone to prepare a place for us, a palace. So all the way through His eternal career and His earthly career and all the rest of it, He is building, building, building. You get it in the Book of Ephesians. Joint by joint, member by member, and so on." But why did God bring Jesus into a carpenter shop down here in His earthly home? Ketcham thought perhaps the Heavenly Father was simply "giving Him a little something to help Him think of home."

Another Ketcham characteristic was his ability to illustrate. Sometimes an illustration would become the cornerstone of a sermon, as in the case of his message "Did You Leave Something on the Stairs?"[8] At other times it was simply to drive home a point within a message. For example, his message on Psalm 1:2: "But his delight is in the law of the LORD; and in his law doth he meditate day and night." When preaching on this verse, Ketcham would point out the fact that the word *meditate* means to ruminate. He drew the parallel of a cow chewing its cud. He would then demonstrate *how* a cow chews it cud—to the absolute delight of his audiences. His listeners would never forget the meaning of meditate.

Usually Ketcham would imitate the cow three or four times and then go on with the rest of his sermon. When his son was a student at Baptist Bible Seminary, Bob Ketcham went there for a chapel series. He had just obtained false teeth. He preached on Psalm 1:2 and demonstrated how a cow chews its cud. But he seemed to go on endlessly. Donn began to get embarrassed. "He chewed and he chewed and he chewed and he chewed. I thought he'd never quit! I thought, 'You're overdoing it!' I found out later that on the first chew, his upper plate had fallen down and gotten stuck crossways in his mouth. All the rest of this chewing was simply trying to get that crazy plate back into position, which he finally managed to do."[9]

8. See pages 301-312 for the text of that message.
9. Donn Ketcham, *taped reflections*, n.d.

Any man who spent as many years in the ministry as Bob Ketcham was bound to encounter occasional embarrassing situations. Certainly the problem with his false teeth ranked high on Ketcham's list of embarrassing moments. However, it could not match an experience he had in New York City. Ketcham was in New York to speak at the First Baptist Church. While there he purchased a new, brand name suit with two pairs of trousers. His new suit was altered and ready to wear on Sunday morning. The pulpit of First Baptist Church was located in a rather lofty and exposed position. While Dr. Ketcham was sitting on the platform prior to speaking, he crossed his legs, putting one ankle upon the other knee. As he did so, he glanced down and noticed that the inner seam of his trousers was missing! A hasty inspection revealed that indeed the seam was split on each leg from the knee up; so he kept his legs pressed tightly together. When it was time for him to preach, he made one swift motion and got behind the pulpit.

For one of the few times in his entire life, Bob Ketcham did not budge from behind the pulpit until his sermon was concluded! At the end of the sermon, he asked one of the deacons to pray. While the deacon was praying, Ketcham beat a hasty retreat to the church basement where his suitcase and another pair of pants were waiting. He decided to change into the other new pair of trousers, but he discovered that they were also seamless. Finally, the frustrated preacher had to borrow some safety pins until he could get to someone's home and get his trousers repaired!

Ketcham had a ministry not only to adults, but also to children and youth. He enjoyed spending a week in camp with junior-high or senior-high young people. Though he was limited in the number of times he could do this, whenever possible Ketcham would accept a Bible conference with the youngsters. One year while ministering at Lamoka Lake Bible Conference with senior-high young people, he chose as his subject sanctification. To illustrate what sanctification involved, Ketcham walked down into the group of teenagers gathered for the meeting. He took a chair from its place in the front row and carried it back to the platform with him. Then he looked at the young people and said: "Now, kids, this is my chair. I'm sanctifying this chair. I'm putting it over here and setting it apart for my use. The choir director can't take this, and the camp director can't take this, and your counselor can't take this because it's mine! I have separated it; that's what sanctification means. It means separation. Sanctification means you are set apart for somebody to use."

Unbeknown to the young people in the congregation, Ketcham had picked out his chair beforehand. He also had placed a thumbtack in the bottom of the chair. His reason for doing this was to further his illustration. No matter where the chair might be moved, he would be able to find it. Thus he could illustrate that God seals His own and knows who His own are. The morning after Ketcham had "set apart" the chair, a young girl came running to him and said, "Dr. Ketcham, some of the boys took that chair last night and put it down in the audience somewhere so you wouldn't know which chair it was!" Of course, none of the campers knew about the thumbtack.

When his message began that evening, Ketcham picked up the chair that was sitting there and said "No, sir, this is not my chair." The young people were quite surprised because all the chairs in the camp looked pretty much alike—wooden, folding chairs. Naturally, the campers wondered how Ketcham knew it was not his chair. Soon Ketcham was in the audience going chair by chair, row after row, looking for his chair. Everyone had to stand as the preacher carried on his investigation. Finally, in the third row he found the chair with the thumbtack. He carried it back to the platform, saying, "This is my chair. This is the chair set apart for my use." None of the young people knew how on earth Dr. Ketcham had managed to find his chair, but they all knew that sanctification meant set apart! When they asked Ketcham how he knew which chair was his, all he said was, "I told you yesterday the Lord knows His own, and He has a seal on them. That's how I know that chair. I have my seal on it." In reflecting on that week in camp, Dr. Ketcham said, "I had a great time on sanctification that week with those young people."

Dr. R. L. Matthews (at one time a field representative for the GARBC) recalled asking Dr. Ketcham on one occasion: "Doc, if you were to have just a few minutes to spend with a half dozen preachers and they asked you to give them a final word of exhortation, what would be your reply?" Without hesitation, "Doc" gave a pastoral theology course in five statements: "(1) Preach Christ. (2) Give the whole counsel of God. (3) Expose error—neoevangelicalism especially. (4) Obey God. (5) Be available to your people." Dr.

Matthews commented, "What a tremendous word for men entering the ministry!"[10]

Thus, in his years as National Representative, Bob Ketcham did much more than fight. While defending the Faith in obedience to the Word of God, he was also faithful to the whole counsel of God. He preached the Word consistently, seeking in every message to give Christ the preeminence. His pulpit ministry helped thousands of people throughout the country to know their Savior more intimately. His God-given ability to make even the most complex truths simple was used by the Holy Spirit to instruct many.

10. R. L. Matthews, transcribed from tape of Ketcham memorial service in Pennsylvania (1978).

The preacher making his point

IN HIS MINISTRY to local churches and national audiences, Robert T. Ketcham gained the reputation of being absolutely loyal to the cause of Jesus Christ. The leadership of the General Association of Regular Baptist Churches recognized him as a man in whom they could place the utmost confidence. After his sixth year of leadership, in recognition of his faithful service as their National Representative, the Council of Fourteen passed the following expression of gratitude:

> Because our beloved brother, Dr. Robert T. Ketcham, has been a faithful witness for the Lord Jesus Christ, a loyal soldier for truth and righteousness, and a devoted crusader for the upbuilding of the Fellowship of the GENERAL ASSOCIATION OF REGULAR BAPTIST CHURCHES from its very beginning, we the Council of Fourteen, in this year of our Lord 1954, desire to express to him our warm love and lasting gratitude for his service to God on behalf of our Fellowship. Likewise, we would express our deep gratitude to God for his faithful and gracious companion in these labors of love, particularly in her faithfulness in prayer for us all. We have confidence in Dr. and Mrs. Ketcham as two of God's most useful servants of the Lord in this day and age.[1]

1. This resolution was signed by the entire Council. *Ketcham Papers.*

The years slipped by quickly for Bob and Mary Ketcham in the ministry that they loved so dearly. It seemed to Bob that he was just getting a good start when he sat at his desk to prepare his ten-year report! Though he recognized that statistics could not tell the entire story, he nonetheless presented to the Council and the Association some of the things that had been accomplished in the previous decade. He had delivered 2,836 messages, an average of 283 a year. This number did not include Sunday school lessons, radio messages or appearances before young people's groups. To the best of Ketcham's knowledge, over half a million people had listened to him. His smallest audience was eight, while his largest was forty-two hundred. This reflects the fact that Ketcham was willing to involve himself in churches both large and small. It gave him a tremendous thrill to visit a tiny congregation in a small community and encourage a young pastor's heart. He recalled very vividly his days in such places as Roulette and Brookville.

During the decade he had seen 881 confessions of Christ. He had traveled 449,101 miles, an average of 44,910 miles per year. He ministered in 560 different towns and cities, an average of 56 per year. During the ten-year period, approximately 370 churches had entered the General Association of Regular Baptist Churches. He then discussed in detail the financial growth in the churches of the Association and the development of Regular Baptist Press, both of which gave him tremendous satisfaction.[2] Ketcham realized more was involved than mere statistics. He expressed the burden of his heart in these words:

> I realize that figures are cold things, and statistics have little of human interest in them, but as helpless as they are, they are the only means at my disposal to give you an overall picture of the ministry of these ten years.
>
> The long, hard and tiresome days, often stretching far into the night—the hours of intercessory prayer engaged in in the privacy of pullman quarters, airplanes, and automobiles—the moments of deep anxiety and concern (although I trust free from worry) as I have watched this beloved fellowship in all of its

---

2. The above statistics appear in a two-page typed report prepared by Ketcham. *Ketcham Papers.*

ramifications move on for God, often in the face of threatening onslaughts, cannot be captured in mere figures.

The hours of near heartbreak as I have seen an occasional church fall by the wayside, and desert the battle; the tears and soul sympathies which I have shared with scores of our beloved pastors and their families as they have gone through deep waters; the endless hours spent in correspondence and consultation with pastors and churches who are seeking to find their way out of difficult entanglements with old Convention ties; the counsel and guidance I have sought to give to pastors and churches who are caught in this ever increasing maze of confusion which characterizes the religious world are matters which cannot be tabulated. The occasions (almost innumerable) when I have had to draw hard upon the wisdom that cometh from above in order to avoid any appearance of lording it over our churches or interferring in the slightest degree in the internal affairs of a local church, and while avoiding all of this, to be as helpful as possible, under God, in the solving of difficult problems and the safeguarding of the harmony and happiness of the Association, have taken their toll of energies and emotions, and no figures or statistics can possibly reflect such ministries.[3]

Ketcham then sought to impress upon his brethren the importance of continued faithfulness. He saw new dangers on the horizon, and he urged his colleagues to be alert:

We must constantly remind ourselves of our own position on the matters which the Lord led us to take and to incorporate into our Constitution 26 years ago. I am sure that none of us realized at that time just how insidious and pronounced the battle would become, but if our position was right 26 years ago, it is right today. If it was to be abided by then, it is to be abided by now. Granted the cost is getting higher and higher with each passing year, but obedience is still obedience and is the price of a good conscience before God and men.[4]

As Ketcham penned these words, he was approaching his sixty-ninth birthday. Indeed, the years as National Representative had taken their "toll of energies and emotions." His eyes continued to deteriorate, and his body grew weaker. But his spirit was indomitable.

3. Ibid.
4. Ibid.

In the spring of 1959, Ketcham visited his son, Donn, in medical internship in Decatur, Illinois. During the visit, Donn took his dad to the office of a medical friend, an internist, for an electrocardiogram. "Pop" Ketcham was nearing seventy years of age, but he insisted on knowing why his son wanted to do such a thing. Donn indicated that when the Lord called his dad Home, the device He would probably use to "shake him loose from this old earth was going to be a coronary." Donn told his father that when that time came, he wanted to have "a baseline EKG so we'd know what was happening." The senior Ketcham protested, but acquiesced to his son's demand.

When he returned to the younger Ketcham's home, he said, "All right now, smart young doctor, you say that I am going to kick off with a coronary someday. Now tell me how I'll know when I have my coronary."

Dr. Donn described in detail a coronary. The older Ketcham nodded and absorbed the details. The visit concluded, and both father and son returned to their responsibilities. Neither realized how soon they would be reunited.

On May 5, 1959, Ketcham was in Detroit, making arrangements for the 1961 GARBC conference. While there, he realized he was experiencing the very symptoms his son had explained just weeks earlier! Ketcham concluded his work in Detroit, made his way to the train station and boarded a train for Chicago. By the time he reached the Windy City, he realized that his symptoms were growing more severe. But instead of entering a hospital in Chicago, Ketcham went to a phone booth and called Donn. He offered no warning of his fears, knowing full well that his son would order him to a hospital in Chicago. Instead, he simply told Donn, "I'm coming down to see you; meet me at the train." Donn could not help but inquire as to why his father was paying this unscheduled visit. The reply was simply, "Well, I'm not feeling very good, so I just thought I'd come down and see you."

Ketcham made his way through the LaSalle Street Station and boarded the train for Decatur. When Donn met the train, he knew in an instant that his father's situation was serious. Describing that moment, Donn said: "Dad got off the train looking like death warmed over, and then I got the story. He took a train clear from Detroit to Decatur, all after having had his coronary. And the reason for all that was that he wanted to be in the hospital where his boy was—so that I could make sure that the doctors were doing justice by him, I guess!"[5]

From May 5 to 12, Ketcham showed steady improvement. But on May 13 he suffered a severe relapse and almost died. For two days he lingered at death's door. Then he began to rally. In the week ahead he continued to improve. After spending almost three months in the hospital, Ketcham was released.

During his hospital stay Robert Ketcham received 2,961 expressions of love in the form of cards, letters and telegrams. Many of these were kept in a large file which he treasured throughout the remainder of his life. These letters came not only from members of the General Association of Regular Baptist Churches, but also from friends in other fundamentalist organizations. One letter came from the general director of the Conservative Baptist Association of America, B. Myron Cedarholm. A portion of Cedarholm's letter expressed the respect of the Conservatives for Ketcham. Though they did not agree on the issue of separation, both groups recognized the problem of modernism and were seeking to battle it. Cedarholm wrote:

> You can be sure of our deep concern over your welfare, and we'll be praying for the healing ministry of the Lord in your body. You probably need a little rest, too. You are known everywhere as a dedicated servant of the Lord without sparing yourself. There are not too many leaders on the scene today who have taken the uncompromising stand that you have. In these closing days before our Lord's return, we need men like you around more than ever before—so we are trusting God for recovery in your body. You have been a real blessing and encouragement to me and countless numbers of others. God richly bless you.[6]

The Regular Baptist community was stunned by Ketcham's heart attack. Though he was close to seventy when the attack occurred, the "grand old man" of the Regular Baptists had seemed indestructible. During the months he was flat on his back, the prayers of thousands went heavenward in his behalf. People continued to pray as Dr. and Mrs. Ketcham took an extended trip to the mountains of Pennsylvania. The doctors said he could not return to his desk before November, and then only for limited activity. But it soon became clear that no amount

5. Donn Ketcham, *taped reflections,* n.d.
6. B. M. Cedarholm to R. T. Ketcham, May 7, 1959; *Ketcham Papers.*

of rest would enable Ketcham to resume the previous pace.

With his activity limited, Ketcham hoped to devote more time to writing, particularly to getting some of his sermons into print. He expressed the desire that with time he would be able to take a limited number of speaking engagements. But when Ketcham published his open letter to Regular Baptists in the November issue of *The Baptist Bulletin,* what had been suspected by many became clear to all: Their tireless leader would never again be able to resume a full schedule. His physical limitations would not permit it.[7]

Through the winter months and on into spring of 1960, Bob Ketcham became increasingly aware of his limitations. After much prayer, he determined the leading of the Lord to resign as National Representative of his beloved Association. He addressed his resignation to the Council of Fourteen and the General Association of Regular Baptist Churches in these words:

> Beloved:
>
> It has been my high joy and great honor to serve you as your National Representative for nearly twelve years.
>
> As I walk through the halls of memory, I find its walls hung with some of the richest pictures of my forty-eight years in the Gospel ministry.
>
> These have been perilous years. We have together come through crisis after crisis, as we have moved in one solid phalanx against the enemies of God, His Son, and His Word. We have had the constant joy of standing together in a great and growing Fellowship, as we have raised and maintained a witness to the glory of Christ, our Savior. The high and holy privilege of being one of your leaders in these glorious years has been accepted by me as a blessed commission from God Himself. The ministry of these years together will linger always as a sweet perfume of memory sanctified by the touch of His hand of blessing.
>
> Since the founding of the GARBC in 1932, we have seen it grow from twenty-two churches to 932. We have seen the missionary giving of the churches reach the peak of almost four million dollars per year. We have seen many hundreds of new

7. In "An Open Letter From Dr. Ketcham" dated September 9, 1959, and published in the November 1959 issue of *The Baptist Bulletin,* Ketcham also conveyed his gratitude for the many expressions of love the family had received and for the prayers of God's people in their behalf.

churches established and multiplied millions of dollars spent in the erection of new church buildings and the enlargement of old ones. And best of all, instead of a tapering off in all of these blessed accomplishments for our Lord, there is an increasing tempo of sacrifice, giving, and service in every area of our field of witness. For what small share God has given me during these twelve years in helping to bring this to pass, I am indeed grateful to Him and to you.

As an Association, however, we have not yet even come close to the possibilities of accomplishment which lie all around us. We must gird ourselves with even greater determination to arise and possess the land than has characterized us in the past. Because of the increasing responsibility which rests upon all of us, I am convinced that I am no longer able to carry the terrific load of leadership which must rest upon your National Representative. As you know, one year ago a heart attack nearly took me Home. God, in His grace and in answer to your prayers, saw fit to restore me to practically a normal state of health. Severe damage was done to the heart, however; so while I feel well, I know I am not well. If I preserve my strength for less strenuous duties, I can have several years of active service in less responsible fields.

In view of my own somewhat limited capacity for the arduous tasks of the past, and realizing that someone else should be selected for this post, I hereby tender my resignation as your National Representative, at once. This does not mean that my love, prayers and service on behalf of this blessed Fellowship will cease. If I can be of service in any way whatsoever, I am yours to command.

Since you, as a Council, must now address yourselves to the task of selecting and recommending a new National Representative, and as an Association, you must prayerfully seek to know God's will, you shall have a constant and large place in my prayer ministry, that God's man for this hour will be made apparent to you and to him.

With every good wish, I am
Yours and His,
R. T. Ketcham
National Representative[8]

The chairman of the Council was Dr. Paul R. Jackson. Jackson, the highly respected president of Baptist Bible Seminary in Johnson

---

8. The text of Ketcham's resignation appeared in *The Baptist Bulletin,* XXVI (August 1960), 20.

City, New York, had just announced that he would leave the seminary to assume a Bible conference ministry. The Council requested that Chairman Jackson leave the room. Dr. Ketcham then presented to the Council his burden for his replacement. Ketcham informed the Council that he was "neither indispensable nor indestructible," and expressed the conviction that Jackson should be named his replacement. In a series of actions, the Council voted first to "accept Dr. Ketcham's resignation with extreme regret and with love and appreciation of his tremendous ministry to our Association." Second, to "extend to Dr. Ketcham an invitation to become the National Consultant." Third, to "draw up an appropriate statement of appreciation of Dr. Ketcham." Fourth and finally, to "extend an invitation to Jackson to become National Representative."[9]

Jackson was then called back into the room and informed that the Council of Fourteen had unanimously voted to invite him to be the new National Representative. It was their desire to present his name the next week to the meeting of the Association. The Council then shared in a time of prayer. "It was the unanimous opinion of all present that this was one of the most blessed sessions ever held by the Council of 14. The sense of the presence of God, the melting of hearts by the Holy Spirit, the so evident unselfishness of everyone involved, and the sense of being strangely bound together in heart dedication to God's holy cause, made this a high point in the history of the Council."[10]

The following Monday evening Ketcham read his resignation to the assembled messengers of the General Association of Regular Baptist Churches. This statement was then unanimously adopted by the messengers:

A STATEMENT REGARDING DR. ROBERT T. KETCHAM

In the course of normal human events, it must needs be that some of us serve our God for His appointed years. Then, by reason of failing strength, we find it inevitable that high and holy

9. Wilbur C. Rooke (Secretary of the Council), *Minutes of the Meeting of The Council of Fourteen of the General Association of Regular Baptist Churches*, (June 1960), pp. 8, 9; *Ketcham Papers*.
   10. Ibid.

responsibilities must be passed on, as a sacred heritage, to the hands of others. Such experiences often cause great shock and sorrow to those who have loved, served and rejoiced together in the blessed ministries of God-ordained leaders in holy causes. Such a time has come to pass in the affairs of the General Association of Regular Baptist Churches in the resignation of our beloved and long-cherished leader, Dr. Robert Thomas Ketcham.

Having received the resignation of Dr. Ketcham as our National Representative, and being forced by circumstances beyond our control to act upon same, it seems most fitting that we should try to express to him, and to the entire brotherhood, our deep sentiment in regard to such a step.

We record herewith our abiding love of, and deep respect for, this man of God. Under Divine providence he has led the forces of independent Baptists for well over a quarter of a century. This leadership has eventuated in a New Testament fellowship of true believers, known as the General Association of Regular Baptist Churches.

We count it a joy that in the mercy of God, this man came "to the kingdom" for such a day as we have been passing through. He has shown great spiritual discernment through these years as he has rendered glorious service to God and his brethren. All of us are better Christians, better servants of our Lord and better warriors in the holy crusade for Truth because of God's rich bestowments upon and through him.

Our acceptance of Dr. Ketcham's resignation is with the deepest sense of loss. Yet it is tempered with the joy that God has spared him to us by bringing him back from the brink of the grave. This has been in answer to the fervent prayers of thousands of faithful servants of our glorious Savior.

We are happy to announce that he has consented to remain in a position of blessed service with us. He will be assuming at our request a place of employment more in keeping with his limited strength—that of National Consultant. We thank God for His gracious providence in allowing us to have our dearly beloved brother in our hearts and Fellowship a while longer.

It is altogether fitting on this occasion that we, the Council of Fourteen, bring to the entire Fellowship the sentiments which we all feel for our brother, Dr. Ketcham. Words are inadequate vehicles through which to convey deep emotions; but as best we can, we do, on behalf of this Baptist body, express to him our abiding love.

As a group of Regular Baptists we also extend our expression of continued love and appreciation to Mrs. Ketcham. We trust that the future days of ministry for both of these dear servants may be rich and fruitful under God.

Unanimously adopted at G.A.R.B.C. conference in Long Beach, California, June 20-24, 1960[11]

Thus, just a few short days before his seventy-first birthday, Dr. Robert Thomas Ketcham concluded his ministry as the National Representative of the Association that he loved so dearly. Though he had been assigned the responsibility of National Consultant, Ketcham still did not know how active he could be. He realized that his threescore years and ten had been completed. But he was convinced that God had not raised him from death's door following his heart attack simply for him to retire. Though he could no longer carry the schedule of National Representative, he continued to have a burden for the Word of God, the testimony of Jesus Christ, and the defense of the truth.

11. This unanimous action of the Association was presented to Dr. Ketcham in scroll form, with a typed copy for his files. It was also printed in *The Baptist Bulletin*, XXVI (August 1960), 21.

27

BOB KETCHAM began his career as National Consultant of the General Association of Regular Baptist Churches at an age when most men have been retired for several years. But Ketcham had no desire to retire. Indeed, following his heart attack he longed to get back into the flow of Regular Baptist life. At the same time, he was more than happy to pass the mantle of leadership to a person like Paul Jackson. Jackson was a man of firm convictions and a loving spirit. Hundreds of students who had passed through the halls of Baptist Bible Seminary regarded him as a dear friend. He was a humble yet forthright man of integrity. Without question, having a man of his caliber available made Ketcham's decision to step down much easier.

Ketcham was anxious to continue serving his Lord in any capacity that he could. As his health improved, he began to accept more and more speaking engagements. He also continued to be involved in the battle for freedom from conventionism. In the early sixties when the First Baptist Church of Wichita, Kansas, voted to withdraw from the American Baptist Convention, a small minority in the congregation sued for possession of the multimillion dollar property. The main body of the congregation, which had voted to withdraw from the modernistic convention, was awarded the property in the lower courts. However, on May 5, 1962, the Kansas Supreme Court overruled the lower court and turned the church grounds over to the minority.

The Supreme Court ruled that the only way a church congregation could withdraw from a convention and maintain its property was to do so unanimously. In so doing, the court in essence was ruling that every different Baptist organization represented a different denomination.

Ketcham studied this case very carefully. He was deeply concerned over the fact that the judges had equated the American Baptist Convention with a denomination. "Every Baptist knows that to move from one Baptist *convention* to another is not moving into another *denomination*. And furthermore, no one knows this better than the American Baptist Convention officials themselves."[1] Ketcham studied the problem in detail. He considered this case to be of paramount importance for the future of the Baptist fundamentalist movement. Therefore, he prepared an amicus curiae (friend of the court) brief to present to the Kansas Supreme Court. Ketcham was authorized to file this brief in behalf of the General Association of Regular Baptist Churches in May 1962.

Meanwhile, by the summer of 1962, Pastor Elwyne Cooper and the members of the First Baptist Church of Roulette, Pennsylvania, were completing plans for a special week in honor of Dr. Ketcham's fiftieth anniversary as a minister of the gospel. A Bible conference was scheduled from Sunday, September 23, which was the anniversary Sunday (his first day in the ministry was September 22, 1912), to Sunday, September 30. The week was to feature members of Ketcham's family. Donn was to have charge of the music and bring messages on Tuesday and Friday afternoons. Don Moffat was to preach on Monday and Wednesday afternoons, and Lois Ketcham Moffat was scheduled to be the conference pianist. Bob's wife, Mary, and Donn's wife, Pauline, both were to speak to ladies' sessions. Also to join the Ketcham family was Bob's brother, Harry. Interestingly, Roulette was Harry Ketcham's first pastorate too. Harry Ketcham was approaching the conclusion of his forty-second year in the ministry. Thus, at the

---

1. R. T. Ketcham, "What Lies Ahead for Baptists," *The Baptist Bulletin*, XXVIII (August 1962), 22.

time of this conference, the Ketcham boys had amassed almost ninety-two years in the gospel ministry![2]

As the fiftieth anniversary approached, Merle Hull asked Ketcham to record some memories of his fifty years in the ministry. In an article prepared for *The Baptist Bulletin,* Ketcham reflected his characteristic humor:

> September 22, 1962, will mark fifty years in the ministry of the Word of God as a *Baptist.* I emphasize that word because I am not ashamed of it. I am a *Christian* and I am a *Baptist.* It is possible, you know, to be both of these at the same time! I hear some people say "I am a *Christian first* and *then* a Baptist." I have discovered that one can be both, and at the same time.[3]

Ketcham reminded his readers that many of his friends had viewed his poor eyesight as a handicap. From his standpoint however, it was "one of God's greatest blessings in my life. It has forced me to 'look unto Jesus' instead of looking to myself."[4] Indeed, in that comment may be seen the key to Robert Ketcham's effectiveness. Throughout the fifty years he recognized that it was God's ministry and not his own:

> Whatever has been wrought through this life of mine has been *all* of God. I had nothing fifty years ago and I have nothing now to give my Lord but *obedience. That* I could give Him and *that* I still can give Him. The rest is *His* responsibility. As His children we are responsible for only *one thing* in relation to God and that is *obedience.* Give Him *that* and that *always* and what happens must be all of Him. There will be no room or place, or desire for boasting.[5]

In spite of the fact that his article was less than two pages in length, Ketcham came back to the theme of obedience again at the conclusion:

2. Program, "50th Anniversary Bible Conference," The First Baptist Church, Roulette, Pennsylvania; *Ketcham Papers.*

3. R. T. Ketcham, "These 50 Years," *The Baptist Bulletin,* XXVIII (August 1962), 8.

4. Ibid.

5. Ibid.

"These fifty years!" I stand at the end of them utterly amazed at what *God* has done with such a terribly poor instrument. My only qualification which I could offer Him was *obedience.* The rest has been all of Him.[6]

The Roulette church spent over a year in preparation for the Fiftieth Anniversary Bible Conference. Consequently, when September 23, 1962, arrived, the people of Roulette awaited Dr. Ketcham's first words with a keen sense of anticipation. Obviously moved by the circumstances, Ketcham warned his audience of two grave difficulties that could be encountered during the week. First, he confessed that it would be a real strain on his emotions to preach from the pulpit where a half century earlier his ministry had started. "The second problem of which he reminded us was that he did not want this conference to degenerate into a 'Ketcham glorification week.' His desire was that through the week the Lord Jesus Christ should be glorified."[7]

A popular feature of the conference was Dr. Ketcham's brief reminiscence during each evening service. He would describe some incident from his early ministry, such as his ordination, one of his battles with the forces of modernism, his coming to the Roulette church to candidate, or his encounter with the old preacher who donated him a book of sermons. These moments were a real delight to the congregation.

The Ketchams were presented with several gifts during the week, including a large cake prepared for the fiftieth anniversary. A touch of humor was added on Tuesday evening when Ketcham was awarded a fifteen-dollar check by Pastor Cooper for "back salary." Cooper indicated that in preparing the history of the church he had discovered Ketcham had been shortchanged in 1915 when he left for the Brookville church!

On Tuesday evening the Galeton church—where Ketcham was saved—sent a delegation to the conference. Thursday evening, members of the First Baptist Church of Smethport sent a large delegation to the service. Smethport, of course, was the church

6. Ibid.
7. Elwyn Cooper, "Dr. Ketcham's Anniversary Conference," typed report; *Ketcham Papers.*

Ketcham had aided in its struggle to keep its parsonage out of the hands of the Convention. Though the struggle was ultimately unsuccessful (the church eventually was forced to purchase their parsonage back from the Convention due to the reversionary clause attached to the Convention donation), the congregation deeply appreciated the ministry that Ketcham had had in their lives at that time. Throughout the week people came from all over Pennsylvania to fellowship in the Bible conference. It was a rich and rewarding time for all, and it was deeply appreciated and enjoyed by the Ketcham family.

Throughout the week tributes arrived from all over the country for Dr. Ketcham. These expressions of love on the part of his friends throughout the nation greatly moved him. Keying on the theme of "fifty," one tribute said in part:

> It wouldn't take *fifty words* or *fifty seconds* to tell what that lump of clay was *worth* when it fell into the Potter's Hands many years ago. It wouldn't take *fifty minutes* (even for you) to tell what Bob Ketcham has accomplished during the other 26,262,670 precious minutes (besides staggering mathematical minds with the astronomical problem of shovelling the atoms in a postage stamp into one pile), but *fifty years from now,* you will still thrill with fresh revelations of what God hath wrought for eternity through a yielded life. . . . I have been personally blessed by your ministry at least *fifty times* and more than *fifty ways.* [8]

Another friend expressed his love in these terms: "We are glad that you were born and born again! Also that in your constitution was placed a backbone rather than a wishbone. We do thank the Lord for you and for your ministry and fellowship from the first and it is a joy to say so!"[9]

Still another expression of love came in the form of a poem:

TO THE GRAND OLD MAN OF OUR
FELLOWSHIP OF BAPTISTS,

> Because of your strong faith, we kept the track
> Whose sharp-set stones our strength had well-
> nigh spent.
> We could not meet your eyes had we turned back;
> So on we went!

8. R. E. Crotty to R. T. Ketcham, September 23, 1962; *Ketcham Papers.*
9. C. M. Keen to R. T. Ketcham, September 20, 1962; *Ketcham Papers.*

Because you would not yield to doubt or fear—
The threat'ning wave of unbelief we braved,
And forward moved with vision true and clear,
          Truth's cause to save.

We now salute you in this golden year!
And take fresh courage for the darker days.
Inspired by your example, as we hear
          "Stand Firm! It pays!"

The letter containing the poem concluded: "You have meant a lot to us, Dr. Ketcham. In precept and example, your stand for separation has put more iron in our backbones. God help us not to let down the bars—ever!"[10]

Shortly after returning to Chicago from the fiftieth anniversary conference, Ketcham once more experienced difficulty with his eyes. His schedule again had to be curtailed, but he steadfastly looked forward to returning to a preaching ministry. With a patience born out of years of experience and years of fellowship with his God, Ketcham awaited God's time to resume his ministry.

Throughout their life together, Bob and Mary Ketcham had a deep and abiding interest in missions. One of the great joys of their life was when Lois and Don had gone to Brazil. Both were thrilled when their only son, Donn, and his wife, Pauline—better known as Kitty—decided to go to Bangladesh (then East Pakistan). Through the years of his life at home, Donn had learned of his parents' burden for missions. Around the family altar at breakfast time, he heard them pray for missionaries and for the field. In describing the influence of his parents on his decision to enter a missions ministry, Donn said:

As for the matter of home life being an influence toward being a missionary, I rather imagine it was the prime influence. There was never a time when my parents said, "You should be a missionary"; but there was also never a time when it wasn't plain that this was the thing that would please them most. Many is the time I heard them plead with the Lord to take their boy to the mission field. They pleaded with the Lord and not with me. The Lord could be more persuasive with me than they could.[11]

10. H. K. Miller to R. T. Ketcham, October 2, 1962; *Ketcham Papers*.
11. Donn W. Ketcham, a three-page, typed personal testimony, apparently prepared on the mission field, n.d.; *Ketcham Papers*.

Donn and Kitty left for the mission field in June 1963. It was a teary farewell for both children and parents. Dr. Bob knew that he was not getting any younger, and he knew that Dr. Donn would be gone for four years. The possibility that they might never meet again on this earth was real to both of them. As they said good-bye they committed one another to the Lord and anticipated the will of God.

When Donn and Kitty arrived on the field, they found the following letter from Dad Ketcham waiting for them:

My darling Kids:

WELCOME HOME!

You are now at your God-called destination. *It and He* will be your "dwelling place."

New experiences, new methods of doing familiar things, new modes of life, new climates, new foods, new faces, new necessities for accommodation to circumstances, new languages, new frustrations, new daily routines, new dangers—yes, just about everything *new* but *Him!* He is the same, yesterday, today and forever. The God Who called you to East Pakistan and Who has now landed you there "will perfect that which concerneth you."

Live much with *Him,* my darlings. The temptation will be to rush here and rush there. The pressure of *things* will crowd in upon you. Don't make the mistake of Martha. Learn *daily* the blessed fact that if you will go into your "kitchen" from the feet of Jesus the work will be a joy. Your "kitchen" will prove to be a thousand different things—but take Him into them and it will go down in history that "Donn and Kitty served" (John 12:1-2).

Don't let *anything* interfere with your personal and family daily—yes hourly—communion with Him. I had to learn this the hard way. I found myself increasingly loaded with local, national and international obligations. I found that I was not "living in the Spirit." I argued that I didn't have *time* to spend with the *Word,* both written and living. I found that I must not *work less* but read, pray and commune *more.* The sense of lost spiritual power vanished and I lived again in the sweet realization of His empowerment.

My darlings, I am not preaching. I am just telling out to you the utter longing of my heart that you, His servants, and my precious ones, may make this Pakistan experience one of not *only blessing to the Pakistanis,* but TO YOUR OWN HEARTS ALSO.

Again I say, "WELCOME HOME."

Okay now—step out there with your little jack knife and your big black Book and get going.

Love in Chunks,
DAD[12]

Ketcham's letter to his "kids" reflected the warmth and love of a half century of walking with the Lord. The years had left their mark on the Allegheny mountain preacher boy. His wisdom had been gained in the school of experience, and he was beginning to realize that age was no respecter of persons. He began to reminisce more and more. In his writing and his conversation, he demonstrated an awareness that the end of his life could be near at hand. At the same time, his brother Harry was experiencing similar thoughts. As a result, Harry addressed a letter to "Bob and Mayme"—the nickname by which most of the family knew Mary. Bob responded quickly to Harry's letter. These letters reflect the warmth and love that was shared down through the years by this family. They are reproduced here because they tell so much about the personalities of both men. They show the love these brothers had for each other and for the Lord they served.[13] The first letter was from Harry and Claudia to Bob and Mayme:

Dear Bob and Mayme:

As I write this letter, I am thinking back over the years that have come and gone. I think of them with mixed emotions. I think so often about what God has done for us and our families. Putting what He has done, and is doing, over against our sinful natures, and total unworthiness, it is so unbelievable, and yet stands out a glorious fact.

What would have been the course of our lives if our own mother had not died, and if Dad had not married Louise Coolidge? Suppose we had always been brought up in the Methodist Church. In view of what the Methodist Church is today, how I

---

12. R. T. Ketcham to Donn and Kitty Ketcham, June 27, 1963; *Ketcham Papers.*

13. Harry and Claudia Ketcham to Bob and Mayme Ketcham, January 1, 1964. R. T. Ketcham to Harry Ketcham, January 6, 1964; *Ketcham Papers.*

thank God for watching over us, and guiding us into the truth that Baptists believe and rejoice in.

Then as I think of our so unusual call into the ministry, so unorthodox, as some of our most educated friends might say, and yet so like the work of the blessed Holy Spirit, the Song of the Lord starts ringing in my heart, and I sit and weep tears of joy, to think that God would trust me to handle and proclaim His Word, for 43 years, and that I am still able to do it even though I shall begin to unwind my 80th year the 19th of this month.

And then to think of His marvelous grace toward you, and the ability He has given you to proclaim His word for over 51 years in a state of almost total blindness. To think of the wonderful memory He has given you to make up for your lack of eyesight, and love and esteem He has given you in the hearts of fellow saints, makes me weep so I can hardly see the keys on this typewriter.

Another thought comes to my mind as I am writing, and that is the goodness of God toward our children. When I think of what an awful life Martha lived for so many years and then of how God delivered her from it, and gave her five years to live for Him before she went to heaven is just about too much for me. Also I praise Him for the wellbeing and good repute of all the rest of them. They had a good and wonderful mother, and I marvel at the grace God gave her to live with me for over 50 years. And then to think that He would love me enough to give me such a wonderful wife as Claudia for these last years of my life, and ministry, I am absolutely speechless before Him.

And then to think of His goodness to you and your family. What a wonderful man Donn Billy is, and that wife and family of his, one cannot find adequate words with which to praise Him. What a wonderful pair Don and Lois are, and then to think of Peg being back in fellowship with the Lord. It is no wonder we are going to have to have new bodies before we can stand the full inheritance we have in Christ, because, right now, if I had any more of it, I would burst wide open. What a wonderful wife Mayme has been to you, and will be now, as she becomes, among all the other things she is, eyes to you.

Although I know you don't want sympathy concerning your waning eyesight, and that you are not sitting around feeling sorry for yourself, nevertheless I am sorry that your sight is getting dimmer, as anyone should be sorry for others who are afflicted in any way, but on the other hand, I have to thank God for your limited eyesight all these years, for I know it is the thing that God has used to keep you close to Him, and that you would not have been the man and preacher you are if you had had perfect vision, physically speaking.

I trust that now since He is permitting the light to slowly fade out that He will give you a ministry, in the years that are still allotted to you, that will transcend, to His glory, all the past years of your ministry.

I wish that you and Mayme would plan to come and spend at least a week with us this spring or summer. Look over your plans, and see if you can't give us maybe an 8 day meeting, Sunday through Sunday, and you name the dates. If you can't do that we will settle for however long you can be with us. We want you to come. We are getting old and I think we ought to try and get together, at least once more on the pilgrim journey.

The Lord bless you and give you peace.

Yours in the bonds of Calvary

Signed: Harry and Claudia

Five days later Bob penned his response to Harry's letter:

Dear Harry:

Thank you so much, my dear brother, for the lovely letter I have just received. It unlocks a train of memories which go back over the years, and as I take stock of them, I find them laden with the sweet perfume of the precious power and grace of a sovereign God. When the song writer said, "When He saved my soul, and made me whole, it took a miracle of love and grace," he was making the understatement of all time. When I think of what the two "Ketcham kids" were by nature and by *action*, I can only marvel that we were not beyond His *grace* and His *power*.

You spoke of God's sovereign guidance in the taking of our own precious mother and giving us another. I have said the same thing in public messages. Of course we don't know what would have happened if what did happen hadn't happened. But from our pure human vantage point, we would have every reason to believe that we would have been caught up in the Methodist apostasy, and probably never have entered the ministry. But God threw the switches and shunted us over onto another track, and today we find ourselves Baptist ministers, and thank God, on the right side of that crowd.

I think, Harry, all of this is God's answer to the prayer of a little dying mother in a Blossburg, Pennsylvania hospital, when realizing that she was going to be with her Lord, her heart and mind leaped back 70 miles away to a farmhouse where two little boys—one 10 and one 6—were romping across the fields of the open farm, and as she thought of us, her last recorded words, according to the nurse, were "Into the hands of God and Charlie I commit my boys." Both God and Charlie have been faithful to that committal. Dad held the lines pretty strict and straight in his insistence upon Christian life and deportment on the part of his boys. As you know, it was this insistence that caused me to walk out of his home at the age of 16, rather than to stay and be under the discipline of a Christian father. Talking these matters over with Dad in later years, he told me what he did the morning I walked out of his yard, even refusing to let him kiss me good bye. He had gone up into the haymow of the old horse barn, and there, with his face buried in the hay, wetting it down with his tears, he had said, "Oh God, there goes my youngest born. Follow him and bring him back to thyself and to me." *And He did!* Our Dad had every right to see both of his boys either strung up by the neck or imprisoned for life, but instead he lived to see both of us ordained into the Baptist gospel ministry. Hallelujah!

My mind goes back to the companionship you and I had in sinning. The fact that God saved either one or both of us is still a marvel in the minds of the old residents of Galeton, and it is a marvel in our own eyes. We sure were a couple of unadulterated messes. I remember one time in Elmira a few years ago, I needed something at a jewelry store, and Grace said, "Why don't you go down to Bob Smith's store on Water Street." I said, "Who is Bob Smith?" She informed me that he was one of the fellows that you and I used to run around with in Galeton. So down to the store I went. As I opened the door and walked in, Bob looked up and immediately recognized me and called me by name. It had been, at that time, at least 48 years since he had seen me. During the conversation he said, "Where is Harry?" I told him that you were a pastor in Sioux Center, Iowa, and he said, "Now, let me see, you had three other brothers—where are they?" I told him that we did not have three other brothers—that there were just the two of us. He replied, "Well, I thought there were five of you Ketcham boys," to which I replied, "No, Bob, it just seemed that way!" Yes, the days of companionship in sin were by a miracle of God's grace changed into days of fellowship in the gospel ministry, and Harry, you will never quite know what an inspiration you have been to me. Things haven't always broken easily for you, and there has been a burning, fiery faith in your heart that would never let go. You have made yourself a student of the Word of God so that I have said on many occasions that I have a healthy respect for any opinion my brother expresses concerning any portion or doctrine of the Word of God. What a joy to be traveling along this road together for His glory.

Well, I don't think we are going to have to travel much farther, Harry. Seems like to me I can hear the Angel Gabriel tuning up his trumpet for the great day. And if the trumpet should sound before I see you again, you lean over this way, and I'll lean over your way, and we will go up together. Bye, my precious brother. Rejoicing in all the love of God's great heart for both of us, I am

With every good wish,

Yours and His,

By the time the above letters had been exchanged, both Bob and Harry had experienced their share of physical trouble. For Bob it had been the heart attack in 1959 and the continuing eye difficulty that had plagued him since youth. Harry's physical problem of long standing was diabetes. Following the exchange of letters, both men continued their ministry for several months. Approximately a year and a half later, in the last week of October 1965, Bob Ketcham visited his old church in Waterloo. During his Bible conference at Walnut Street, Harry and Claudia drove from Sioux Center to Waterloo for the Monday night service. Bob and Harry visited throughout the day Tuesday, and Harry stayed for the Tuesday evening service before returning to Sioux Center for his own prayer meeting on Wednesday.

When Bob said good-bye to his brother in Waterloo, it marked the last time he would see him alive. After preaching both services in his own church on October 31, Harry became ill. He went into the hospital on November 3 with a serious case of diabetes. By Saturday the doctors felt they had the problem under control. His physician left the room after telling Harry the good news. When he returned about fifteen minutes later, Harry was with the Lord. He died of a severe coronary thrombosis.

Bob returned to Iowa for his brother's funeral. He preached Harry's funeral message from the fourth verse of the beloved Twenty-third Psalm: "Yea, though I walk through the valley of the shadow of death, I will fear no evil: for thou art with me; thy rod and thy staff they comfort me."

DURING THE thirty-fourth annual conference of the General Association of Regular Baptist Churches, Bob Ketcham announced his second retirement. The next year, he indicated, would be his last as National Consultant. The years gradually had sapped his strength. His dim eyesight necessitated that someone guide him as he walked. Even the process of walking had become a chore at the age of seventy-six, and he seldom moved without the aid of his cane. If he did not recognize friends by voice, he could not identify them. But the years had not dimmed his sense of humor. He announced his retirement by saying: "This next year I'll be seventy-seven and I'll become a Regular Baptist with the right to vote at the 35th Annual Bible Conference." In recording that statement in *The Baptist Bulletin*, Edgar Koons said: "Great men have a sublime way of announcing events of major significance. . . . What better expression could have been spoken to announce that he was stepping down from his position of National Consultant to assume his position and place as a loyal Regular Baptist."[1]

Immediately upon Ketcham's announcement of his impending

1. Edgar R. Koons, "A Worthy Tribute," *The Baptist Bulletin*, XXXI (March 1966), 7.

retirement, the Council of Fourteen swung into action. They organized a special committee to plan an extended expression of appreciation to Dr. and Mrs. Ketcham. In line with the predetermined course of action, Dr. Robert L. Powell sent a letter to all pastors in the Association. He reminded them of Ketcham's planned retirement and said:

> The entire Association will surely want to take proper notice of this significant event. We all feel a sense of gratitude to God for giving us such a master workman as our National Consultant, and because of the sense of gratitude, many of us feel some worthy recognition should be given this warrior of the faith. The occasion of his retirement is that he will have reached the age of seventy-seven, and in the course of human events that begins to tell on one's strength. And while he retires officially from his present position, yet he will never retire in the sense of quitting the work of the Lord as long as he is able to serve.[2]

Powell went on to describe Ketcham's life, indicating that it read "like a romance of service to the Lord."

Powell indicated that many felt it would be appropriate for a love offering to be provided for Dr. and Mrs. Ketcham on the occasion of their retirement. It was the desire of the Council that this be a well-planned offering which would enable every Regular Baptist to have an opportunity to "share this token of love." The suggestion was made that a special Sunday be set aside, perhaps early in May. Powell expressed the hope of the Council that the congregations of the Association would respond generously. He concluded:

> And, of course, the whole matter is strictly on a basis of a voluntary principle, as is always the case among us "independent Baptists." But we believe that such an opportunity will be gladly and enthusiastically accepted by all of the fine people called "Regular Baptists," because to Dr. Ketcham more than any other man alive is the credit for keeping the cause of the GARBC alive and going at a good rate of growth. Hundreds of pastors and missionaries have felt that he is really their "father" in the scriptural sense of the word. All of us owe him a debt of gratitude for the work God has done through his surrendered life.[3]

2. Robert L. Powell to GARBC pastors, February 4, 1966; cited by Koons, ibid.
3. Ibid.

In addition to planning the love offering for Dr. Ketcham, the Council of Fourteen also decided that an issue of *The Baptist Bulletin* would be dedicated to an expression of appreciation for the Ketchams. In his lead editorial in the March 1966 issue, Merle Hull announced the significance of the special issue:

> For the first time in the BULLETIN'S thirty-three year history, the major portion of an issue is being dedicated to one person—Dr. R. T. Ketcham. Should anyone harbor even the momentary thought that in this we are exalting a man instead of the Lord, he has only to read the material presented this month to be set straight. It will be evident that what we are doing is *honoring* a man who has *exalted* the Lord. For such an act, there is clear scriptural precedent.[4]

The cover of this special issue of *The Baptist Bulletin* carried an expression of Regular Baptist appreciation. It was entitled simply "In Appreciation":

> Occasionally God thrusts upon some man more than ordinary responsibilities and then demonstrates to and through that man His sufficiency for every task.
>
> Members of the Council of Fourteen have had the opportunity of co-laboring with such a man in the person of Dr. Robert T. Ketcham. In the close contacts afforded in such a relationship the Council members have gained a new insight of his devotion to the Person of the Lord Jesus Christ, of his dedication to the Word of God, and of his courage to dare to stand for what he believes is right in the sight of God. Through more than fifty years of a rich public ministry these very qualities have enabled him to leave a vital spiritual impact on his generation. Without question the cause of evangelical Christianity has been enhanced because God chose and enabled this man to stand in the gap.
>
> In view of Dr. Ketcham's announced retirement in June from active leadership in the General Association of Regular Baptist Churches, the members of the Council of Fourteen, in behalf of our national constituency, wish to express their appreciation for his dedicated life and energies, his courageous stand for truth, and his thirty-four years of leadership in our GARBC.[5]

---

4. Merle R. Hull, "A Special Issue," *The Baptist Bulletin,* XXXI (March 1966), 6.

5. Council of Fourteen, "In Appreciation," *The Baptist Bulletin,* XXXI (March 1966), front cover.

When Bob Ketcham was asked to prepare a message for that issue of *The Baptist Bulletin,* he immediately knew what sermon to present. There was only one choice. Colossians 1:18 was the text, and the message was "The Preeminence of Christ." In explaining his text he said: "I am using this text (Col. 1:18) because of the precious way it got tangled up in my life during the early months of my ministry."[6] He then described for his readers the battle that had raged in his own soul over that verse many years before when he had inscribed the reference in the flyleaf of his Bible. In reflecting on the years of his ministry he said:

> I frankly admit that had I known that day where obedience to that verse was going to take me, I would not have had the courage to commit myself to it. Had I known the raging battlefields that verse would lead me into; had I known the dear friends who would turn away from me in the years ahead; had I known the many, many nights of weeping upon my pillow—had I known all this, I doubt if I would have left it there. But do you know something, dear reader? If we know WHO is out there ahead of us, we do not need to know or fear WHAT is out there.[7]

Bob Ketcham was not only grateful for the leadership of God and the preeminence of Jesus Christ in his life; he was also grateful for his Heavenly Father's provision of a godly wife who shared over a half century of ministry with him. He insisted on writing a tribute to his beloved Mary for the special edition of *The Baptist Bulletin.* In it he reminded the readers that the road had been a difficult one for her. She had spent much time alone while he was away. But her spirit of willingness to endure this made his work much easier.

> They have been blessed years as Mrs. Ketcham and I have walked together through brilliant sunshine and deep shadow. No one but I will ever know what her faithfulness in the home, her loyalties in the battles, her delights in my victories, and her ministry in prayer have meant to me. Whatever of blessing and success I have enjoyed in these years of service for God has been largely due to her.[8]

6. Robert T. Ketcham, "The Preeminence of Christ," *The Baptist Bulletin,* XXXI (March 1966), 13.

7. Ibid., pp. 13, 14.

8. R. T. Ketcham, "My Partner in Service," *The Baptist Bulletin,* XXXI (March 1966), 15.

In particular, Ketcham indicated that the sustaining influence of his wife's prayer had been very precious to him: "Without overstatement I can say that when I am in need of special help from God, I would rather have the prayers of my wife undergirding me than those of any other person on earth. One reason for this is that I know she LIVES where she PRAYS."[9]

Indeed this was a fitting tribute to Mary Ketcham. Those who have heard her teach a women's group or a Sunday school class, those who have prayed with her or experienced her loving concern in their lives, have recognized her as a woman of God. Her gracious spirit and tender heart have warmed the lives of thousands.

Through the early months of the spring, gifts poured in to the Association office for the love offering for Dr. and Mrs. Ketcham. Literally thousands of people contributed to this venture, and the Association leadership watched with interest as the figure mounted.

The 1966 annual conference of the GARBC was held in Grand Rapids, Michigan. Wednesday night was set aside for Ketcham's appreciation service. He was invited to preach, and following his presentation of the Word of God, Dr. and Mrs. Ketcham were given a check for $13,643.42. In addition, they were told that the Council of Fourteen had voted to provide them with $100 per month for life from the general fund of the Association. (The Council did this because the Association did not have a pension program of any kind at that time.) It was one of the most moving scenes ever to occur in a Regular Baptist conference. The tears flowed freely from both Dr. and Mrs. Ketcham and from the 4,500 people who attended the service.

On July 11, 1966, Bob Ketcham sat down to write a thank-you note to all those who had contributed to his retirement gift. By this time the figure had reached $14,110. The money meant a great deal to him because it met a real financial need. But it was not the dollars that overwhelmed him. Instead he was deeply moved by the manifestation of love on the part of Regular Baptists throughout the country. For a man who had been preaching the Word of God over fifty years, it was difficult to be speechless, but that was how he felt.

9. Ibid.

> There are times when one comes to such a place in his emotions as he thinks upon the goodness and grace of his fellow believers in the Christian family. The emotions are so deep that old words and phrases just won't do. The heart cries out for some *new* words from which he can create a *new* vocabulary which expresses what his heart is *really* saying.[10]

The love gift enabled the Ketchams to make a dream come true. More than anything else, the Ketchams wanted to visit Bangladesh to see their son and his family. Had it not been for the gift of God's people in the Association, they would not have been able to do so. Dr. and Mrs. Ketcham had nothing in the bank. They had spent virtually every penny for eye operations and other physical needs. But when the love offering was provided, they immediately determined that a portion of it would be used to finance an overseas trip, with visits to the Philippines, Japan, Hong Kong and three weeks in Bangladesh with Donn, Kitty and the grandchildren.

The ministry of medical missions in Bangladesh overwhelmed Bob Ketcham. He rejoiced in the modern hospital and its conveniences. He wept over the tattered "mass of humanity huddled on the ground waiting to be brought in to see the doctors." Tears welled in his eyes as he said, "It just takes the heart out of you to see them."

But observing was not enough for Bob Ketcham. He was an active seventy-seven-year-old, and he wanted the chance to preach. When Ketcham arrived in mid-December, the mission was just concluding a short-term Bible school. Missionary Jay Walsh invited Dad Ketcham to speak to the students; so Ketcham delivered his series on Psalm 23, with Walsh serving as his translator.

During one of Dad Ketcham's messages, Daniel, a young Muslim convert, left the meeting. A short time later he returned. As he walked back into the room, Ketcham was saying, "I will fear no evil for thou art with me." Ketcham pointed out that if a tiger or lion came after the sheep, all the sheep had to do was look up and make sure he was near the shepherd. If he was near the shepherd, there was nothing to fear;

---

10. R. T. Ketcham to "The Churches and Individuals Who Contributed to My Retirement Love Gift," July 11, 1966; *Ketcham Papers.*

he could leave the fighting to the shepherd. Thus, Ketcham continued, when the Christian is beset by evil forces or evil people, "all he has to do is make sure he is close to the Shepherd and that should suffice." As Ketcham said those words, tears started streaming down Daniel's face. Through the tears, the former Muslim began to shout, "Hallelujah! Hallelujah!" Ketcham was surprised to find a shouting Baptist in Bangladesh. Later he discovered why Daniel had been so vocal.

The converted Muslim had been called out of the room by a delegation from his local village. The delegation insisted Daniel recant. If he did not, they would kidnap his wife and children and exile them to an island in the Bay of Bengal. Then they would kill him and burn his home. Daniel looked at the delegation steadily and replied: "I am a Christian, and with my Bible I will stand." He turned and walked back into the meeting—just in time to hear Dr. Ketcham describing how to handle that very situation! In the months ahead, there were several attempts on Daniel's life, but all of them were unsuccessful.[11]

Donn recalled Dr. Ketcham's continuing interest in Daniel: "Every five minutes he had to have another report as to what was going on with Daniel. 'Look, I've told him that he doesn't have to worry; the Shepherd will take care of him. God's got to protect him. If He doesn't, then I've got to rethink the whole Twenty-third Psalm.' It was an interesting experience for Dad to be involved in something like that right on the mission field. He had heard many many of these stories, I'm sure, from other missionaries, but here he was right up to his earlobes in one himself."[12]

The Ketchams (and Ruth Ryburn, who accompanied them on the trip) stayed in Bangladesh the last three weeks of December (1966), spending both Christmas and Donn's birthday with the younger Ketchams.

When the Ketchams returned home, Dr. Ketcham had to face the reality of retirement. His solution was simple: Keep preaching! Though

11. For the full story of Daniel, see Jay Walsh and Patricia C. Oviatt, *Ripe Mangoes: Miracle Missionary Stories from Bangladesh* (Schaumburg, IL: Regular Baptist Press, 1978), pp. 59-69.
12. Donn Ketcham, *taped reflections,* n.d.

of necessity his schedule was more limited, he continued to faithfully proclaim the Word of God. When he reached eighty, he preached at the Bible conference of the Grand Rapids Baptist College. The day following his message, a gentleman came to see him. "Dr. Ketcham, I think you would enjoy what happened last night." He went on to explain that on the way home from the service, his seven-year-old had said to him, "Daddy, that man can't be eighty years old." The father assured the youngster that indeed Ketcham was eighty years old, to which the child replied, "No, Daddy, he can't be! No man eighty years old can shout that loud!"

Indeed, the years did not diminish the voice that spoke out so clearly for God. Nor did the years diminish his convictions. One of the greatest messages Bob Ketcham ever preached was preached in the last decade of his life. It was not a sermon delivered from a platform, but rather it was the message of his life. It was a sermon preached so eloquently, yet so tenderly.

Throughout the years Ketcham was the subject of much criticism for his strong separatist stand. Many thought he was unkind or harsh in his stance. But he spoke what he felt was God's will for him, and he stood by it. He defended the truth of the Word of God with unwavering faithfulness in spite of what anyone said. But in all his stand for the truth, he stood in love. And when he stood for the truth, he stood against the errors of modernism and apostasy.

In the later years of his life, Ketcham was deeply troubled by the fact that some of his beloved brethren did not seem to understand the nature of the battle for the truth. Some lost sight of the fact that the war was with those who denied the validity of the Word of God. It was an understandable lack of focus. Ketcham fully realized that it was easy to lose sight of the real enemy and become accustomed simply to fighting a war. But to see this literally occur broke his heart. He did not believe it glorified God or aided the cause of reaching people for Jesus Christ. Therefore through his life and his actions, he sought to instruct his brethren.

Bob Ketcham was a Baptist—a thorough-going, one-hundred-percent, couldn't-be-prouder Baptist! Yet, throughout his ministry, he recognized that the battle was not just a Baptist battle. His early involvement in the American Council of Christian Churches and the International Council of Christian Churches demonstrated his willingness to work with other Bible-believing fundamentalists of a separatist persuasion in spite of the fact that they had doctrinal differences.

The explanation for this was very simple. He based his belief in separation on 2 Corinthians 6:14-17 which ordered him not to be "unequally yoked together with unbelievers." It was in the context of unbelievers that verse 17 stated: "Wherefore come out from among them, and be ye separate, saith the Lord, and touch not the unclean thing; and I will receive you." Clearly, separation was to be from the unregenerate. Thus, Ketcham had no hesitation whatsoever in separating himself from Baptists who denied the truth of Scripture, while continuing to have fellowship with members of other denominations who maintained the truth of Scripture. Interpretations of the truth might vary, but belief in the verbally inspired Word of God and other fundamentals of the faith could not. Consequently, it deeply troubled Bob Ketcham when his brethren began to argue over interpretations.

In the late 1960s when some in the General Association of Regular Baptist Churches sought to positionalize on the day-age theory of creation, Ketcham was opposed. He demanded that people recognize creation as the direct and instantaneous act of God. He rejected any concepts of theistic evolution. Though he maintained a firm, twenty-four-hour-day position, he realized that many who held to the day-age theory maintained those same principles. To him, this was an area of interpretation. The Association did not positionalize, though it made a strong statement on Biblical creation.

When the Calvinist question became an issue in the GARBC, Ketcham was deeply concerned. Disagreement on this theological issue had been in the Association from its inception. "We have had two views of election in our Fellowship for forty-three years, and we got along as happy as two bugs in a rug."[13] He was particularly sensitive to the attempt on the part of some to label him.

> For 43 years we have believed what the Bible has said to us about Election and we have all been happy. Now why this sudden confusion? Dr. Good quotes me on what I say in my books about

13. R. T. Ketcham, *personal interview,* 1975.

Election and then he winds up his paragraph by saying, "Therefore, Dr. Ketcham is a Calvinist." I made these statements not because I am a Calvinist, but because I am a Biblicist. I believed what I taught years before I ever heard of John Calvin. I emphatically deny that I have built my theology around what Calvin or any other man has said or taught. I have built it around The Book. Now, why must I be labeled as a Calvinist? I am a Biblicist. I have thought all my brethren were, too. Let us not run off now and follow a man who insisted that the State have a part in controlling the church. Why should we insist upon being called by the name of a man who engineered the burning at the stake of a man named Servetus? I have always given invitations to the unsaved to confess Christ. Not to do so would be like slamming the door in the face of one who was ready to come.[14]

Once more Ketcham's main concern was the matter of making election a test of fellowship. He had no quarrel whatsoever with the doctrinal position, but he did not believe that it was a basis for separation.

Ketcham went through a heartbreaking experience in the late 1960s as he watched Carl McIntire become less and less willing to cooperate with anyone who in any way disagreed with him. In a series of letters, Ketcham urged his longtime friend to be more gracious in his dealings with other Christians and to be receptive to their attempted contributions to the ACCC and ICCC. Ketcham was unable to effectuate any shift in McIntire's position. Instead, the two drifted farther apart. Ketcham continued to hope for a change in attitude on the part of McIntire. But such was not the case. Indiscriminate charges were hurled at men of God in the *Christian Beacon*. A conflict over International Christian Relief found several Regular Baptist men strongly disagreeing with McIntire, and the GARBC withdrew from the International Council of Christian Churches.

McIntire continued his attack on the ACCC, which had rejected his leadership. Finally, in October 1970, McIntire interrupted a meeting of the ACCC, from which he had withdrawn two years earlier. Before the delegates were properly certified, he usurped the floor, had

14. R. T. Ketcham as quoted in the *Fundamental Baptist Fellowship Information Bulletin* (May-June 1975), p. 2.

himself elected president by a delegation he had brought with him, and refused to yield the podium to the duly elected representatives of the ACCC. Ketcham, an eyewitness to the drama, was heartbroken. In his account of the events of that day he said: "Really, I never expected to live to see the day when this kind of procedure would be witnessed in a group of fundamental Christians. It was amazing and shameful to the nth degree. It was piracy at its worst!"[15]

Bob Ketcham's later years provided an important lesson for the future of fundamentalism. He knew the battle was real and had to be waged to the utmost—but only against the enemy! God's people were to relate to one another in love. They had to learn to handle legitimate disagreement. Ketcham believed that the basis for coping with disagreement rested in a man's ability to handle success and failure. He learned to do this in the dark hours following his eye surgery in 1946. He described what God taught him at that time with these words:

> These days we need to know the secret of being occupied only with Him, and not with "things." Martha got into trouble worrying about "things." Mary got into blessing by being occupied with Him. As a faithful shepherd our Lord *must* lead us into the shadows as well as into the sunshine. It is how we react that makes the difference between defeat and victory. If we become pre-occupied [sic] with the shadows, we will become cynical, bitter, discouraged, and defeated. If we become preoccupied with the sunshine, we will become self-satisfied, self-centered, thoughtless of others and, worse still, forgetful of Him. But if we remain preoccupied with the Shepherd, regardless of shadow or sunshine, we will survive the peril of both with Victory.[16]

This important lesson, recorded over thirty years ago, was Ketcham's message for the future. When the child of God is "preoccupied with the Shepherd," he is able to withstand both success and failure; for he recognizes that man is only the vehicle through which Christ may be seen.

---

15. R. T. Ketcham, "Piracy At Its Worst," p. 2; a three-page typed report circulated by the GARBC; *Ketcham Papers.*
16. R. T. Ketcham dictated to Mary Ketcham (1946). Mrs. Ketcham's handwritten copy is in the *Ketcham Papers.*

Mrs. Robert Ketcham

Dr. and Mrs. Robert Ketcham

Harry Ketcham, Grace Ketcham Canavan,
Robert Ketcham—Roulette, Pennsylvania, 1961

IN THE TWILIGHT of his life, Dr. Ketcham's activities were limited by his physical condition. Though seldom able to preach, his love for his Lord knew no boundaries. His final messages were delivered from a stool. One of his last messages was in 1974 in Grand Rapids, Michigan, at the annual Bible conference of the Grand Rapids Baptist College. On Friday, February 22, he preached a message entitled "Declaring the Word of Truth." His text was Galatians 5:1: "Stand fast therefore in the liberty wherewith Christ hath made us free, and be not entangled again with the yoke of bondage." In defining liberty, Ketcham said, "Well, it means that something has been done to me which makes it possible for me to do something which I could not formerly do. Namely, obey Christ."

This was the key to Robert Ketcham's life. Liberty to him meant obedience. It was obedience to God that he sought to demonstrate in his home, in his life and in his ministry. Every morning around the breakfast table, the Ketcham family spent time in the Word of God. "At our house it was understood that if you did not have time for breakfast and devotions, you went without breakfast."[1]

This obedience to the way and will of God enabled Ketcham's

---

1. Donn Ketcham, *taped reflections,* n.d.

children to see a consistency in his life which they could not escape. On the basis of the example of their home, Lois and Donn entered Christian service. Both served on the mission field, though Lois's time was limited. Nonetheless she remained in Christian service with her husband, Don Moffat. But for the third Ketcham child, the influence of a godly home was resisted. Margaret struggled spiritually for many years. Dr. and Mrs. Ketcham prayed for her daily and sought in every way they could to encourage and restore her. The influence of a godly home eventually paid dividends in her life. She returned to fellowship with God, and after doing so she sent her dad a Father's Day card. On it she penned a note that summarized not only her entire life, but also her father's:

TO MY FATHER

Who saw pitfalls and tried to guide me around
them (I fell in).

Who was there to pull me out, put me on my
feet and set me out to try again (I did,
and failed).

Who prayed always that I would see my need of
trusting in my Heavenly Father (I heard,
but did not listen).

Who practiced what he preached—leaving no
question that His way was the better way
(I saw, and could not deny).

Who has lived to rejoice with me, that now we
are truly daughter and father in the bonds
of the loving care of Him who is *our*
Father (Thank God you persevered!)!

Peg 'o your heart

Ketcham sensed that he was nearing the end of his life. In response to a birthday telegram from Donn and Kitty in 1972, Ketcham wrote: "As I go a little closer to the end of my journey, I am so thankful for what God allowed me to have to present to Him at the throne someday. There is my precious son and his family. There is Lois and her wonderful husband. There is the tremendous woman of God, Peg, who is the darling returned to her Heavenly Father and to her earthly one. Thank You, dear Lord, for what You have given to this old man."[2]

During the last few years of his life, it was increasingly difficult for Bob Ketcham to leave home, though he loved to go to God's house and listen to the Word when possible. But in the quietness of their home, Dr. and Mrs. Ketcham continued a ministry which had been theirs for over a half century: the ministry of prayer. They prayed for their children and for the people in the local congregation. They prayed for the missionaries and for the pastors in the Association. "Over and over I have heard Dr. Ketcham pray, especially on Saturday, for the pastors in our Fellowship all across this land. He prays that they will not go into their pulpits discouraged and defeated, but that they will go with the realization they have the power only the Lord Jesus Christ can give. He prays that they will always exalt the Lord and show Him forth."[3] High on Ketcham's prayer list were the 608 people who had been called into Christian service during his years of ministry. He greatly cherished this statistic. He prayed much for those people and for others around the world who served his Lord.

On December 19, 1976, Dr. Ketcham suffered a severe stroke. After thirty-five days in the hospital, he was able to return to his apartment, but the stroke had affected his whole body, including his speech. He became dependent on a walker or a quad cane. His memory was affected for a time, but to a certain extent came back to him. By late 1977 it was no longer possible for him to leave his Chicago apartment.

On June 30, 1978, he experienced another severe stroke and became almost helpless. The second stroke affected his limbs and throat. He could not swallow without choking, and his efforts to speak were ineffective. He was in Swedish Covenant Hospital in Chicago for almost a month, after which he was moved to an extended care facility.

Though communication was almost impossible, Mary Ketcham stood daily vigil with her beloved husband as long as the hospital permitted. He knew she was there, but could not speak. She thought

2. R. T. Ketcham to Donn Ketcham, July 31, 1972; *Ketcham Papers.*
3. Ruth Ryburn, *taped reflections,* n.d.

of his many hospitalizations and realized that the conclusion of this one would be different. On Sunday, August 20, Mrs. Ketcham, accompanied by Ruth Ryburn, returned to the hospital. Her husband's condition was unchanged. But on Monday morning, August 21, hospital officials urged her to come immediately. She was taken to the hospital by a neighbor. By the time she arrived, Bob Ketcham had been ushered into the presence of his Lord. As she looked down at him, her sorrow was mingled with a peace that "passeth understanding" as she saw contentment and radiance on his face. She knew her husband was where he longed to be. He no longer faced the limitations of his earthly body. He was with his Lord, and in the face of his beloved Savior he had found the reward of obedience.

Within hours, Joseph M. Stowell, National Representative of the General Association of Regular Baptist Churches, had sent a letter to pastors throughout the nation informing them of the funeral arrangements. The service was held at the Belden Regular Baptist Church in Niles, Illinois. (This was the church which had hosted the first meeting of the General Association of Regular Baptist Churches. Though urban renewal had forced it out of the city of Chicago and into the suburban area, Ketcham remained a part of that historic church.)

Members of the Council of Eighteen of the General Association of Regular Baptist Churches and friends from throughout the nation gathered to pay their respects to this great warrior in the cause of truth. It was a dreary, cloudy day, but Robert Ketcham's funeral service was one of joy and triumph. God's servant had gone to his reward.

In speaking for the General Association of Regular Baptist Churches, Dr. Joseph Stowell paid tribute to Ketcham as a man of God:

> He was a warrior at the battlefront for truth. He stood solidly for the Scriptural teaching for separation from liberalism, and was one of the great hearts in the fundamentalist-modernist war. Yet in the midst of that, he was different from some other leaders.
>
> First of all, in his ministry, even in the heat of the battle, he hardly preached a sermon but what the Savior was lifted up and the glory of the cross, the wonder of the redemptive work of Christ was foremost. And when some others might have been bitter and harsh and unrelenting, there was a fiber of warmth and heartfelt spirituality about his preaching. He was a man with a great heart of sympathy for human beings. He related to people. His sermons evidenced that.

Beyond that he differed from many great leaders in that the preacher of the smallest church always had access to him. He was willing to sit down with the least among us. Further, if you felt he was wrong, he would listen carefully to what you had to say. And if he sensed you were right, he would change.

Many leaders are unrelenting. They have the attitude, "I am right. I will not change." That was not characteristic of our dear brother. And that is really the heart of greatness. But when he had learned what was right and was convinced of it, he could not be deterred. There was not an ounce of compromise in him. There was no giving in when his convictions were settled.[4]

In his message, Dr. John Balyo said, "He was a great man, one of God's tall men. And today there is a great empty space against the sky."[5] In an editorial, Ketcham's longtime friend and associate, Merle Hull reflected: "If institutions are indeed lengthened shadows of men, then the shadow of Dr. Ketcham would be the clearest of all those represented in our Association. No other man stands out as prominently in the total record of our Fellowship."[6]

Bob Ketcham never wanted such honors for himself. Several years earlier, following his heart attack in 1959, Ketcham had prepared a three-page document with a suggested order for his funeral. He indicated that he had no desire to be eulogized. He wanted his service to tell for Christ. Through his life he had attempted to live in obedience to the command of God. His one, all-pervading desire was to fulfill the principle of Colossians 1:18: ". . . That in all things he might have the preeminence." Thus, in his mind there was but one fitting epitaph to his life. It was found in the opening words of Ephesians 2:4 —

"BUT GOD"

4. Joseph M. Stowell, "God's Hand Was Upon Him," *The Baptist Bulletin,* XLIV (October 1978), 10.

5. John G. Balyo, "Lead Me to the Rock," *The Baptist Bulletin,* XLIV (October 1978), 9.

6. Merle R. Hull, "Editorials," *The Baptist Bulletin,* XLIV (October 1978), 7.

Margaret Ketcham Yover

Don and Lois Moffat

Donn and Kitty Ketcham

Appendixes

A Chronology of Events

July 22,	1889: Robert Thomas Ketcham born in Nelson, Pennsylvania
	1896: Death of Ketcham's mother
March	1898: Ketcham's father married Louise Elliot
	1900: Ketcham family moved to Galeton, Pennsylvania
	1905: Ketcham's "unscheduled" trip from home which interrupted his education
	1910: Publication of *The Fundamentals*
February 16,	1910: Robert's salvation experience in the Galeton Baptist Church
September 22,	1912: Ketcham began pastorate, First Baptist Church, ← Roulette, Pennsylvania
August 30,	1913: Ketcham went to Philadelphia for treatment of eye problem
January 12,	1915: Ketcham ordained at the First Baptist Church of Roulette
July	1915: Ketcham began pastorate, First Baptist Church, ← Brookville, Pennsylvania
	1916: Formation of the World's Christian Fundamentals Association
November	1918: Flu epidemic; Ketcham spent two months in bed
January	1919: Ketcham began pastorate, First Baptist Church, ← Butler, Pennsylvania
	1919: Northern Baptist Convention launched New World Movement
	1919: Ketcham published pamphlet against the New World Movement
	1920: Meeting of fundamentalists prior to the Northern Baptist Convention conference; formation of National Federation of Fundamentalists of the Northern Baptists

	1920:	Deaths of Robert's cousin, grandmother, wife (Clara) and father
June	1922:	Ketcham married Mary Smart
	1922:	Indianapolis convention of the Northern Baptist Convention; fundamentalists decided to form a permanent structure
May 10-15,	1923:	First conference of Baptist Bible Union of America held in Kansas City, Missouri
May 14,	1923:	Ketcham addressed the Baptist Bible Union
	1923:	Ketcham began pastorate, First Baptist Church, Niles, Ohio
	1925:	Seattle convention of the Northern Baptist Convention; the final great effort of fundamentalism within the Convention
	1926:	Baptist Bible Union formed its own mission agency
	1926:	Ketcham began pastorate, First Baptist Church, Elyria, Ohio
	1927:	Northern Baptist Convention meeting in Chicago; fundamentalists prepared Foreign Mission Board ballot and were defeated
	1927:	Michigan Baptist Bible Union formed completely independent Union of Regular Baptist Churches
	1928:	H. O. Van Gilder, Earle Griffith and Ketcham decided to withdraw from the Northern Baptist Convention; formed Ohio Association of Independent Baptist Churches at Central Baptist Church, Columbus; Hebron Association of Churches formed in Elyria
May	1929:	Student riot forced closing of Des Moines University (operated by the Baptist Bible Union)
	1931:	Ketcham received honorary doctorate from Los Angeles Baptist Theological Seminary
May	1932:	34 delegates met at Belden Avenue Baptist Church—last meeting of Baptist Bible Union; first meeting of General Association of Regular Baptist Churches
	1932:	Ketcham began pastorate, Central Baptist Church, Gary, Indiana
January	1933:	*The Bulletin* first issued; H. G. Hamilton, editor

May	1933:	Second meeting of GARBC; Ketcham made vice-president
	1934:	GARBC met in Gary; constitution, bylaws and confession of faith adopted; Ketcham elected president
	1935:	Ketcham reelected president
	1936:	Ketcham reelected president
	1937:	Ketcham reelected president
November	1937:	Don and Lois Moffat left for Brazil
January—June	1938:	Ketcham took leave of absence from Gary church to travel for the GARBC
April	1938:	GARBC reorganized; Council of Fourteen established
July	1938:	Lois stricken with beriberi; Ketcham became editor of *The Baptist Bulletin*
August 27,	1938:	Lois arrived in Norfolk
March 10,	1939:	Son born to Lois and Don Moffat
September	1939:	Ketcham began pastorate, Walnut Street Baptist Church, Waterloo, Iowa
	1942:	Formation of the American Council of Christian Churches
Fall	1944:	H. O. Van Gilder became the first National Representative; offices rented in the Manhattan Building, Chicago; Ruth Ryburn became secretary
September	1944:	Ketcham became president of ACCC
January	1945:	Van Gilder became editor of *The Baptist Bulletin*
January	1946:	Ketcham's first corneal transplant
March	1946:	Two more eye surgeries to save the transplant
May	1946:	Third surgery to save the transplant
Fall	1946:	Second corneal transplant
January and May	1947:	Meetings between Regular Baptists and Convention Fundamentalists
	1948:	Conservative Baptist Association formed
October	1948:	Ketcham became National Representative and editor of *The Baptist Bulletin*
	1949:	Publication of Ketcham's *The Answer*
December	1949:	The Smethport case
	1950:	Establishment of the Baptist Builders' Club and Regular Baptist Press
	1952:	RBP moved to Hayward, California
	1953:	Publication of Ketcham's *I Shall Not Want*

	1954: RBP moved to Dayton, Ohio; Mr. and Mrs. Hull added to the staff
	1955: All offices consolidated in Transportation Building, Chicago; Merle Hull became editor of *The Baptist Bulletin*
May	1959: Ketcham suffered major heart attack
June	1960: Ketcham resigned as National Representative and was succeeded by Paul R. Jackson; Ketcham became National Consultant
	1961: Ketcham awarded honorary doctorate by Bob Jones University
September 23-30,	1962: Fiftieth anniversary Bible conference, Roulette, Pennsylvania
June	1963: Donn and Kitty Ketcham go to Bangladesh as missionaries
January	1965: Association offices moved to Des Plaines, Illinois
June	1966: Ketcham retired as National Consultant
November—December	1966: Ketchams and Ruth Ryburn take Far East trip
November	1969: Joseph M. Stowell became National Representative
December 9,	1976: Ketcham suffered major stroke
December 27,	1976: Association offices moved to Schaumburg, Illinois
June 30,	1978: Ketcham suffered second major stroke
August 21,	1978: Ketcham died
August 24,	1978: Ketcham's funeral

DID YOU LEAVE SOMETHING ON THE STAIRS?
Robert T. Ketcham

(A message first delivered in 1949 in Cleveland at the annual conference of the General Association of Regular Baptist Churches.)

Did you leave something on the stairs?

Please read the second chapter of the Song of Solomon. This book is so often misunderstood. It is unjustly and unfairly criticized for some of its language. When you understand this book, your basis for any criticism of it immediately goes out the window. The Song of Solomon is very largely a dialogue between the lover and his beloved, the bridegroom and his bride. It is intended to show in the most intimate terms the blessed fellowship and relationship between the Lord Jesus Christ as the Bridegroom and the Church which is His Bride. Naturally there are intimate statements made, but they are perfectly in order when you consider that it is the Bridegroom and His Bride who are speaking. Sometimes the dialogue is a bit difficult to follow. It slows up in places, and in other places it steps up its tempo. Sometimes I am not dead sure which one is doing the speaking. For instance, the opening verse says, "I am the rose of Sharon, and the lily of the valleys." I know tradition has said that it is Christ speaking, but I am not so sure but what it might be the Bride speaking.

May I give you an outline of my message? I want to speak about the Position of the Church, the Possession of the Church, the Product of the Church and the Peril of the Church. The Church's Position, Possession, Product and Peril.

Let us first examine the position of the Bride of Christ, the Church. According to the fourteenth verse of the second chapter, the Bride has a twofold position. She dwells in the clefts of the rock and in the secret places of the stairs. It is the secret places of the stairs that I am particularly interested in.

However, I cannot get the consent of my conscience to pass over without some comment (even though it is very limited) about that first position of the

Bride. She is in the clefts of the rock. This Hebrew word *rock* lives in beauty and warmth and glows with infinite and precious spiritual significance.

Let me give you just one illustration. In the seventeenth chapter of the Book of Exodus, the Israelites came up to a place in the wilderness where there was no water. People and herds were in danger of dying of thirst. And so a complaint committee went up to the Reverend Doctor Moses, pastor of the First Baptist (or Presbyterian) Church of the Wilderness, and entered a complaint. The Board of Deacons, the Board of Trustees, the Christian Education Committee and the Ladies Aid Society all joined in. They said, "Now this is a pretty fix. You brought us out here to kill us. You brought us out here to die. Here we are—no water—we're going to die."

There is one thing I like about dear old Brother Moses. He didn't resign. You know—it doesn't take any backbone to resign and fold up like a piece of wet spaghetti.

Moses took it to the Lord. That's a good thing to do. He said, "Now what am I supposed to do?" And the Lord answered, "That is very simple, Moses. That's easily fixed. You just take your rod and strike that rock out there, and it will all be fixed."

So Moses took that trusty old rod that he had used to split an ocean of water wide open, and a lot of other things, and he went out and struck the rock—and the water flowed. It was a sizable river too. I think it was that river that the Amalekites were after in this same seventeenth chapter. It was so big they wanted it. At any rate, the water flowed, and everyone got their drink. The flocks got their water, and that was that.

Then in the twentieth chapter of Numbers, the same thing happened again. I rather doubt if it was in the same place—I don't believe it was. But it was the same situation. Flocks and herds and people were going to die of thirst if they didn't get a drink. They had no water. So the committee waited on the pastor again, and this time the Reverend Doctor Moses got just a little irate. I don't blame him. He went to the Lord again, and the Lord said, "Moses, that is easily fixed. Just speak to the rock."

Moses still had not quite cooled down. He was still angry, and instead of speaking to the rock, he gave it a whack with that rod of his. Again the water flowed, and the people got a drink—so did the livestock. But Moses got spanked and put to bed for that little fit of temper. The Lord said, "Now you just come on up here. You'll never take the people into the Promised Land. You disobeyed. You did not do it the way I told you to do it. In grace, I am going to let the men, women, boys and girls and the livestock have the water, but I am not going to let you lead the people into the Promised Land because you didn't do what I told you to do. I told you to speak to the rock, and you smote it with the rod."

Every Bible student knows that these two rocks are beautiful, beautiful types of our lovely Lord: first, in His humiliation, and second, in the fact that He has been crucified *once,* and you do not have to bring Him down and have Him crucified all over again. He is *the Rock.* Paul says that rock was

Christ—that is, it was a figurative Christ, a type of Christ. The first time the rock had to be smitten. And so in order to get the rivers of salvation, our Lord had to come down from the Glory and be smitten upon Calvary, and the waters of salvation flowed.

Now the second time it happened, all that was necessary was to speak to the rock. Whenever a sinner gets saved, he doesn't have to put in an application and wait for the Lord Jesus to come down and be crucified again before he can be saved. All a sinner has to do is *speak,* and immediately the river of salvation is his because the Rock was smitten once.

Moses spoiled that beautiful type by striking the rock the second time. Christ died *once,* and because of that all we have to do is speak to Him, and He will hear us and save us. "Once in the end of the world [age] hath he appeared to put away sin by the sacrifice of himself" (Heb. 9:26). Moses, in anger, spoiled that beautiful type by his disobedience.

The word translated "rock" in Exodus 17 is a word which means a low, submerged rock. It is not a little stone. It is a mammoth rock, but most of it is covered with earth, and you only see a little of it. It is embedded in the uncomfortable environment around it. That is the rock that was smitten. How beautiful the picture of our lovely Lord! We read in Philippians that he "being in the form of God, thought it not robbery to be equal with God: But made himself of no reputation, and took upon him the form of a servant, and was made in the likeness of men" (2:6, 7). He did not lay aside His deity—only the form of it. He was found in form and fashion as a man, "and became obedient unto death, even the death of the cross" (2:8). There He was—God incarnate—walking this earth, and men were calling Him the Devil incarnate. Even today men in some seminaries still say that He was the son of a blond, German soldier. Nels Ferré, a professor in Andover Newton, an American Baptist Seminary, says that you cannot deny that Jesus was born of Mary, but that His father was a blond German soldier. Well, I *can* deny it, and I *do* deny it!

What humbling! He looked like any other man. Isaiah said, "There is no beauty that we should desire him" (53:2). Think of it! He, Who was high above the heavens, came down in the form of a man to look things over on His earth, and He was dealt with by His people as though He were a sinner. In fact, God, His Father, dealt with Him in His substitutionary position for us as though He were a sinner, counting that our sins were on Him, and God put Him to death. There He is—the humbled Rock, the embedded Rock, the submerged Rock—surrounded by all the dirt of the world.

The definition of the word translated "rock" in this passage is exactly that. However, in Numbers 20, when you again run on to that word *rock,* it is a different word. The word translated "rock" in the Numbers passage is the word which means a high, lofty, craggy, towering height. Here again, how beautifully fitting is the type. The Rock that was smitten for you and me, the humbled Christ, the despised, the lowly One, the One whose glory was hidden, was smitten. But in the Philippians passage He became obedient unto death. Therefore God highly exalted Him and gave Him a name which is above every name, that at the name of Jesus every knee should bow, and every tongue shall confess that Jesus Christ is Lord, to the glory of God the Father (2:8-11). There He is—the great, towering, rocky, craggy height—and He is the One you speak to. How beautiful is this word!

Does anyone wish to guess which one of these Hebrew words is in that fourteenth verse: Oh, my dove, my fair one, that dwelleth in the clefts of the rock? "Rock of ages, cleft for me. Let me hide myself in Thee." If you are a believer, you are there in the risen, exalted, glorified Christ in the Glory. You are in Christ Jesus. You are down in the rocky cleft, hidden from all possibility of attack.

Back in Isaiah you have it again: "He shall dwell on high: his place of defence shall be the munitions of rocks: bread shall be given him; his waters shall be sure" (33:16). That word rock is the one for towering, craggy heights. You are sure of your sustenance up there. When you are in Christ Jesus, you don't have to get outside. Do you know why? All you have to do is speak to the Rock and it becomes bread—the Bread of life. All you have to do is speak to the Rock—and it becomes the Water of life. Your munitions of rock is Christ—He is your Bread and your Water. What a blessing!

That is one of the Church's positions. Now for the one we want to discuss in particular. The text says she dwelleth "in the secret places of stairs." Stairs—that is an interesting word. What are stairs for? The better translation here is "dwelleth in the secret ascending places." But whether it is ascending places or stairs, the word secret is there. Stairs—what are they good for? Well, you're down here and you want to get up there, so you have to have a stairway. A stairway is a way of exit.

He says that His beloved lives in the secret places of these ascending stairs. I think this is a reference to her daily communion. When I say "her," I mean each individual member of the Body of Christ. Each has a private stair. It's this place of communion and fellowship with your precious Lord Jesus that He is speaking of here.

There are still some old-fashioned houses left, but if they keep on building ranch houses, I am going to run out of illustrations. In most of these old houses there are two stairways. There is one in the front of the house, and it is lovely. There's a twenty-eight or thirty-two-foot-wide front room, and over on one end, sweeping up in a lovely symmetrical curve, is the ivory painted stairway with its polished mahogany rail, reaching to the second floor. Those stairs are so spotless you could eat your dinner off of them. They are polished and swept and scrubbed and rubbed and mopped. The reason for that is that they are the ones all of your company sees. When the pastor comes to call, that is the stairway he sees. Oh, isn't it lovely! When you have overnight guests, that's the stairway you use to take them up to their bedroom. You're so proud of it! It's beautiful, and you keep it clean as a hound's tooth.

But there is another stairway that goes up out of the kitchen. That's your own private stairway. That's the one you use to run up and down. You never take the preacher out there and take him up those stairs. You never take your overnight company up those back kitchen stairs.

Now I want to ask you—did you leave something on those stairs? Those private stairs of yours? Dad has gotten up and gone to work, and the kids have gone to school. You, Mother, are trying to get the morning work done. You're running the Hoover in the dining room, and it hits something. It goes rolling and bangs up against the wall. You retrieve it and discover it is a marble. Johnny left a marble on the floor, and it doesn't belong there. It belongs upstairs in Johnny's marble bag in his room. Well, you're not going upstairs just yet; so you open the back kitchen door and lay the marble on the steps, and say, "I'll take it up when I go."

You get your old Hoover going again in the front room, and something goes clickety-click. You look down and there is Susie's little lead pencil. She laid it there and forgot it. It doesn't belong down here—it belongs upstairs in Susie's room in her pencil box. You're not going upstairs just yet, but you'll take it when you go. So you open the kitchen door and lay it on the steps and shut the door.

Then you get around to vacuuming Dad's den, and there are his slippers and lounging robe which he should have taken upstairs; but he didn't. Soon you'll be going upstairs, but not just now, so on the back stairs they go. So goes everything else you find. You finish your dustmopping and your sweeping, but you're not going upstairs to use them just yet—you have some other things to do. So you open the back kitchen door and put the Hoover and dustmop there on the stairs. There they all are. "I'll take them up when I go," you say.

You go over to the sink and start washing the dishes. You're in water and detergent clear up to your elbows. All of a sudden you hear a familiar cry from upstairs. Little Junior has stood up in his crib, and you know he has learned how to lift the little latch on the side. The side of his crib has dropped down, and he has fallen out and broken his neck—maybe. "I've got to get up there. I've got to get up there! He is yelling bloody murder—I've got to get up there." You rinse the suds off, yank that door open, take a step and start up. The ball of your foot hits that marble, and you go flat on your pretty little nose on about the fourth step. Your knee bumps on the first step, and you're all banged up. That little tyke is still yelling. "I guess his neck isn't broken—he can still yell, but he is hurt. I have to get up there. I have to get up there." So—you get up on your feet and take another step, and this time your foot lands on that little rolling lead pencil. And down you go again! This time you really do hurt yourself. You cut your lip and skin your knee and get runners in your stockings. While you are trying to undo yourself and get up, you knock the sweeper and dustmop over, and one bangs you on one side and the other bangs you on the other side. You're all banged up and in a real mess. There was an emergency at the top of the steps, and you had to get there—but you couldn't because you had left something on the stairs. You couldn't get through.

Now I want to talk to you about your own *private* stair. That is, your back stair, you know. I am not talking about your public stair—the one you take to prayer meeting with you. I am not talking about the public stair that you take to your Sunday school class with you. I'm not talking about your public stair that you take into your pulpit with you. I am not talking about that showcase stair that you have. That one is as clean as a hound's tooth. Everyone looks at you and they say, "Oh, my, what a lovely Christian," because they don't see anything else. I am asking about that private stair. "Thou that dwellest in the secret stair"—that secret place which you and you alone use. No one else has access to it. It is *your* stairway—it's not mine. I have one of my own.

Every believer has a secret stair in his life which he can use to reach the Lord Jesus Christ and have fellowship and blessed communion with Him. It's *your* secret stair. I can't go up and down your stair. You can't go up and down mine. The only stair you can go up and down for access and intercession and fellowship with the Lord Jesus Christ is your own. It's the secret stair. It is not even the stair that you use in morning devotions with your family. It is not the stair you use when someone drops in and says, "Let's have a word of prayer." The stair I am talking about, my brother and my sister, is that stair that you use when there is absolutely no one there but you and Jesus Christ. It's the place where you do not have to pay particular attention to nicely formed phrases and get all of your nouns, pronouns, verbs, adverbs and split infinitives in the right place. All you have to do is open the secret place of your heart and talk to the Lord Jesus Christ, and He talks to you. This life of personal fellowship and communion with the Lord Jesus Christ is what I am talking about.

Now, did you leave something on your stair which is going to impede your use of it? You see, you do not know when you are going to need it. There is an emergency. Something has happened, and you want to get up that stair and pillow your head on the bosom of the Lord Jesus Christ and sob your heart out to Him. You race to the stair, and you can't get up. Why? Because you have left unconfessed and unjudged sin on it. Under divine inspiration, the psalmist declares: "If I regard iniquity in my heart, the Lord will not hear me" (66:18).

Our churches are full to overflowing of real, born-again Christians who have the silly notion that they can play along with known sin in their lives. God has spoken to you about the cigarette habit. He has spoken to you about this business of running off to "good" movies. He has spoken to you about that gossipy tongue of yours. He has spoken to you about a lot of little things in your life. No, no, no—they are not baby elephants. They are little foxes. It is not huge, big packing boxes that you have on the back stairs. It is just a little marble. It's a very small thing. You say, "Well, I know it is just a little thing, and I will take care of it someday."

And then before that someday comes, you need that stairway in a hurry.

The doorbell rings, and the Western Union boy is standing there. He hands you a telegram. You open it and read: "Dad and Mother killed in an auto accident today." Or it may be a telegram from Uncle Sam saying, "Regret to inform you that your son was killed in action." You want to get up there to Jesus Christ, and you want to get up there in a hurry. And you know the only stair you can use is your private, secret one. You take a run for it—and there they are—all those little hindrances that you put there and didn't take care of. You are trying and trying to get up, and the Lord is saying, "If you regard iniquity in your heart, I can't hear you. I have been talking to you about these things which displease Me, and you haven't changed one thing. You have not paid one bit of attention to it." You say, "Oh, I know I ought not to do this, and I ought not to do that. I ought to quit this gossiping and backbiting. I ought to stop. Someday I will. Someday I will." And that is all you have said. You have not taken those things off the stairway and there they are. You can't get up. "If you regard iniquity in your heart, I can't hear you." He not only can't—He won't.

Have you left something on the stairs? I don't mean great, open, bold sin. I am not talking about the things everyone would see on your front stairs. I am talking about that sin in your life that nobody but you sees. No one in the world knows what is on that back stair in your life except you and the Lord. That is the one I am talking about. Have you some unjudged and unconfessed sin there on that secret place of access into the presence of the Lord Jesus where you can go for fellowship and communion?

When I was a young fellow in the old Baptist church in Galeton, Pennsylvania, we had a deacon whose name was Earl Playfoot. He was quite a young man, and I remember him giving this testimony one night in prayer meeting: "I've had a real shaking experience this week. God has really shaken me to pieces." He continued, "Right across the street from me lived a man named Bill. He was not saved. I had talked to him several times about the Savior. Night before last (about one o'clock in the morning) my doorbell rang. I answered it, and there was his wife. She said, 'Mr. Playfoot, Bill is dying. The doctor is there and says he can live just a short time. He is asking for you. He wanted me to ask you to come over and pray with him and tell him about Jesus. Will you come?' Why, of course I'll come.

"Bill's wife went back home, and I went upstairs to dress. While I was dressing, the Lord said, 'Now, son, what are you going to do over there?' I am going to talk to Bill and pray for him that he might be saved. 'Son, do you remember about seven months ago you let a sin come into your life, and you have played with it ever since? Every time you have come to pray and talk with Me, I have put My finger on that thing, and told you to take it out of your life. Thus far you have refused to do it. Son, it has been seven or eight months since you have had contact with Me. Oh, you have said words; you prayed in prayer meeting, and you even supplied the pulpit one Sunday for the preacher. But your private stair—you had some iniquity on it that I was talking to you about, and you refused to do anything about it, Earl. And since you have regarded iniquity in your heart, I can't hear you.'

In the emergency I knew I had to do something. So I knelt down beside my bed and wrestled with the Lord, and He with me. Finally, after at least a half hour, instead of battling this thing, I said, 'Lord, Lord, I give it up. I confess it and put it away. Now use me.' I went across the street and rang the bell. Bill's wife came to the door sobbing, 'Oh, Mr. Playfoot, where have you been? What took you so long? Bill died just ten minutes ago.' "

Do you hear what I am saying to you, Christian? You cannot afford to have your secret stair—your place of contact with and access to the Lord Jesus Christ—all cluttered up with a lot of little things. Little things, little marbles, little pencils that can throw you. You don't know when you are going to have to get up there in a hurry. It may be this very day for some of you.

You may get a sudden call, informing you of the death of a loved one. Do you have a quick place of access to the comforting heart of your Savior? Are your stairs clean? When the calamity falls, will you have to remove a sweeper, a dustmop, marbles, pencils and so forth from your spiritual stairway before you can go and lay your head on the heart of Jesus Christ and be comforted? Did you leave something on your stairs?

These stairs are very interesting. The Lord Jesus Christ wants us to use this secret stair by ourselves—not in company with anyone else. Each has his own. He wants us to come to this stairway where we can have access to and communion with Him for some definite, specific reason. He is saying: "Thou that dwellest in the secret places of the stair, let Me see thy countenance, let Me hear thy voice; for thy countenance is comely and thy voice is sweet. Oh, my dear child, I have bought you with My precious blood; you are so precious to Me. You mean more to Me than all the earth. Come to the stair. Just lift your face and let Me look at it. Speak, speak to Me. Talk to Me in prayer."

There is a passage in Revelation 8 which sets forth a precious principle. When the incense was being offered which the Word specifically says was the prayers of the saints, God just stopped every angel—right in the middle of a measure of music, perhaps—and asked for a period of silence while He listened to the prayers of His people. The sweetest sound in Heaven today is not the angels singing, "Holy, holy, holy, Lord God almighty." The sweetest sound in Heaven is not the twitter of birds. No, no—the sweetest sound in Heaven is when one of His blood-bought, born-again ones comes to his own private stair and talks with Him up there. Oh, how sweet! "Thy voice is sweet."

You may have a face as homely as a mud fence after an eight-day rain—I don't know. But you are the most beautiful thing in all His universe to Jesus Christ. To Him, you are more beautiful than all those angels. The angels didn't cost Him anything. All He had to do was speak, and they were there. But to get you, He had to die—He had to suffer. He loves you so. Oh, how He loves you! He longs to talk with you and have you talk with Him. He longs to hear your voice. He longs to see your face so He can have fellowship with you. He says: "Come away, my dove. My fair one, come, come, come to the secret places of the stairs. Let's have some sweet and wonderful fellowship." That is one reason. But there is also another reason. There is transformation. Looking unto Him, we are changed from glory to glory, image to image, until we become more and more like Him.

There is still another important thing about these stairs. I think He wants you to come to this stairway for the purpose of rebuke. When I was a young fellow, my father ran a milk route in Galeton, Pennsylvania, and I helped him deliver the milk. In those days I liked to read what they called "Diamond Dicks"—Nick Carter, Buffalo Bill, Frank Merrywell and so forth. They cost a nickel apiece, and they were taboo in Deacon Ketcham's household. None of that blood-and-thunder stuff was allowed around there.

But the deacon had a son who liked them, and there was only one drugstore in town that sold them. Every day on the milk route I would finagle so that Dad would take the left-hand side of Main Street, and I would take the right-hand side where the drugstore was located. When I delivered the milk there, I would buy one of those blood-and-thunder books. So that Dad wouldn't see it, I would raise my jersey sweater, stick the book in it, pull the sweater down over it, and go on with the rest of the morning's delivery of milk.

The first thing I did after I got home would be to run upstairs to my bedroom and put Diamond Dick under the mattress. Then at night I would go to bed, blow out the light and be as still as a church mouse. I would wait until I was sure everyone else was in bed. (I recognized everyone's snore.) When I was sure everyone was asleep, I'd sneak out and light the old oil lamp, pull Dick out from under the mattress, and read. I could read the book in about forty-five minutes. I didn't dare leave Diamond Dick lying around because Dad would come to my room about four-thirty every morning to call me to get up and help with the chores. And he'd see to it that I did! So I would put Dick under the mattress again. Then when I dressed in the morning I would stick the book in my sweater again. We had one of those big, pot-bellied stoves in the front room. When I came downstairs, I would step over to the stove, pull Diamond Dick out of my sweater and toss him into the fire and let him burn up.

One morning I forgot Dick. It is as vivid as though it were yesterday. My mother had a routine. She would get up when the rest of us did and eat her breakfast. Then she would prepare ours. We would have buckwheat pancakes. I'm not talking about those cartwheels that you can roll down an aisle. They won't fold up, and they are so thick and tough. No sir—I am talking about the old-fashioned, homemade buckwheat pancakes that you could hold up to the light and see through them. We also had homemade sausage, sliced in thick slices and browned to a crisp, and our own homemade maple syrup. Boy! Mother made a huge stack of those delicious pancakes with a big platter of sausage, and Harry and Dad and I would come in. She would pour our coffee, and we'd get started. Then, while we were eating, Mother would go upstairs to make the beds.

I will never forget that awful morning. I was eating and heard a sweet, little voice say, "Robert, come here."

"Dad, give me some more pancakes, please. Put on some more sausage."

"Robert."

"I want some more cakes, Dad."

"Robert!"

"Son, do you hear your mother calling you?"

"Oh, was she?"

Then I got up and got started. It was like trying to walk seven miles right down the middle of a freeway! My feet dragged as though each one of them was carrying a 150-pound weight. I dragged them over to the foot of the stairs. There I stood. Mother was up at the top. She said, "Look up here, Robert." I couldn't look up. "Robert, look up here!!!" Oh, how I dreaded to look, for I knew what I would see. I would see the sweetest little mother standing at the head of the stairs with that red, ugly book in her hand, with tears streaming down her cheeks.

Did you leave something on the stairs which the Lord Jesus Christ found? You know what it is. Don't tell me what it is. I don't care. Did you leave something on the stairs that the Lord told you to get rid of? He found it, and He is calling you by name right now: "Joe, Pete, Kate, Susie, Bill. Come here. Come here." You know what He wants. You know jolly well what He wants. He has found that thing in your life, and He wants to talk with you about it. He wants to rebuke you and cleanse you and get it out of the way so He can hear your voice and see your face.

Now, look in your Bibles and notice the construction of this passage. I have already dealt with the Bride's position and her possession. She has a lovely voice and a lovely face. I am not going to deal with her product. You know what the product of a Christian should be. You know that without my telling you. It ought to be other Christians.

I want to make a short comment on the Bride's peril. Verse 15 says: "Take us the foxes, the little foxes, that spoil the vines." Note that it is the *little* foxes. It isn't great big public sins. No sir. Your public stairway looks to everyone around you as though it is clean. They think that your back stair is clean, too, and it isn't; and you know it isn't. Christ knows it, and He says, "Come here." He holds it before you—and may God give you grace. You don't have to walk the aisle of your church. Right where you are you can say, "Lord Jesus, it's gone. I give it away. I give it up."

I don't know what it is. Perhaps it is bitterness in your heart about somebody. Perhaps there is someone in your church you won't speak to. Perhaps there is someone you like to "dig" all the time. These are evil habits. I don't care what it is. If it is iniquity, the Lord won't hear you. He has found it in your life, and you haven't had fellowship with Him. You have said prayers a yard long, and He never heard a word because you haven't dealt with known, unconfessed sin in your life.

Now let us look at the little foxes. Read verses 14 and 16 and skip verse 15. The Word says: "O my dove, that art in the clefts of the rock, in the secret places of the stairs, let me see thy countenance, let me hear thy voice; for sweet is thy voice and thy countenance is comely. . . . My beloved is mine, and I am his: he feedeth among the lilies." Isn't that a beautiful sequence? Here it is. Here is what it ought to be, and here is what it can be. The Lord is saying to you and to me: "My dove, my fair one, come away. Come to the secret places of the stairs. I just want to look at you. I just want to feast My eyes on you, My precious possession. I just want to look at you, and I want to hear you say something to me."

And you, the Bride, answer back: "My beloved is mine, and I am his." This does not refer to a sinner coming to the Lord. This refers to one who is already saved—coming in full, utter, complete and total abandonment and surrender to his or her Lord. This *ought* to be the response. He pleads, "Come, my dove, my fair one, come away. You that dwell in the clefts of the rocks, and you that dwell in the secret places of the stairs; let Me hear your voice, and let Me see your countenance; for your countenance is comely, and your voice is sweet." You, as an individual, can answer back, "My beloved is mine." You *can* say, "Jesus, all I am—body, soul, spirit, time, substance, talent, will, plans, purposes, ideas, opinions—are all yours. Whatever I am, whatever I have, dear Lord, is yours." Isn't that a sweet relationship?

But you see, it is broken. I left out verse 15 which says, "Take us the foxes, the little foxes, that spoil the vines: for our vines have tender grapes." You cannot say verse 16 until you have done what verse 15 tells you to do. The Lord is crying in such pleading tones for you. In the dark days at the close of this apostate age, He is saying to those of you who do know Him, "Won't you come a little closer? I am getting so lonely. I am so lonesome to have some real fellowship with My own. Come, My dove."

But before you can say, "My beloved, you are mine, and all I have is thine," there are those little foxes on the stairs which have to be dealt with. There is no use kidding yourself now, brother or sister. With the back stair of your life all cluttered up with a bunch of junk, you come and say, "My beloved is mine and I am His," and you know it is not true. He saved you. You are His born-again child—but He doesn't possess you. He doesn't own you. He doesn't control you. You are not *all* His. Because of that, all He is and wants to be to you is not yours because there is a blockade. Oh, how sweet that was when you read it without verse 15, right?

Well, if that is the way you want it, then you will have to deal with verse 15. Dear heart, if this is the relationship you want with your lovely Lord, you will have to take care of the little foxes—those little unconfessed sins and rebellions that you haven't given up—those little surrenders that you won't make. No, I am not "unsaving" you. I am not "unchristianizing" you. But I am telling you that you are a sorrow to the heart of the One Who died for you.

Just now do you see Him standing at the top of your little, secret stairs with utter longing in His voice as He says: "My dove, My fair one, come. Come here. Let Me see your face. Let Me hear your voice." Oh, what longing there is in His heart to have fellowship with you and with me. How can we hurt His heart by not taking away the little foxes!

This portion of Scripture is rough medicine, but it is good for us. May the Lord help us to take our portion, whatever it may be, so that verse 15 can be left behind.

MEMORIAL SERVICE
for
Robert Thomas Ketcham
August 24, 1978
Belden Regular Baptist Church, Niles, Illinois
Pastor Gerald P. Safstrom, Officiating

ORGAN PRELUDE: Miss Gladys Hawkins

PASTOR SAFSTROM:
   We are met here today in memory of Dr. Robert T. Ketcham who some sixty years ago bowed to his sovereign Lord and said: "Lord, I have absolutely nothing to give you except obedience. That I can and will give You. What You will do with this absolutely useless vessel, I do not know. All I can do is obey. The rest of it is in Your sovereign hand." History has recorded much of the favor of God upon his life. Eternity will reveal the complete story of God's sovereign grace in the outworking of obedience. The words "but God" as stated by the apostle Paul in Ephesians chapter 2, verse 4, are the fitting epitaph to his life.
   If our beloved Dr. Ketcham were here today, he would no doubt pray thusly—and I quote from a message of his years ago: "Precious Savior, help these dear ones to find out something about Thyself which they could never have known apart from this experience." And we trust that this experience today will be a means to the end of knowing something more of the greatness and grace of our loving Lord.
   At this time, we're going to ask Dr. David Moore, pastor of Cedar Hill Baptist Church in Cleveland, Ohio, to read the Scripture.

DAVID MOORE:
   The whole Bible was Dr. Ketcham's Book, but we're choosing today to read just a few portions of Scripture that we believe express the great hope we have in Jesus Christ.
   (Portions of Scripture read were: Romans 8:14-39; 1 Corinthians 15:20-28, 51-58; 2 Timothy 4:1-8; Ephesians 6:10-18; Psalm 23.)

PASTOR SAFSTROM:

Dr. Ketcham was not only a faithful pastor, but for many years served in the capacity as National Representative and National Consultant to the General Association of Regular Baptist Churches. Our present National Representative is Dr. Joseph Stowell. We've asked him to come at this time and share a few words with us. Dr. Stowell.

DR. STOWELL:

It is my privilege to bring a tribute from our Association to our dear brother, Bob Ketcham, and to his family. This morning in *Daily Light*, the first words from the Scriptures that were given are these concerning our Lord: "He knoweth their sorrows." And isn't it wonderful that those of us who know Christ, even though we sorrow, sorrow not as others which have no hope? Our confidence is in Christ, and our upward look reminds us that the resurrection is coming, and the parting may not be long, and we will be united together again when our Lord appears in the sky at the rapture of the Church. What a wonderful reunion that will be! And it might be even yet today. That was the confidence in which our brother was put to sleep in Jesus, his body sealed now by the Holy Spirit, awaiting that glad morning when our Lord will come for His own and the saints go marching in.

I suppose that more than any other one man, Dr. Ketcham was responsible for the building of our Association. Now with more than fifteen hundred churches, it was his life and his heart, in the latter years of life. He gave his very best for it. He guided its direction and established it structure and was used of God to maintain its position, which still continues to this very hour.

It was my privilege to first meet Dr. Ketcham, I believe, in 1933 and be introduced to him. Some of you here have known him longer than that. But through all of these forty-five years, I have watched him, rejoiced in his testimony, reveled in his ministry and been greatly blessed by his counsel and his guidance. And as I think—even though he was a warrior at the battlefront for truth and stood solidly for the scriptural teaching for separation from liberalism and was one of the great hearts in the great fundamentalist-modernist war, in the midst of all that—he was different from some other leaders. I think of these wonderful things.

First of all, in his ministry, even in the heat of the battle, hardly a sermon was ever preached but what Christ was exalted and the Savior was lifted up and the glory of the cross, the wonder of the redemptive work of Christ, was foremost and at the very center. And after all, that's what it was all about. And when some others might have been bitter and harsh and unrelenting, there was a fiber of warmth and heartfelt spirituality about Doc's preaching. He was a man with a great sympathy for human beings, and he related to people. His sermons manifest and evidence that.

Beyond that, he differed from many great people—great leaders—in that the so-called smallest preacher always had access to him. He was willing to sit down and listen to the least among us. Further, if you felt he was wrong, he would listen carefully to what you had to say. And if he sensed you were right, he would change. Lots of leaders are so unrelenting. They have the attitude, "I am right. I'll not change." That was not characteristic of our dear brother. And that is really the heart of greatness—the wonderful ability that he had. But when he had learned what was right and was convinced of it, he could not be deterred. There was not an ounce of compromise in him. There was not an ounce of giving in when he knew for sure what was right. He was wonderful. God gave him a great gift and ability to preach.

Most of you know, he came from a very humble beginning—not a great deal of education. In the early days he was a rough railroader, he had told me. But when he was saved as a young man, that all changed, and it wasn't long until God called him to preach. His eyesight was bad. His education was minimal. And, as the pastor has indicated, it was his saying he had nothing to give to God but obedience—which he did.

In his first pastorate God wonderfully gave a great revival. His first baptismal service was some seventy people. And before he had finished in the brief span over two hundred had been baptized in the little tiny village with its small church. From the very outset, God's hand was upon him with fruit that remained all through the years.

And I suppose that if there is any one outstanding characteristic of his ministry above others it was his great heart for Christian missions. How many missionaries, I wonder, are there out on the field today who are there because they yielded their lives to Christ for service under the ministry of Bob Ketcham? I know! That great theme of missions in his life and ministry affected my own life and ministry and gave a pattern of great interest for Christian missions.

He served on the board of Baptist Mid-Missions in the early days until he became emeritus. His own daughter Lois and son-in-law Don went to the mission field. His own son, Donn, is out on the field. The Great Commission was at the very heart of his preaching, pleading with young people to lay their lives upon the altar of living sacrifice. That characteristic has been transferred to our Association which he headed for many years—the great spirit of missionary zeal and outreach. All around the world our Regular Baptist movement has taken root with probably more churches in distant lands beyond the sea than we have here in the homeland. A great deal of that is due to the vision that God gave this man.

So my heart is full of all the good things that could be said, but you know them too. I've come to pay tribute from our beloved Association; from our pastors whom he loved and counseled; from the people in the pew who felt that he was their friend; and from the missionaries scattered all around the world who look back to a day at camp or a missionary conference or in the churches where he served when life-determining decisions were made, and they turned their backs upon personal plans and their own will and yielded everything to the will of God to go out to the regions beyond where the name of Christ, in many instances, had not yet been given.

This man, who is now in the Glory, was humanly responsible under God for all of that. How we all thank God for Doc Ketcham and what he has meant in our own lives and to our churches and to our missionaries scattered everywhere. Amen.

PASTOR SAFSTROM:

Dr. Stowell has made mention of the fact that Dr. Ketcham was for the pastor. In the year and nine months that it had been my privilege to be his pastor, I can stand and testify that he's for the pastor. Always encouraging him; always saying, "Go on, preach the Word." And I appreciate the encouragement.

Another one who knows something more than I do of this encouragement in the life of the preacher is Dr. Gordon Shipp, who was his pastor for many years. Now we ask Dr. Shipp to come and share a few words with us at this time.

GORDON SHIPP:

This is a very special privilege for me to be here today. In my mind's eye—in these pews right down here—rests much of the memory that I have of Dr. Bob Ketcham. He was an excellent church member and a fine example to any believer as to how one should elegantly inhabit a pew and work for the Lord within the confines of just being a church member.

The first time that I ever remember becoming closely akin to Dr. Ketcham was when he came to the school that I attended in Minneapolis, Minnesota. It was many years ago, Northwestern College. He was asked by the president at that time to come and bring a series of messages. All of the young men in my dormitory began to let me know that "fighting Bob Ketcham" was going to arrive to preach a series of messages. But when "fighting Bob" got there, he was "feeding Bob," and he fed the students at Northwestern College in a wonderful way. Before the week was over, the president was petitioned by the student body to allow him to continue on for more time. He could not do this because of other commitments, but there was a warmth in his preaching and a blessedness in his preaching that thrilled my soul.

I remember so well the illustration he often used of the Good Shepherd Who carried the sheep on His shoulders. Not shoulder, not in His arms, but on His shoulders, with one omnipotent hand here and one omnipotent hand there and handkerchief in between around his neck. That was an illustration that blessed my soul and warmed my heart and will continue to do so as long as God gives me breath in this body.

I was his pastor for seven years. And during that seven years we watched the transition from a man who was preaching all over the country most every Sunday to a man who could no longer preach. I was with him shortly after the doctor had visited with him in his hospital room to say that he had to terminate his ministry of preaching to churches around our country. I really had mixed emotions when I went into his room. I really did not know how Bob Ketcham would respond to such a decree from his doctor that he no longer could travel and minister. But when I got there—you might have already sensed the fact—I did not have to be concerned. He said to me, "If I cannot adopt what I've been preaching all these years to people, then my God is less than I think He is and know Him to be. And if this is God's will for me, while I may chafe under it, I'll accept it and thank God for it." I appreciated that.

One humorous incident that I remember was the time when Dr. Ketcham was hospitalized in Swedish Covenant Hospital. I went to visit him shortly after he had been hospitalized. I said to him, "How are you doing today, Brother Ketcham?"

"Oh," he said, "I'm doing fine. I've been up and around the room, and up and down the hall out here, and just having a good time. Feel great. Don't know why I'm here, but they tell me I have to be."

And then the doctor came in the room, and I offered to leave. But the doctor said, "No, no sit down. We'll talk with him for a while. Now," he said, "Dr. Ketcham, you must be very careful. You've had another slight attack, heart attack, and you must be very careful. You can have a little exercise, but don't overdo it."

Dr. Ketcham said, "Yes, yes, I know. I can be up and down the hall."

"Oh, no, no," the doctor said; "you cannot be up and down the hall. You must just confine yourself to the room. And be very careful because your strength will just not allow you to go up and down these halls."

He listened to what the doctor said the rest of the time; then when the doctor left, with a twinkle in his eye, he said, "I guess what he doesn't know won't hurt him."

I so appreciated this man just because of his excellence, not only as a leader in our Association, but also as a kind, considerate and loyal gentleman in the pews of the church that God allowed me to pastor during the time I was here in Chicago. It will be a blessing I will never forget, and my ministry will never be the same because I've had the opportunity to be encouraged by someone that God gave me the privilege to preach to.

I remember as I came to this church, Dr. Ketcham was not in the habit of giving his pastor advice. He was in the habit of following the advice that the pastor would gain from the Word. But I remember saying to him shortly after I came, "Dr. Ketcham, I hope I can feed your soul as well as the souls of the people here."

He said, "You don't have to be a great scholar to do that. All you have to do is have a warm heart and sit down and listen closely to what the Lord has to say."

We tried to do that. And a few years after that God gave me a message one day that I entitled "The Secondhand Saint." It had to do with John chapter 13 where Simon Peter beckoned to John. He said, "John, what is

Jesus saying?" It's in John 13:24: "Simon Peter therefore beckoned to him, that he should *ask who it should be* of whom he spake." I *see* here that Simon Peter could well have asked the Lord himself. But he missed the blessing of getting the answer from the Lord himself and asked John to get the answer. Thus he became a secondhand saint.

During the years that I pastored here, I tried to be a firsthand saint. And I was encouraged to be one by a man who was a good "amen corner." Years ago Dr. Carl Elgena used a statement that I have used over and over again. He was referring to one of his choice laymen at Grandview Park Baptist Church in Des Moines. He was referring to the fact that that layman was faithful in his service to Christ. The great church that Grandview Park Baptist Church in Des Moines is could be so because of people like this man. Dr. Elgena said to me one time, "With men like that (referring to this gentleman at Grandview Park) in your pew, if you cannot preach, you ought to hang up your ordination certificate and get out of the business."

And I say this, in the seven years that God allowed me to preach here, Dr. Ketcham was my "amen corner." And if you can't preach with Dr. Ketcham in your "amen corner," hang up your ordination certificate and get out of the business. I praise God. And I extend my sympathies to this dear family, but I know that they wouldn't want him back here. He's with his Savior.

PASTOR SAFSTROM:

If time allowed, many more of you, I'm sure, could add tribute upon tribute to the testimony of Dr. Ketcham. Seated behind me in the choir area today are members of the Council of Eighteen of the General Association of Regular Baptist Churches. We thank the Lord for these men whose lives have also been touched by the ministry of Dr. Ketcham.

I would like to read a public tribute today, one from the Pennsylvania Association of Regular Baptist Churches:

> We from the state of Pennsylvania feel very deeply over the Homegoing of Dr. Ketcham. While his ministry was worldwide, his roots were in Pennsylvania and affected all of us in a very personal way. He will be greatly missed by his friends and neighbors in the Keystone State. Darris Hauser, Chairman, Council of Ten, Pennsylvania Association of Regular Baptist Churches.

And then from the American Council of Christian Churches:

> The American Council of Christian Churches owes a great debt to Robert T. Ketcham for his insight of issues, his inimitable manner of presenting truth and his spiritual power. His clear and uncompromising convictions will be long remembered and always treasured by the American

Council of Christian Churches. The officers and executive committee express their deepest Christian sympathy to Mrs. Ketcham and the family. Yours in Christ, L. Duane Brown, President, American Council of Christian Churches.

At this time we are going to be led in prayer by Dr. William Kuhnle, who at one time served with Dr. Ketcham in Iowa as his assistant and now is the assistant to the National Representative of our Association. Dr. Kuhnle.

WILLIAM KUHNLE:
Let us unite our hearts in prayer.

Our loving Heavenly Father, on an occasion such as this we pause to thank Thee for the grace of God by which sinners are saved. And as we thus come to Thee this morning, we come not hopeless but in hope, not with tears but in triumph. We come, O God, to thank Thee for the memory of one long loved and now lost just awhile; one who's gone on just a little while ahead; and one who with blinded eyes through life now has beheld the Savior Whom he loved and Whom he served.

We thank Thee, Heavenly Father, for the memories of Dr. Ketcham, for the joys of working with him, for the learning experiences that were ours under him. But we come to Thee, O God, to thank Thee above all for the Christ Whom he preached and for the Book from which he preached, that Sword of the Spirit which he so gallantly and valiantly defended. We give Thee thanks.

And so, this morning, although our hearts are mixed with sorrow, yet there is a song of triumph. We come to Thee not in a time of defeat but of victory. We thank Thee, dear Father, for this pilgrim whose journey is over and who has arrived at the city whose Builder and Maker is God; for him who loved as a son has now reached the Father's house; a soldier who has laid down the sword that he might pick up the crown which awaited him.

And thus, our Father, we come with gratitude rather than with gloom for the glory of the Lord which is our strength and which Thou hast promised to Thy people. And, our loving Father, we pray this morning Thy special strength upon dear Mrs. Ketcham. We thank Thee for the fortitude Thou hast given through these long years of illness, for her loving-kindness and care and concern for Doc. We pray, Lord, that in the days ahead Thou wilt sustain her, and may she realize that underneath are the everlasting arms. We pray Thy blessing upon Peg and upon Lois and upon Dr.

Donn over in Bangladesh especially. Lord, sustain this young surgeon. Thou knowest the strength he needs. Bless him, we pray. And we pray for other members of the family. Through the Homegoing of this dear loved one and this dear leader of our Association, speak to our hearts. May we be drawn Heavenward. Make Heaven more real. And may earth truly recede in our own thinking and the glories over yonder shine more brightly because of this one who has just gone on a little while ahead. These things we pray in the name of Jesus Christ our Lord, and with thanksgiving. Amen.

PASTOR SAFSTROM:

I still see in my mind's eye Dr. Ketcham sitting in the third or the fourth row down here and saying on many a Sunday morning, even with a feeble voice: "Preach it. Amen. Preach it." And the hour would never be complete without the preaching of the Word. Dr. John Balyo, member of the faculty of Grand Rapids Baptist College and Seminary, is the speaker of the hour. May the Lord bless you, Dr. Balyo, as you preach the Word at this time.

JOHN BALYO:

Psalm 61:2: "Lead me to the rock that is higher than I." Why did not David say, "Lead me to the rock that is higher than a mountain or higher than a star"? Did he think of himself as the highest thing by which he might measure One Who is above him? I think the answer is an emphatic yes! He thought of himself as higher than a mountain and greater than the stars.

The greatest thing God ever made is human personality. Man alone is made in the divine image, and by God's grace and power has awesome potential. But man has to get to the Rock that is higher than he. There alone he finds security and satisfaction. The world in which we live is simply not enough. Its pleasures are phantoms; its power is fancied; its glory is vain. The bird is satisfied with its nest. The cow is satisfied with its pasture. But man can never be satisfied simply with food and a temporary home.

Carlisle once said, "Not all the financiers, upholsterers and confectioners joined together in a stock company could make one shoeblack happy for more than an hour or two, because the shoeblack has an immortal soul, quite other than his stomach, which would require an infinite universe to fill."

Now, our Christian forebearers knew that. They confessed themselves to be owners of a vast and satisfying eternity. They called it the Promised Land, and they said that was what they were heading for. They were marching to Zion, and that for them made all the difference.

Vance Havner once wrote, "It was hope in the sweet by-and-by that gave courage to our grandparents and dried up their tears and made their sad hearts sing."

That is true. They knew, of course, that all that was bad would pass, and all that was good would last; and the best was yet to be. Don't ever say of a Christian, "He's seen his best days," because that is not true on the planet earth. *The best is yet to be!* Someday we will be living on such a wide and magnificent scale that the imagination reels and staggers at the thought of it.

Paul himself waxes eloquent in Romans 8 when he thinks about our future. He looks around and he says, "The whole creation is groaning and travailing in pain together until now." He says, "Not only it but we ourselves also groan within ourselves, waiting, waiting for something—the adoption, the redemption of our bodies, for we are *saved unto hope.*" Paul looks at a groaning universe and forward to the glory to come, and says, "This is what salvation anticipates." Hope means anticipation.

What is hope? Well, go back to Genesis 1 and read, "In the beginning God created the heavens and the earth. And God said, Let there be light." And there was a universe flooded with light and life. But leaf through Genesis and come to the last chapter and the last verse. What you find is an obituary notice. Joseph died at an hundred and ten years of age and was put in a coffin in Egypt. What a vast difference between the opening verse of Genesis and the concluding verse!

Well, is that the end of the road for Joseph? Joseph said not. He said, "When God leads you out of Egypt, will you please take my bones along?" That seemed an extraordinary request. But Joseph is mentioned in Hebrews 11 for that very statement, as having extraordinary faith. Joseph was saying, "I want everybody to know that I belong to the people of God; and when resurrection day comes, I want to rise from Canaan Land." We read, "Moses took the bones of Joseph with him," carried them around for forty years in the wilderness, and buried them finally in Shechem, in the heart of Palestine. A grave in the Holy Land holds the bones of Joseph and a shining promise of a future resurrection.

Perhaps we ought to stand at the graves of some of God's great men. Maybe we ought to remember what they believed and what they fought for and how they suffered and how they triumphed.

Have you ever seen a great tree stand tall against the sky? But then age and weather finally felled it. You passed by, looked where the tree used to stand and there was only a great empty space against the sky.

I am told that the Japanese produce dwarf trees which are only a few feet high. You may see a pine tree or a maple tree in a dish, and the tree is only about three feet in height. They stunt the trees by continually cutting the roots. I think we live in a world of mostly little men, midgets, dwarfs, because they are not *deeply* rooted in *great* principles, *great* loyalties, *great* truths and *great* faith.

Dr. Ketcham *was.* He was a great man, one of God's tall men. And today there is a *great* empty space against the sky. He was a man of integrity. He was a man of great compassion. I shall never forget the warmth of his messages when he spoke about tears gathered by God in a bottle. I shall not forget in Council meetings, hearing him sob sometimes when he prayed for pastors or missionaries. I shall not forget the tenderness of a genuine compassion. I shall not forget his great ability.

If he was limited in education, he became an educated man; for he read omnivorously, and he was eloquent in his presentations of truth. God endowed him richly; he stirred up the gift that was within him. He was a man of courage. That is a rare virtue, it seems. If he believed in something, he never stopped to count the cost.

As I thought of him, I thought of that passage in Malachi when it was another dark and evil day. People were saying, "It's a vain thing to serve the Lord. It doesn't really pay. People who are proud are set up and exalted, and people who put God on trial are delivered."

But there were those who gathered together in a fellowship, those who reverenced the Lord and thought upon His name and spoke one with another. As they talked in this blessed fellowship of a minority group, the Lord hearkened and heard.

God listens to our talk. He said, "Bring me a book." And he said, "Now, I want you to record the conversation of those in this fellowship in a book." He said, "Someday you are going to know the difference between the righteous and the wicked, and those who reverenced My name and those who did not. This is a book of remembrance, remembering these who revered Me, and they shall be Mine in that day when I make up My jewels!"

Someday God is going to put the pearls on His own string, and the pearls are not anything of His magnificent creation of the universe. They are human personalities.

And if you think of some men like the prophets of the Old Testament or the apostles of the New, you can think also of those who have been continuing in church history to represent Jesus Christ faithfully. And I can see God, in imagination at least, as He strings His pearls, adding the human personality of Robert Thomas Ketcham. "They shall be mine in that day when I make up my jewels."

Yes, there were a faithful few in Malachi's day. And Dr. Ketcham wanted to bring such people of our day into a fellowship. I have heard him say, "I want the GARBC to be a haven for pastors and churches in this dark day."

Well, now for him the battle is over. And he fought because there was something worth fighting for. And there still is. For him the race is run, and it was an obstacle course. But God laid it out for him, and he finished the course, and the bells of Heaven ring.

Some time ago, in a country church where I was asked to preach, I heard an old-fashioned tenor sing in a style reminiscent of other years, "When They Ring Those Golden Bells." It took me back to Grandmother's house and the old record player in her living room. I would wind up that ancient machine, put that record on, "When They Ring Those Golden Bells," and sit on the sofa right beneath the picture of my grandfather with his white hair and little white goatee. And I would listen to the tenor sing. He would sort of coast through the stanza, and then he would take off for the skies on the chorus. He would just keep climbing and climbing until he struck those last high notes, and I felt inside of me something of the tintinnabulation of the music of the bells; golden bells for you and me. The golden bells of Heaven are ringing now.

I can only imagine what Dr. Bob would have done with a text like mine. I can imagine at times he would have thundered about the Rock. Oh, with a deep conviction he could do that. He would talk about the Rock that is higher than I. And I can sort of feel his own heart in some measure, I believe, for I heard him preach enough, that I think he might mellow a bit and say, "Lead me, lead me to that Rock. Nothing else is enough. There is no security in the world. There is no satisfaction in the world. I need the Rock! Will you lead me, just lead me, just lead me to the Rock that is higher than I."

Oh, how I loved him. He was a great man and a dear friend, and now he is with the Lord he loved so much. And I am looking forward to the time when I am going to say "Hello" to the Lord Jesus and greet Dr. Bob again. Amen and hallelujah!

PASTOR SAFSTROM:

Dr. Bob would want you to pay tribute not just to him, but above all to the One he loved and served so faithfully through the years. Please take your hymnals and turn to number 37. And let us join together in singing a song that probably was one of his favorites, "How Great Thou Art."

(Congregational singing.)

I want to read the last paragraph in the booklet *I Shall Not Want* that Dr. Bob wrote some years ago.

> Wonderful, blessed, sweet, eternal communion to go on and on endlessly with the One who endeared Himself to us here in these changing scenes below. Never another hill to climb. Never another dangerous mountain passage. Never another scalding, bitter tear. Never another pang of heartache and heartbreak. Never another disappointment. Gone—gone forever are these, and now, *forever, only Him.*

Let us pray.

> Now the God peace that brought again from the dead our Lord Jesus, that great Shepherd of the sheep, through the blood of the everlasting covenant, make you perfect in every good work to do His will, working in you that which is well-pleasing in His sight through Jesus Christ, to Whom be glory forever and ever. Amen.

ORGAN POSTLUDE: "Great Is Thy Faithfulness"

HAT ON HIS HEAD, CANE IN HIS HAND
Donn W. Ketcham, M.D.

(Reprinted from *The Baptist Bulletin,* October 1978.)

How does one distill the intimate experience of years of living together? How do you condense into a paragraph the lessons learned from a lifetime of watching, listening and savoring the life of a godly man? How do you explain the depth of the heritage that is mine in being the son of Robert Thomas Ketcham? Let me just skim a few observations about my father.

One of the deeply seated character traits of my dad was his total commitment and devotion to the Word of God. We often hear of people who claim the Word as their sole guide; but how often do we see a person who actually guides every facet of his life by the Word? Such a person was my dad. He knew the Word intimately. At every turn of life, at every hurdle, at every idle moment, you would hear him say, "Mother, get the Book." I cannot think of a phase of his life that was not consciously aligned with the guideline of the Word.

In all the years of my observation, I never once saw my dad act in a petty manner, say an unkind word or behave in a "small" way. He was far too secure in his relationship to the Lord to have to resort to anything at all bemeaning. It wasn't that he saw himself as too "big" to behave "small"; but he saw himself as the child of a "big" Heavenly Father Whom he tried to emulate. Back in the years when Dad was leading the fight against modernism in America, it was his fierce devotion to the Word that caused him to fight. At no time did he engage in a vendetta against personalities. Few realize the tears he shed over former friends with whom he had to part when those friends departed from the principles of the Word.

How shall I describe life at home? The atmosphere was permeated by love. There was a never-ending flirtation with my mother. There was a rollicking good sense of humor which made our house a place where all my friends enjoyed gathering. There was a sense of fair play that assured you against being exploited or treated imperiously. There was a sense of "all is well" as you found Dad always shouting through the radio speaker at the White Sox manager as to how to handle the game. There were the zany moments in which Dad composed and sang a whole cantata to the words of "Hey diddle diddle, the cat and the fiddle." Life was warm, secure and fun in his house.

Being a preacher, Dad was always early for his engagements. It never failed that if we were scheduled to leave the house at 6, Dad was ready at 5. I well remember our last furlough when Mom and Dad would come to Grand Rapids and spend a week or two with us. After a while Dad would get anxious to get back home to Chicago. We would agree to leave for Chicago the next morning at 9. Upon arising at 7, we would find Dad in the front room, shaved and dressed, hat on his head and cane in his hand, saying, "Let's go home."

As his years wound down toward the end, Dad often prayed for a soon Homegoing. Our daughter, Becky, put it well. She said, "He's got his hat on his head, his cane in his hand and he's saying, 'Lord, let's go Home.' "

CHAMPION OF GOD
Paul N. Tassell

(Reprinted from *The Baptist Bulletin,* October 1978.)

What Thomas Jefferson was to the United States of America, Dr. Robert T. Ketcham was to the General Association of Regular Baptist Churches. As Jefferson was the major force in the writing of the Declaration of Independence, so Ketcham was the major spokesman and writer for hosts of Baptists declaring their independence from the tyrannical infidelity of the Northern Baptist Convention fifty years ago. As Jefferson's thinking was prominent in the writing of the United States Constitution, so Ketcham's incisive and precise thinking is interwoven throughout the constitutional and organizational genius of the General Association of Regular Baptist Churches, which had its official beginning in 1932.

Dr. Ketcham was a many-faceted man. He was a warrior who knew that the pen is mightier than the sword. His opponents were often made to feel the sharpness of his inky sword as he defended the doctrinal positions of the GARBC. In correspondence, in editorials, in pamphlets, in booklets and in Associational literature items, Dr. Ketcham could parry and thrust with an expertise born of the Spirit of God and perfected by the constant use of the Sword of the Spirit, the Word of God.

His pen was not just an instrument of spiritual warfare, however. He often used that pen as a shepherd's rod or staff. His treatises on Ephesians 6 and Psalm 23 are just two examples of how edifying, how encouraging and how enlarging his expositions could be to our hearts.

But Dr. Ketcham was first and foremost a preacher. How he could preach the Word! How he could exalt Christ! How he could expose error! He had the God-blessed ability to make Old Testament characters live before his listeners. He could make New Testament incidents absolutely unforgettable. (Do you recall his exposure of the modernist's foolish attempt to explain away the miracle of the feeding of five thousand?) Dr. Ketcham believed in the inerrancy of God's Word, and he preached that Word confidently, courageously and compassionately. Like a farmer, he plowed a straight furrow. Harvests have many times followed his patient sowing. Heaven is already peopled with many of his ingathered sheaves and shall be even more so through the coming years.

The words spoken by Pastor A. G. Brown at the funeral service of Charles Haddon Spurgeon may be aptly applied to Robert Thomas Ketcham: "Champion of God, thy battle long and nobly fought is over! The sword, which clave to thy hand, has dropped at last; the palm branch takes its place. No longer does the helmet press thy brow, oft weary with its surging thoughts of battle; the victor's wreath from the Great Commander's hand has already proved thy full reward."

Dr. Ketcham was an evangelistic example and a pastoral pattern. Our Regular Baptist churches need to exercise that scriptural zeal which so wonderfully characterized his missionary vision and vitality. We as pastors need to feed and guard our sheep with the same scriptural faithfulness that demanded separation from doctrinal degradation and denominational deceit. By the grace of God, we will preach the same gospel and exalt the same Christ he preached and exalted until that day when we join him in the Glory.